ACKNOWLEDGEMENTS

Thanks to Des Gibson of Paperweight for suggesting this project and for his help and support. My thanks also to Gerard Colleran for his guidance and assistance throughout the writing of this book.

Many friends and colleagues helped, corrected, encouraged and supported. These include Aoife Ni Lochlainn, Brian Murphy, Michael O'Regan, Fionnan Sheahan, Carl O'Brien and Liam Reid.

My thanks for guidance exclusively in matters of Mayo football history to Sean Rice, Tom Shiel, Terry Reilly and James Laffey. I'm grateful also to the people who helped with invaluable archive material: Ursula Halligan of TV3; Paddy McDonnell of Newstalk; Killian Murray of Today FM; Henry McKean of Newstalk; Michael Kealy of RTE's Late Late Show; Richard Crowley of RTE's Prime Time; and Sean O'Rourke of RTE's News At One; Martin Long of the Catholic Communications; and Fr Michael Kelleher CSsR (CSsR).

Mo bhuiochas freisin le Sinead Ni Uallachain, Radio na Gaeltachta.

Thanks to James Laffey and many others for their help in sourcing photographs.

Helping someone write about a senior politician still active in public life is a tricky business. My thanks to all those I approached from the worlds of politics and public affairs past and present.

I'm especially grateful to those two dozen people who spoke to me, some at great length and on a few occasions. All were asked to speak in confidence on the basis that no names would be used. I trust they find I have respected that confidence and relayed their contributions fairly.

I'm grateful to my wife, Bethan Kilfoil, as well as Mari and Denis, for their understanding and support. Thanks to Dafydd and Pam Morris of Glyn Ceiriog and Nick and Nia Bennett of Cardiff, in whose homes in Wales large chunks of the later chapters were written.

John Downing,
October 2012.

ENDA
KENNY
THE UNLIKELY TAOISEACH

POLITICAL BIOGRAPHY
by JOHN DOWNING

Paperweight

First published in 2012 by Paperweight Publications, Level 4, Building 5,
Dundrum Townhouse Centre, Dublin 16, Ireland.

Enda Kenny - The Unlikely Taoiseach
© John Downing

9781908813084
Enda Kenny - The Unlikely Taoiseach

9781908813138
Enda Kenny - The Unlikely Taoiseach e-book

Printed and bound by CPI Group
(UK) Ltd, Croydon, CR0 4YY

Paperweight Publishing Group, Level 4, Building 5,
Dundrum Townhouse Centre, Dublin 16, Ireland.

www.paperweightpublications.ie

INTRODUCTION

RISING WITHOUT TRACE

"A BOOK about Enda Kenny? A whole book?"
"So, a political biography of Enda Kenny. A short volume I shouldn't wonder!"
"Enda Kenny. A book? Why?"

Those were the immediate reactions, from three people of different political party backgrounds, who were among those who agreed to be interviewed for this book. One of the speakers admitted to not especially liking, though not actually disliking, the man.

But the other two were kindly disposed towards him, and one of these was also a life-long staunch member of the same party as Kenny. All three doubted whether he was a truly serious politician capable of doing the huge job he has been given as Taoiseach at a time of enormous crisis.

Well into his second year in the highest political office in Ireland, deep-seated doubts persist about Enda Kenny. These doubts enrage many of his close collaborators and supporters who argue that the man is the victim of lazy media stereotyping which panders to his opponents.

These supporters insist that Kenny has battled through a decade of adversity as leader of Fine Gael and won the office of Taoiseach to prove his personal mettle and ability. They argue that the naysayers should now leave him a clear field in his efforts to lead the restoration of Ireland's prosperity.

Unyielding critics often counter-argue: "What did he ever do in his political career? He was over 35 years in the Dail before he was elected Taoiseach. Name just one thing he did or said."

These critics add that he has been an exceptionally lucky politician who got to be Taoiseach due to a huge economic crash and the total implosion of the opposing party, Fianna Fail.

It is true that Enda Kenny's political rise has been gradual and sometimes unremarkable. He was a TD for 11 years before he got his first taste of government as a junior minister and 19 years at Leinster House before he entered Cabinet.

He astonished all his Fine Gael parliamentary colleagues in February 2001 when he told them he wanted to be their leader after 25 years in public life. Before being elected Taoiseach he never held office in a ministry with major economic responsibility.

It is also true, as this book details, that he has been lucky at several crucial junctures. But as we look back over a remarkably long political career spanning five decades, we also see him suffer reverses and persist in the face of difficulties.

This book looks in some detail at the central role of Enda Kenny's wife of 20 years, Fionnuala O'Kelly, whom he met in the Dail while she worked for 'the enemy', Fianna Fail, as press officer and later as head of the Government Information Service. They conducted a sercret romance during her nine years working in Charlie Haughey's party, a period among the most fraught in Ireland's political history.

All who know the couple agree that she has been an important influence in changing his attitude and sharpening his focus in politics. It also looks at the back-up provided by other family members, notably his brother Henry Kenny, who passed up an opportunity to step into his late father's shoes in favour of his younger brother.

The people of Mayo have few doubts about Enda Kenny and have elected him 12 times, more usually with a resounding vote. In February 2011, voters in five-seat Mayo constituency did him the honour, unprecedented anywhere in the country's political history, of electing four Fine Gael TDs.

Scenes from his triumphant return to his home county as Taoiseach have been compared with the welcome given to Pope John Paul II on his visit to Knock in 1979. In Mayo, and many parts west of the

Shannon generally, the criticisms of Kenny are often resented as being founded mainly on snobbery.

The book details Enda Kenny's long journey from his childhood home in Islandeady, near Castlebar, Co Mayo, which began in April 1951, and was completed in March 2011 when he was installed in Government Buildings as Taoiseach.

It considers the life and times of his much-loved father, Henry Kenny, a football star recruited by Fine Gael, and who cadged lifts, walked and bicycled his way about Mayo canvassing his first election in May 1954. It recalls Henry Kenny's tragic death and the by-election in November 1975 which brought his son Enda into politics. It highlights the role of sport and the GAA in the Kennys' lives and in Irish politics generally.

The book looks at Kenny's life-long loyalty to the political party which adopted his father and which he has also served unswervingly for most of his adult life. It looks at the many internal rivalries, both local and national, which characterise Irish politics.

Along the way it evokes the huge characters of Mayo and national politics including Padraig Flynn of Fianna Fail and the ever-combative Michael Ring of Fine Gael. It recounts marathon media battles with journalist Vincent Browne and also explains Kenny's own very pragmatic, low-key approach to the business of politics.

Neither critic nor supporter has doubted Kenny's skill as a political operator. His career as a TD, which made him the 'Father of the House' or longest-serving deputy in the Dail after his election in February 2011, speaks for itself.

Doubts have centred on his fitness to hold higher political office – to lead a major political party and finally lead the Irish people as Taoiseach. He has at times fed these doubts by poor judgement, a lack of application and by too often portraying himself as a happy-go-lucky person when a more serious attitude was required.

But he has also shown some finer political qualities, including loyalty, doggedness and courage, which deserve more attention and are explored in this book in some detail. His finest political achievement to date has been the revival of his party's fortunes, bringing it from the brink of extinction and into government.

The doubts about him as Fine Gael leader were revived just eight months before the February 2011 general election when the majority of his own front bench tried to oust him as leader. His own hand-picked team members said he was not capable of leading them to government because he did not project a credible image as a future Taoiseach.

In that leadership heave, he showed skill and courage few people knew Enda Kenny possessed. He went on to lead Fine Gael to a historic and unprecedented election win and become Taoiseach.

These developments were all good for Enda Kenny and Fine Gael and were an understandable source of pride for people of his native Mayo. They also arguably carry some benefits for Irish democracy and political pluralism.

But the bigger and more important question still remains: can he deliver in Government Buildings?

Those close to him believe he will continue to serve his full term to spring 2016. He has pledged to lead the transformation of Ireland's current parlous situation over the coming years.

This is 'a whole book' about Enda Kenny, detailing how and why he became Taoiseach. It is a story that also offers some pointers as to what lies ahead.

CONTENTS

PART 1

Political Football

CHAPTER 1

Family Business

The young man sent from headquarters to boost the by-election effort was struggling to make conversation with the grumpy old stager who collected him off the train at Castlebar Railway Station.

"By the way, who is the Labour candidate?" the youngster finally ventured as affably as he could – in another effort to break the silence.

"Labour candidate? Labour candidate, is it? This is Mayo, boy. In Mayo we don't do 'fringe' parties," the veteran Fine Gael man replied.

That truncated conversation took place in June 1994, when Fine Gael got the better of Fianna Fail in a by-election. By then the pattern was emerging of Fine Gael being nicely ahead in their decades of local struggle with their old Civil War rivals in Mayo.

The struggle between these two giants left little room for smaller political operations in Mayo for a very long time. But if you check back a little further you'll find that Mayo not only 'did fringe parties' – the county was a veritable home for one fringe party in particular.

And, in an irony of history, it was Mayo voters' love of that 'fringe party', Clann na Talmhan, which began a chain of events that would ultimately help propel Enda Kenny to the job of Taoiseach at this crucial time in Irish history.

Among Fianna Fail's many successfully promulgated myths was

the notion that they 'owned everything west of the Shannon'. This could not always be said of Mayo, where Fianna Fail were strong – but rarely all-conquering.

But between 1943 and 1961 both big parties, and especially Fine Gael, suffered at the hands of Clann na Talmhan in Mayo. At one stage, from 1945 to 1948, 'Clann' held three seats in what was then five-seat Mayo South. Their long-time leader, Joe Blowick from Belcarra, Co Mayo, was twice Minister for Lands, in the 1948-51 and the 1954-57 Inter-Party Governments.

Henry Kenny was a much-loved icon of Mayo Gaelic football when he was recruited by Fine Gael in the spring of 1954. The 40-year-old national-school principal and farmer had no track record in politics and took a lot of persuasion to let his name go forward.

The persuader was Willie Munnelly, who ran a bicycle shop in Castlebar, lived well into his 90s, and was a Fine Gael true believer all his adult life. He had told his party colleagues that he had the ideal candidate who could stop the Clann na Talmhan havoc being wreaked upon them.

But when he went to unveil his 'mystery man' to a party meeting, the would-be candidate was nowhere to be found. Munnelly had to go back to Henry Kenny and do some more persuading over the succeeding days.

There was still another hurdle to be cleared. Some party members felt that Dr Philip Cawley from Swinford, a good friend of Henry Kenny, would be the ideal candidate. In that case Henry would not seek a party nomination against his friend.

But the doctor's wife had issued an ultimatum: "You can have me – or the job." So, ultimately, Henry got the nomination on the proposal of Dr Cawley, seconded by his 'creator', Willie Munnelly.

Twenty-one years into the future, in October 1975, after the untimely death of Henry Kenny at the relatively young age of 62, the same pair would nominate Henry's third son, Enda, to stand in the resultant by-election.

Football was key to Kenny senior's nomination and football was to play a part in launching his son's second career. Thirty-five years into his own political career, in 2010, Enda Kenny, leader of Fine Gael and soon to become Taoiseach, reflected upon this, saying his party took a leaf from Fianna Fail's book in selecting his father as a hero of Mayo football.

In 1951, three years before Henry Kenny's candidature, Fianna Fail had taken a Dail seat there by choosing Sean Flanagan, the star and captain of two Mayo All-Ireland winning sides, in 1950 and 1951. Fine Gael were matching a current football hero with another, slightly older, football hero of the 1930s and 1940s in Henry Kenny.

"Sean Flanagan was still playing when he was elected in 1951 and that was probably it for Fine Gael. What they wanted was a name," Enda Kenny recalled.

****

Henry Kenny did not even have a car when he faced into the 1954 general election campaign.

At the start, all his canvassing was done on foot or by bicycle. He was friendly with a journalist with the local *Connaught Telegraph* newspaper, PW Leamy, who, unusually enough for those times, did have a car.

The journalist would drop him and his fellow canvassers out the country. They would agree a general canvass route and PW Leamy would drive back along it in a few hours and pick them up.

Later, hackney cars were hired – especially for transport on polling day. Henry's brother John had two hackneys, so they were automatically hired for the campaign.

That 1954 election campaign was tough. Fine Gael had not held even one seat in the constituency of South Mayo since 1943. Fine Gael's last TD there was the renowned barrister James Fitzgerald Kenny, a Gaelic scholar who had been a supporter of John Redmond in an earlier life, and in 1927 succeeded the murdered

Kevin O'Higgins as Justice Minister in the Cumann na nGael Government led by WT Cosgrave.

Clann na Talmhan, translated as Family of the Land, was formed in 1939 and had echoes going back to the 1880s, to Michael Davitt, Charles Stewart Parnell and the Land League. This gave Clann particular resonance for Mayo, which was the founding place of the Land League, Davitt's home county, and whose voters had been among those who elected Parnell to Westminster at the height of his powers, though Parnell never actually sat for Mayo.

More practically, Clann na Talmhan's policies about farming and forestry, land rates and taxes, and the scandalous lack of economic and social development spoke directly to western rural voters' concerns in the 1940s and 1950s. They advocated schemes to enlarge smallholdings, to drain and reclaim poor land, and to create rural jobs by planting more trees.

Henry Kenny winning the fourth and last seat in Mayo South in May 1954 was part of the beginning of the end for the Clan, though they did participate in the ensuing Inter-Party Government. Clann na Talmhan leader Joseph Blowick headed the poll in the same constituency as Henry Kenny and was again appointed to cabinet.

But by 1965, Clann na Talmhan had disappeared as victim to, among other things, continuing rural depopulation. Like many of Ireland's other smaller political parties before and since, its voters had gradually sloped back to the bigger parties.

The Fine Gael Mayo South back-room folk allowed themselves a pat on the back after that important 1954 win. Henry Kenny polled 4,983 first preferences – against a quota of 7,328 – and was finally elected on the eighth count on transfers from his running mate, Michael Dalgan Lyons from Ballyhaunis, who had polled precisely 3,400 first-preference votes.

Fine Gael had defeated two Clann na Talmhan seasoned campaigners, unseating Dominick Cafferky and also seeing off the challenge of Bernard Commins, who was standing in his sixth election and had twice been elected a TD. Henry Kenny's speech was a template for his future ones: short, modest and courteous.

He thanked all who worked with him, thanked the voters – even those who had not voted for him – and admitted the campaign was a bit of an ordeal.

"I am not used to election campaigns and whatever campaign I went through, I hope I will never have to go through it again. I would like to thank everyone and especially those who refused to give me Number 1.

"I know nothing about the Dail but you can rest assured I will do everything I can for the people, and all they have got to do is ask me and I will do my best for them," he said.

Henry Kenny was about to find out a lot about the Dail over the next two decades. His young wife, Ethna, and their growing family, including three-year-old Enda, were also going to learn much about life in a political family.

****

Despite growing up in the town of Castlebar, Henry Kenny had always dabbled in farming. His father, Anthony, was a countryman with farming interests who also helped his wife, Bridget, run her pub and grocery store.

This was first located in Linenhall Street, and later on Main Street. These days the premises on Main Street houses a Chinese restaurant but it is still owned by one of the extended Kenny clan.

As well as the pub and grocery store, Anthony operated the council weighbridge, which monitored load sizes and safety on carts, and got a small fee for that. On fair days they had a licence to sell bottled beers from a tent on the town's Fairgreen.

Henry Kenny was a bright student strongly encouraged by his mother and the only one in the family to complete second-level education. After attending the local St Patrick's National School, he won a scholarship to study at St Gerald's de la Salle secondary school in Castlebar. From there he won another scholarship to train as a teacher at De la Salle College in Waterford.

Until 1939, the new Irish State kept up funding arrangements for the De la Salle Brothers' Waterford training college, originally granted by the British authorities on condition they train lay male teachers as well as religious brothers. Its lay attendance included a host of GAA personalities who honed their sports skills there.

Henry Kenny is often wrongly written about as attending St Patrick's training college in Drumcondra, where his son Enda later trained as a teacher. But the role of St Patrick's Drumcondra, as for many years the sole college for training lay male teachers, came later.

From Waterford, Henry got a job teaching in the Connemara Gaeltacht school of Doire Mhor Iata near Recess, where he put his great knowledge of Irish to use and deepened it. He was already a considerable football talent who became a regular on the Mayo county side from 1932 to 1947, when he finally hung up his boots.

Henry Kenny's heroic status in Mayo owed much to his starring role in their first ever All-Ireland win of 1936. He was a strong man, almost six feet tall and weighing about 13 stone, who played for a time in the half backs and sometimes in the half forwards and was well able to score.

But he is most remembered as a midfielder with enormous, 'magic' hands, who would rise high in the air and collect the ball in one hand, reputedly changing direction before he landed. In 1936 his partnership with his Castlebar near neighbour and friend, Patsy Flannelly, was rated unbeatable in the middle of the park.

That Mayo team was deemed unlucky not to win at least another All-Ireland. Enda Kenny says that listening to his father's lively recall of those games has left him convinced the team were unlucky and sometimes the victims of injustice.

"As a child I was reared in a sporting household. You were reared in that environment in the 1950s and 1960s when football was the issue – when there weren't other diversions like the mobile phones and so on," Enda Kenny said in an interview on Radio Kerry in August 2011.

In that discussion with local sports-enthusiast-cum-journalist Weeshie Fogarty, the Taoiseach showed his abiding pride in his father's and his colleagues' achievements. He pointed out that they won a record six back-to-back National Football League titles between the 1933-34 and 1938-39 seasons and went 53 straight games without a defeat.

"They could have won more – and there were occasions when they should have won more," Enda Kenny emphatically said.

The lack of another All-Ireland win was something which was discussed from time to time by the Kenny family members. The 1937 campaign, when Mayo lost the semi-final to Cavan by a single point, was recalled as a travesty in family discussions.

"We were playing our best form and five minutes from the end we were all over them, coasting home by five points," Henry Kenny later recalled for journalist Raymond Smith. But there were no barriers around the pitch in Mullingar and the fans invaded the field of play twice in those final minutes.

There is a strong sense of lost innocence in newspaper reports of this epic between the 1935 champions, Cavan, and the reigning 1936 champions, Mayo. Cusack Park in Mullingar was thronged, with a record 26,000 spectators paying IR£1,788 at the turnstiles; in pre-match ceremonies Mullingar Town Commissioners presented the teams with a formal address of welcome to which both captains "suitably replied".

"'Ground full' was announced three times but still that human tide flowed on and on, spreading itself from sideline seats to touchline," *The Connaught Telegraph* reporter wrote, mobilising his best purple prose. Crowd encroachment on the pitch was inevitable, all accounts agree, though reports next day by 'The Recorder' in the *Irish Independent* and 'Green Flag' in *The Irish Press* are more indignant about sections of the crowd blocking the view from the press table than about any pitch encroachment.

Amid all the stop-start confusion, Cavan smashed in two very late goals. Woe followed misfortune for Henry Kenny's Mayo, as their usually reliable free-taker, Jackie Carney, missed a final-minute close-in free which would have tied the game.

"Our luck was completely out," Henry Kenny summed up. But there was much muttering in Mayo about the impact on players' fitness of a six-week trip to America just weeks earlier.

This took in New York, New Jersey, Pennsylvania and Boston, with Mayo as reigning All-Ireland champions playing exhibition games which drew crowds of up to 20,000 Irish exiles. The team travelled out and back via Cobh on the luxurious *SS Manhattan* liner in a voyage which took 10 days each way.

There was far more controversy and bitterness surrounding Mayo's failure in the 1939 campaign, after a very bad-tempered All-Ireland semi-final against Kerry which resulted in a draw at the remarkably low score of 0-4 each. Henry Kenny recalled that Mayo had got a last-minute close-in free – but then the referee reversed his decision and gave a hop ball after being approached by two Kerry officials who came onto the pitch.

Henry said he caught the ball from the referee's hop but was being pulled to the ground by Kerry backs when the final whistle sounded. Kerry convincingly won the replay by 3-8 to 1-4, a 10-point margin.

But Mayo's sense of grievance remained extremely deep-seated and Henry Kenny and his teammates were at the centre of national controversy, with suspicion looming large about "an engineered draw" to generate replay gate receipts. Mayo County Board chairman Thomas Forde got his delegates' unanimous support for calls for a full inquiry as things soon headed for a series of rows.

The whole controversy reveals much about the GAA politics of the time in a very authoritarian era. The newspaper reports sit amid accounts of war in Europe, speculation that Germany might seek a truce and Government notices about air-raid precautions.

Mr Forde said the people at this Kerry-Mayo game in Croke Park were left with the impression that a draw "was a foregone conclusion" as the replay date was known even before the game started. He stressed that Mayo went to Dublin that day to win – and would have no part in a "disgraceful intrigue".

The GAA Central Council blasted back at their critics, saying that it was usual practice to fix and publicise a replay date in advance just in case. Thomas Forde backtracked; in a letter to all the papers he stressed that he was expressing the dismay of the Mayo public – and the criticisms were not his personal views.

This in turn drew a big local backlash, with accusations of cowardice. 'Disgusted of East Mayo' wrote a letter to the editor of the *Western People* saying the Mayo footballers had courage – the County Board had none.

Matters concluded at a GAA hearing in December 1939. A Mayo delegate, described in *The Irish Press* as "Mr O'Donnell, chairman of the Mayo Western Board", admitted he had used the word 'racket' but used it in the sense he did in his everyday work of teaching and meant rows or rough play.

"He did not use it in the American sense as that was slang," *The Irish Press* reported him saying. In a climbdown, the Mayo delegation accepted the match referee's report that he had not been intimidated by the Kerry officials into reversing his decision on a close-in free for Mayo.

But weeks before that, Mayo had got their own quiet version of retaliation in by 'retiring' from the 1939-40 National Football League, passing on a chance to win a record seventh back-to-back title. They made no mention of the Kerry match controversy but cited increased transport costs due to petrol rationing brought on by the 'European war'.

It is most interesting to note that of the 30 players involved in those contentious Kerry-Mayo games there were three future TDs spanning the three main political parties. Along with Henry Kenny of Mayo, there was Kerry captain Sean Brosnan, who would represent Cork North East as Fianna Fail TD and for a time as Senator from 1969 to 1979, and Dan Spring, Labour TD for Kerry North from 1943 to 1981, the father of future Labour leader and Tanaiste, Dick Spring.

Enda Kenny says that, then as now, Kerry were the gold standard of Gaelic football and the ones to beat. What clearly galled the Mayo team was that they had proven themselves a match for Kerry on several recent occasions.

In May 1936 Henry Kenny lined out with Mayo when they beat Kerry by seven points at home in Killarney, winning a set of commemorative gold medals at the opening of Fitzgerald Stadium. Later that year they beat Kerry in the 1936 All-Ireland semi-final on their way to that one coveted title. In the spring of 1939 they had also beaten Kerry in a home league match in Tralee.

****

Enda Kenny gleefully recalls his father's tale of the Mayo team's late-night return from Killarney after the Fitzgerald Stadium opening tournament on Sunday, May 31, 1936. "Seven or eight of the Mayo players were in one car when they left to return to Mayo that night. I don't know whether it was the road signs or the driver that was at fault. But they found themselves in Carlow the next morning.

"They were all starving and went into a cafe and ate breakfast, only to find that nobody had any money to pay for it. Paddy Moclair caused a diversion while the rest of them made a run for it," Enda recalls his father telling him.

Another of his father's memories recounted by Enda Kenny shows how a completely different attitude to drink-driving made late-night returns from matches in a car packed with players even more hazardous.

"They were dropping my father off in Connemara very late in the night when the car plunged into a stream. There must have been a few drinks taken because nobody was too worried and they all fell asleep in the car. When they awoke there were 40 or 50 people with shovels around the car. They thought that all the sleeping motionless players inside the car were dead."

When Henry's midfield partner, Patsy Flannelly, died in a

shooting accident while out hunting near Castlebar in October 1939, Henry was so affected that he did not play any football at all for the remainder of the season. The pair had been friends since boyhood; Flannelly's family ran a butcher shop not far from Kenny's pub in Castlebar.

The Kerry GAA fraternity's warm and sympathetic response to Flannelly's tragic death by sending four players to his funeral helped repair relations between the two counties. Mayo entered the 1940-41 League and Henry Kenny captained them to a big win in the final over Dublin on April 27, 1941, giving him a record seventh league medal.

Recalling the 1939 semi-final incident, Enda Kenny stressed that his father spoke only occasionally about such controversies and generally had a great liking for Kerry and its people. But he acknowledged that such incidents were remembered in vivid detail.

"Some things never change – win at all costs," Enda Kenny remarked ruefully of Kerry to Radio Kerry in 2011. He added that he retained hopes that Mayo could still win an All-Ireland in his lifetime.

It is also noteworthy that Enda Kenny's retelling of the 1939 'hop ball' story involved one of the match umpires warning the referee that "if he wanted to make his way home safely" he should not give Mayo a free in these circumstances. In Enda Kenny's retelling of the event on radio, the referee actually awarded a free out to Kerry – not a hop ball.

But apart from the reality of football records, which show Kerry dwarfed Mayo across the decades, there was the added reality that Enda Kenny is married to a Dublin-born Kerrywoman, Fionnuala O'Kelly, whose father, Sean, starred in the 1953 Kerry All-Ireland victory.

Fionnuala's parents retained a holiday home on the original family farm in Kilcummin near Killarney, and holidayed there each year. Enda Kenny, Fionnuala and family kept to that tradition and have been doing the same for the past 20 years.

The harsh reality for the Mayo man is that Kerry have 36 All-Irelands to Mayo's three, the first of which was won by his late father and his teammates in 1936 and the last of which was won in 1951, the year of his own birth.

Despite his hopes of Mayo victories, for Enda Kenny most years, it's a case of Kerry for the All-Ireland – and the holidays.

****

The vast contrast between inter-county GAA teams of his father's era and the current day is not lost on Enda Kenny. "There were no headshrinkers or no dieticians or whatever else. You had to do your own thing – though it was a different style of football," he said.

The Mayo County Board largely contented themselves with telegrams informing players they were selected and telling them to stay fit. Joint training sessions were rare, though training camps were established in advance of really big games. One such telegram in the Kenny family archives was despatched from Claremorris in July 1937.

It read: "It is important that each member of the Mayo team be fighting fit. It is not possible to bring the members of the team together, but the County Board expects each member to do his part. Will you do your part?"

In Mayo Henry Kenny had played with Castlebar Mitchels and won a Mayo county championship with them in 1932. But while teaching in Connemara, he played club football with Oughterard, 18 miles from his school.

In 1938 Henry played on the Oughterard team which won the club's one and only Galway senior title. The final against champions Ballinasloe was not played until March 1939 and Henry Kenny played a starring role in their close-fought win, which finished Oughterard 2-5, Ballinasloe 1-3. Signing on for part-time courses at University College Galway qualified him to play for the college team in the Galway championship and in the prestigious Sigerson Cup.

In the early 1940s Henry transferred to teach in east Galway, near Williamstown, and played club football once more in the Galway championships, first with Poleredmond and later with the more established Dunmore club. With Henry Kenny at mid-field Dunmore had some good runs in the county senior competition but honours eluded them.

When it came to training, the Mayo board had utterly no reason to worry on Henry Kenny's part as he was something of an iron man. He cycled a round trip of 36 miles to and from Oughterard several times each week to play football and often bicycled back to Castlebar at weekends, a trip of almost 70 miles, across the dreadful roads of that era.

On the field he had some famous duels with legendary Kerry player of the 1930s, Paddy Kennedy from Annascaul. All contemporary reports and later reminiscences show that Kenny was a very sporting player who was never sent off during a 16-year inter-county career. After his retirement from football, Paddy Kennedy spoke of Henry Kenny as one of his favourite opponents and "a man who played pure football".

Even when provoked or attacked, Henry Kenny was loath to retaliate and had a knack of sometimes making his attacker feel bad afterwards. Tom McNicholas was the last surviving member of the 1936 Mayo team when he talked about this to GAA writer Dermot Crowe in 2010.

McNicholas, who died in 2011, believed that Kerry midfielder Johnny Walsh followed orders to attack Henry in one match in 1937. "He flattened him and all Kenny said was: 'Johnny, why did you do that?' And Walsh was so humiliated that he didn't play any kind of a game after that. He was so vexed with himself that he had allowed others to influence him," McNicholas recalled.

A similar trait seemed to follow Henry Kenny into political life, where he avoided aggression and sought to disarm with a joke. When he died in September 1975, John Healy, a Mayo-born commentator who had led a new kind of political journalism, caught something of the man's skill and charm.

"He disarmed even the 'crabs' in Dail Eireann who couldn't touch him, for if they did, it was at the risk of revealing their own smallness," Healy wrote.

****

Enda Kenny gets a large store of 'lighthouse' political symbolism from his mother's side of the family. His mother, Ethna, was the daughter of a lighthouse keeper who served all around the coast of Ireland.

Henry Kenny met his future wife, Ethna McGinley, in Oughterard, Co Galway. She had trained as a domestic-science teacher at a college in Kilmacud in south Dublin, and was giving lessons in domestic economy in the schools around Connemara.

Mary Ethna, as she was christened, was almost five years younger than Henry. She was the daughter of lighthouse keeper James McGinley, whose story would fuel many of the future Taoiseach's speeches and anecdotes about lighting the way through perilous rocky seas.

James McGinley came originally from the coastal townland of Malinbeg in south-west Donegal. He was 25 years old when he started in the lighthouse service in 1905.

After training at the Baily Lighthouse near Howth in Dublin, he was posted back close to his Donegal home as assistant keeper at Rathlin O'Birne Lighthouse, separated from the mainland by a small treacherous gorge. He was serving at Beeves Rock in the Shannon Estuary in 1910 when he married Margaret Heskin from Carrick in Co Donegal. The couple shared a home near Askeaton in Co Limerick – when James was not out on the lighthouse.

James served on Tuskar Rock Lighthouse off Co Wexford during World War I, and was there when Margaret returned to her mother's home near Carrick to give birth to Ethna on February 12, 1918. By turns he served in Inishowen and Arranmore in Donegal, and also on Inisheer.

Ethna had two brothers, Andrew and John Joseph, but John Joseph died at the age of five. Her mother died in childbirth when Ethna was eight and her father later remarried, to Myra Crowley, a Dublin nurse whose family also worked in the lighthouse service. They had six children together.

Ethna was with the family when her father, James, was posted to Loop Head Lighthouse on the Clare side of the Shannon Estuary in January 1933. That was where her stepbrother, Joseph, was born in April 1934. In May 2012 Taoiseach Enda Kenny was at Loop Head in the company of his Uncle Joseph to formally open the new visitor centre at the now-automated lighthouse.

The McGinleys were all back where James started in late 1935 when he began his final posting as head lighthouse keeper at Rathlin O'Birne, which would last five years. James retired to a life of farming in 1940, and enjoyed an occasional bottle of stout and regularly played the fiddle.

The life of a lighthouse family early in the last century was materially better than many of their neighbours as it bought regular income and reasonable accommodation, fuel and other essentials. But it could be isolating and demanding, with the father often separated by howling seas from the family for weeks on end.

Ethna Kenny kept up contact with her Donegal home place. The Kenny children all have memories of summer holidays spent at Malinbeg. Her Donegal relatives and friends were present in big numbers at her funeral in Castlebar in November 2011; she died aged 93.

In 2007, after Enda Kenny made a major Fine Gael Ard Fheis speech based on his grandfather's lighthouse career, he recalled for one journalist his mother's family stories of her own father and mother using semaphore communication with flags when separated by stormy seas.

"She could see the lighthouse – he could see the cottage. There were no phones – so semaphore it was," he explained.

Enda Kenny also gloried in recalling his grandfather's skill in curing fish, laying it in a barrel between copious layers of salt.

When later retrieved, the fish was soaked overnight to dispel the salt and plump out the flesh. "It would taste delicious," the FG leader recalled.

James McGinley died in 1962 aged 81, when his grandson and future Taoiseach, Enda, was just 11. Family members insist he was a Cumman na Gael or Fine Gael voter since the State's foundation and would have heartily approved of his grandson's future career and applauded his election as Taoiseach.

In a speech to the Fine Gael Ard Fheis on March 31, 2007, Enda Kenny gave a full public billing to his deceased maternal grandfather as he himself negotiated the jagged political rocks and election rip tides by offering 'a contract' to the Irish voter. It was just weeks away from his first Dail election as Fine Gael leader and potential Taoiseach: his first head-to-head with Bertie Ahern.

"I leave you with the thoughts of one man who kept his contract, kept his word. His name was James McGinley. He was a lighthouse keeper on our west coast. Just a lighthouse keeper. Not famous, not rich, but crucially important," Enda Kenny told the packed auditorium in City West Hotel, Dublin.

"Cross the Atlantic and he was the first and last Irishman, the first and last European. In his ordinary life, with his ordinary family, in his ordered lighthouse, he didn't just keep the light, he kept his contract; that was his job.

"Whatever the weather, he had to. It was up to him. People depended on him for their lives. You see, James McGinley was my grandfather. He kept his contract and he used it to look out for people, to make their journey better, to bring them safely home.

"So tonight, people of Ireland, I give you our light, our contract," Enda Kenny said.

****

Ethna McGinley and Henry Kenny married in a quiet ceremony at the Pro-Cathedral in Dublin on July 16, 1942.

Henry was by then living in Williamstown, Co Galway, close to the borders with Mayo and Roscommon, and much closer to his native Castlebar. He had transferred there from Connemara and was teaching at Leitir School.

Ethna joined Henry in their new family home at Polredmond, near Williamstown. Their first son, John Anthony, was born in a nursing home in Herbert Street, in the centre of Dublin, in their first year of marriage. The family were to continue to reside at Polredmond until the summer of 1948.

But in October 1944 a great tragedy befell them as Ethna gave birth prematurely to triplets at their home in Polredmond. Little Bridget died soon after her birth while the two others were rushed to hospital in Galway in efforts to save them.

The second child, Henrietta, died the following day in the Galway Central Maternity Hospital. Her little sister, Margaret, lived for just a further day. The cause of the deaths was recorded as cardiac failure due to premature birth.

More than 67 years later their loss was publicly recalled in prayers at Ethna's own funeral in Castlebar. But again, it was a common feature of Irish life in the 1940s, where infant mortality was high, around 70 per 1,000 live births. It soared to Europe's highest level by the end of that decade.

While Ethna and Henry still lived at Williamstown, another tragedy struck the extended Kenny family. Henry's brother Denis was killed in Doncaster in England in February 1947. Denis Kenny was a foreman with the British building firm Cementation Ltd and had travelled all over Britain on various contracts as well as working in parts of mainland Europe before World War II.

Denis had been popular with the Irish community in England, with a good reputation for helping Mayo men seeking work and ensuring they got fair treatment. He died in a hotel room and an inquest found that he was asphyxiated by gas leaking from a defective radiator.

Henry's other brother, John, flew from Dublin and brought back Denis's remains by mailboat and train to Castlebar, where hundreds of locals met the coffin at the railway station. Denis Kenny, Enda's uncle, was buried amid a huge outpouring of grief at the town's Old Cemetery.

In February 1948, just six months before the family moved to Castlebar, Henry and Ethna's second son was born. After the devastation of the loss of the triplets, the couple took no chances and Henry Francis was born in the County Hospital, Castlebar.

Just weeks later it was announced that Henry Kenny was returning to his home turf as he was appointed principal teacher in Leitir School in the parish of Islandeady, some five miles from Castlebar. Henry bought a house and smallholding two miles from the school at Derrycoosh.

The couple's third son, James Enda Martin Kenny, was born on April 24, 1951. Irrespective of the names on the birth certificate, he would be called Enda, and would live the next 40 years in Derrycoosh until his marriage in January 1992. The family of five children was completed by Mary Carmel, born in December 1955, and known to family and friends as Maria, and finally the youngest, Kieran, in 1957.

Like most of their Islandeady neighbours in the 1950s and into the 1960s, the Kennys were largely self-sufficient in food, firing and other necessaries. Many of the houses were thatched with locally grown sally rods and rushes.

The same sally trees provided the material to make turf creels, potato baskets and vegetable strainers. Families made their own butter with an old-style dash churn or the newer propelled model.

As well as running a home, raising five children and being lynchpin of a TD's constituency operation, Ethna Kenny ran the small family farm. The children all had their household and farm chores when their schoolwork was done.

Since people walked or cycled for the most part, it was quite safe to play on the roads. The great luxury for young Enda Kenny was a No 4 football, which could be bought from Clery's shop for 15 shillings.

When he had time, Henry took the boys shooting. The area round about was replete with wildlife of all sorts, and wild geese, grouse and partridge were among the fowl which fed from the oats and barley grown for cattle fodder.

Most farmwork was done by hand, with the back-up of horse and cart. The carts were made locally, as were the wheels, and the blacksmiths were kept busy. Two local farmers, Phil Cooney and Joe Keane, achieved some local notoriety by being the first in the area to have tractors.

Few houses had running water or septic tanks. Henry Kenny was among a group, including a neighbour John Carney, who canvassed local houses and persuaded people to take part in the rural electrification scheme of the early 1950s.

Much of the hoisting of electricity poles and stringing of cable was done manually and the Kenny boys were later to recall watching horses hauling the black poles across the fields where gangs of men would dig holes with pick, shovel and crowbar. A lot of the wiring of houses was done by local men, some of whom had returned from England to avail of work at home.

Job opportunities in and around Castlebar in those years were very limited.

Apart from the County Council and the Castlebar shops, there was a hat manufacturer and the bacon factory where Ned Killian, husband of Enda's aunt, worked as an inspector. "Each summer and Christmas brought the return of working men from London, Liverpool and Manchester," Enda Kenny later recalled.

Change came slowly. Enda Kenny recalled the family's first television which was rented for the 1964 Olympic Games. "Its picture was snow-filled and black and white," he said.

The family lived in the original farmhouse on their Derrycoosh holding for all of their children's early years. Henry finally built a new modern bungalow in the early 1970s to replace it.

The Catholic Church played a huge role in everyday life. "The Church wielded huge influence in those days. I was the first child baptised by the late Fr Stephen Blowick PP in Islandeady

Church; he was a kind and saintly man who conducted his business on behalf of the Church with a genuine vocation and interest in his people," Enda Kenny wrote in an article, Reflections Of An Islandeady Childhood, published in 2000.

The parish priest, Fr Blowick, who baptised the infant Enda, was the brother of Henry Kenny's old constituency rival, Joe Blowick of Belcarra, who for two decades was leader of Clann na Talmhan, the party which contributed hugely to Kenny's recruitment to Fine Gael.

Fair days on Castlebar Fairgreen, three miles away, were a big social occasion. His father's brother, John, kept up the family franchise for selling drink to cattle dealers.

"The sounds, smell, bustle and activity of those occasions live sharply in the memory. My late uncle, John Kenny, had the sale of drink on the Fairgreen and many a deal or none were washed down with a bottle of stout," Enda Kenny later recalled.

CHAPTER 2

Dail Wake

Enda Kenny does not really remember a time when his father was not a TD. His third birthday came and went during Henry Kenny's first election campaign in 1954.

For the older family members, John and Henry, the first notable change following their father's election to the Dail was the arrival of the family's first car – a Hillman Minx, registration number ZO 8668. The number is fondly recalled to this day. Soon they had the only phone in the area, a large black Bakelite piece with a wind-up handle to call the local operator.

Several more Hillman Minx cars followed, before Henry moved on to an Opel. Like many men of his generation who took up driving later in life, he had his own idiosyncratic driving habits which were sometimes the focus of family humour.

All the family got used to their father being away quite a lot. When the Dail was sitting he was gone for most of the week, and when back in Mayo there was a non-stop round of meetings and functions to be attended. It was for long periods a one-parent operation with Ethna running the show.

Household and farming chores were shared and so was the political back-up work. As soon as the children could write to any passable standard they were addressing envelopes and, soon enough, even drafting correspondence. At election time the electoral register was divided up and each of them had to address a quota of envelopes for their father's leaflets.

There was also a lot of leafletting and preparing posters, with prints stuck with wallpaper paste on to cardboard backing. Enda Kenny could truthfully say as he faced into the by-election caused by his father's death in 1975 that he knew exactly what he was taking on.

"I have grown up with an understanding of what the life of a politician is really like. After all, I was only a few years old when my father was elected for the first time," he said.

But all the five Kenny children were involved in what was to become the family firm. Enda's birth in April 1951 had followed that of his elder brothers, John and Henry, and Enda was in turn followed by their sister, Maria, and finally Kieran.

The older children, including Enda, went briefly to their own father's school in Leitir. But all of them got the bulk of their primary schooling at another school in Islandeady parish, at Cornanool, which was run by principal John Egan, a man remembered for his love of football and a promising playing career cut short by injury.

Cornanool National School roll book shows that Enda Kenny was formally enrolled there for the first time on October 30, 1955, aged four-and-a-half. He was one of 12 pupils in the infant class and there were two other teachers on the staff, Mary Devaney and Mary Reilly.

"I attended Leitir NS for a short time before my late father entered national politics and we changed to Cornanool NS under the tutorship of the late John Egan known as 'The Master'. I recall writing on a slate in Leitir NS and can still see the huge fireguard and the clouds of smoke swirling back down the chimneys on windy days," Enda Kenny wrote years later.

"Schooldays in Cornanool consisted of books, copies, pens and nibs, sums, spellings, poems and the fear of the cane being produced," he further reminisced.

The school turf shed was not just a place for storing winter fuel – it sometimes also played an important role in supporting the school's academic reputation. "I recall on occasion some children

24

being despatched to the turf house when the annual catechism exams were held," he remembered.

'The Master', John Egan, knew Henry Kenny very well and clearly had affection for the family and for Enda Kenny in particular. Master Egan had also worn the Mayo colours and captained Castlebar Mitchels to successive county championship wins in the early 1930s, with both he and Henry playing on the same winning Mitchels side in 1932.

Golf was to fill the void left by Master Egan's forced retirement from football. At break time, he would practise his swing and drive, and the fleet-of-foot Enda Kenny was among a team of boys who would retrieve the balls. Family members credit this as Kenny's first introduction to the game he loves to play whenever he can.

The day Enda Kenny was elected a TD in November 1975, Master Egan, who had retired just weeks earlier, was at the Castlebar count centre and among the first to congratulate him with a warm embrace. But that was in the future. Back in the 1950s, Master Egan ran a tight ship and, as Enda Kenny later wrote, the prospect of the cane being deployed was ever present.

When Enda Kenny returned as Taoiseach to his old school, in June 2011, former classmate Michael Sweeney recalled Enda being sent to cut a cane from a nearby sally bush. To the great relief of his classmates awaiting punishment, the young Kenny chose and cut badly, producing a weapon deemed by the teacher as not fit for purpose.

In another celebrated piece of heroics, he is recalled as slipping some of the teachers' canes down a hole in the rickety floorboards. Another classmate, John Parsons, recalled the day Kenny and his classmates clambered in the school back window to avoid having to account for lateness to Master Egan on guard at the front door.

****

From their earliest years, the children witnessed at first hand how Irish politics worked.

There were no formal constituency clinics and no such thing as a separate constituency office. On Sundays it was known that the TD was at home to callers and people came seeking help, advice or favours. It was all about medical cards, social welfare, farm grants, school and college scholarships and any chance of 'pull' to get a job.

Henry Kenny copper-fastened his role as 'local fixer' by taking a seat on Mayo County Council in 1955, the year after his Dail election. An election speech in that contest echoed his words of a year earlier. In essence he said: If you are satisfied with my Dail work so far, then please elect me to the County Council.

His determinedly salt-of-the-earth approach was heightened by sharing the platform with Pat Lindsay, who had been also elected TD for neighbouring Mayo North after five previous failed Dail election attempts. Lindsay, a barrister and larger-than-life character, loudly castigated "Fianna Fail nabobs and Gauleiters" who abused their long-time job-giving powers to drive out other parties' supporters, and reassured everyone that everything would be different now his party, Fine Gael, was at the helm.

Once elected, be it to Dail or council, Henry Kenny persisted. He was far too new and unconnected in the business to rate even a very junior government appointment in the 1954-57 Inter-Party Government led by Taoiseach John A Costello on his second stint in the job. When that government fell, Fianna Fail were to return for another 16 years in power, mirroring their 1932-1948 run.

A trawl through the Oireachtas debate record shows that Henry Kenny took quite some time to break his Dail silence – a trend which his son Enda would follow years later. It should be noted, however, that they were each constrained by starting in the Dail on the government backbenches.

As a government backbencher, Henry Kenny for two years confined himself to asking parliamentary questions, chiefly dealing with the Mayo daily preoccupations of land, farming, fisheries, public job allocations, postal and telephone services, buses and railways, welfare schemes and payments.

He made short contributions on various items in 1956 and 1957 but his first major recorded speech came on June 11, 1958, in an education estimates debate which was presided over by then Education Minister and future Fianna Fail Taoiseach, Jack Lynch.

It is a short but very thoughtful speech, covering scarcely two A4 pages, about problems in education which showed his own experience and continuing contact with former teaching colleagues. He pointed to the huge pupil-teacher ratios, where 40 to 60 children per class were common. "I know one case in my own town of Castlebar in which there are 100 pupils under one teacher," he said. In such cases it was impossible to keep order, much less impart any knowledge – and children with learning problems inevitably suffered more.

Henry Kenny then turned to the question of teaching Irish and the vexed question of language revival, both topics dear to him as a fluent speaker of the language. He said too many people were too busy making ends meet to make time for Irish; people who had Irish were too "apathetic" about speaking it; children starting school had enough to contend with without having a language, foreign to them foisted upon them, and parents gave a negative impression of Irish to their children.

"The Department should take steps to abolish compulsory Irish in the infant grades," he said. In this, Henry Kenny was before his time and his dislike of compulsion would in due course be shared by his son Enda.

For Henry Kenny, it was about speaking the language. "In a foreign country a person can make himself intelligible if he has about 200 sentences to get along with," he argued. Each school child should be given a booklet with such a stock of phrases and an explanatory glossary – and let them begin speaking it. Alas, such common-sense suggestions were never listened to.

Apart from such occasional Dail flourishes, Henry Kenny

continued on the opposition Dail backbenches and continued to work in Mayo County Council.

A journey back through the three main local papers of the time shows Henry Kenny as carefully attending functions and meetings across his constituency – and being recorded as doing this. He was a low-key, decent and well-liked professional who was elected a TD at six elections between 1954 and 1973.

In his final tribute in 1975, political columnist John Healy noted: "Henry was not a great verbaliser. He didn't make too many speeches." But Healy saluted his work as a local advocate for the people – it was the only option open to a TD warming the opposition benches.

****

Political change eventually came. After a hectic election in February 1973, the Fine Gael-Labour National Coalition entered government after narrowly winning an election fought on a common programme.

It was a difficult election for Henry Kenny, whose strength was sapped by oncoming illness and a newly configured Mayo West constituency: the county was now divided on east-west lines. Fine Gael had a new constituency director of elections, Frank Durcan, who divided the constituency, and significant resources were put into promoting businessman Myles Staunton from Westport, with a strong message that this town was long overdue a TD of its own.

Henry's campaign suffered from persistent reports and assessments that his vote could be taken for granted. In the event, Myles Staunton headed the poll. But Henry also took a seat, making it a considerable coup of two out of three at the expense of former Fianna Fail Minister Micheal O Morain, who had been a TD since 1938. The seat gain enhanced Henry's chances of a government job.

New Taoiseach Liam Cosgrave did appoint Henry Kenny as

Parliamentary Secretary at the Department of Finance with responsibility for the Office of Public Works, known more popularly as the Board of Works. This was the job he had held as opposition spokesman for almost two years.

In simple terms, it was one of the more senior of the junior ministries, with access to mechanical diggers and other government hardware which could make things happen in rural Ireland. In sum a strong, albeit second-string, government job.

But, by his own admission, Liam Cosgrave had his doubts about Henry Kenny when it came to picking his government team. In a later interview touching on those cabinet choices he made in March 1973, Cosgrave argued that he had to balance appointees' competence and experience while also considering geography to keep regional supporters happy.

Despite his protestations to the contrary, he also had to balance the liberal wing of the party clustered around Garret FitzGerald and his own conservative wing.

Cosgrave said his decision to include Peter Barry from Cork as Minister for Transport and Power was based on Barry's business experience and the need to give recognition to Cork. Then he referred to Henry Kenny.

"And the people from the West, like Henry Kenny, who again was an exceptionally able person, but wasn't recognised as such until he got the position," Cosgrave recalled.

In fact, the Fine Gael leader had not included Henry Kenny in his front-bench team announced after the previous general election in summer 1969. Kenny did appear in the front bench Cosgrave announced in June 1970 and was given responsibility for the Office of Public Works. But he was dropped in April 1972 when Cosgrave once more reshuffled his pack.

As opposition spokesman for the OPW, Henry Kenny operated in his typically personalised way. The Minister he was marking was Noel Lemass, son of former Fianna Fail Taoiseach Sean Lemass, and who was quite friendly with Henry.

Before Dail debates, Henry would be seen quietly leafing

through an advance copy of Noel Lemass's speech. Henry knew the short cuts, but others were also aware of this and suspected his commitment to the job as a result. He was among those who had the reputation of coming to the Dail to quietly deal with constituency correspondence and share a few convivial evenings.

His great wit and easy-going manner suggested, rightly or wrongly, that he was less than serious about the 'Dublin end' of his work. A similar reputation would follow his son for the first two decades of his Dail career.

****

Like most TDs of that era, Henry Kenny's office was his various pockets. He is remembered as forever taking notes on scraps of paper about people he met, things he had to do and quaint turns of phrase or bits of knowledge which might prove useful.

Each day he would turn out his pockets in an untidy mess and assess what he had to do.

After Henry died, there were drawerfuls of these impromptu notes found in his Dail office and at home.

His great friend and inseparable companion, Dick Barry from Fermoy, Fine Gael TD for what was then the constituency of Cork North East, later recalled the vital political role of the TD's pockets. "Our offices were our pockets and one Cork TD had his tailor sew A4-sized pockets to the inside of his mackintosh. He used to say he could stuff as much into them as a pair of creels," Barry said.

Dick Barry was also dropped by Cosgrave in his April 1972 front-bench revamp. It was a tough time internally for Liam Cosgrave, who was facing a number of threats to his leadership, most notably from the wing he had controversially dubbed "the mongrel foxes" in an Ard Fheis speech he had made in Cork.

But both Henry Kenny and Dick Barry, to the surprise of some, made a comeback when it mattered most and got government appointments. Dick Barry was made Parliamentary Secretary, or junior minister, at the Department of Health.

Both Barry and Kenny had strengthened their claims to preferment by bringing in a running mate by good vote management. In Barry's case it was Paddy Hegarty, who retained the second Fine Gael seat out of four in the constituency. But Henry Kenny had gone one better in Mayo West, where his party took two seats out of three – despite Fianna Fail having over 50 per cent of the vote.

Tom O'Donnell from Limerick East was an unexpected choice as Gaeltacht Minister on Cosgrave's team. O'Donnell then faced the problem that he had little to do with Irish since leaving school almost 30 years previously.

The Limerick man had been greeted by Henry Kenny on his first day in Dail Eireann in 1961 and the pair had remained on good terms. Soon after his appointment, O'Donnell sought linguistic advice from Henry Kenny, who was a fluent Irish speaker.

"We talked for a while and then he coaxed me to speak a little in my Irish, such as it was. Then he said: 'Look, you'll have no trouble. Go the Gaeltacht as often as you can and practise as often as you can. But remember the people of the Gaeltacht will have far more interest in what you can do for them than they will have in your language competence,'" Tom O'Donnell recalled.

The incident reveals much about the pragmatism, courtesy and political skill of both men. Henry Kenny, a completely fluent Irish speaker who represented a Gaeltacht constituency, appeared better suited to the job of Gaeltacht Minister while O'Donnell had his own claims to a more suitable cabinet post. They were both just getting on with things, smoothing over and avoiding potential tensions.

Overall, the Cosgrave government was dubbed from the outset 'a government of many talents' as it contained many charismatic and dynamic characters who would loom large in Irish life and also feature variously in the future career of Enda Kenny.

Labour, led by Brendan Corish from Wexford, got five cabinet positions, including the internationally renowned UN diplomat and writer, Conor Cruise O'Brien, and television presenter and agricultural expert, Justin Keating. That pair would soon campaign hard to have Enda Kenny elected to the Dail.

Fine Gael's liberal wing, led by Garret FitzGerald, a future Fine Gael leader and Taoiseach, had to be accommodated by Cosgrave. But observers noted that Cosgrave sought to 'neutralise' Garret by giving him Foreign Affairs and sideline another liberal 'young tiger', Declan Costello, by making him Attorney General.

The more conservative Cosgrave Fine Gael wing was represented by Richie Ryan, appointed Finance Minister ahead of FitzGerald, who was fancied for the job, and Tom Fitzpatrick, appointed Minister for Lands. Curiously, Pat Cooney, who was soon to become a hard-line Minister for Justice, was then deemed to be on the Fine Gael liberal wing.

Cosgrave, in his usual sardonic style, spoke about what observers called a talented team. "I need hardly say that I am glad to have got a place on it," he said.

But amid Cosgrave's mixed reasons for his choices, geographic factors came last. Henry Kenny was the only government deputy west of the Shannon appointed to the government team. By contrast in the previous Fianna Fail Government, Mayo had two senior ministers, with Micheal O Morain in the Department of Justice and Sean Flanagan in the Department of Lands.

The *Western People*, based in Ballina and one of Henry Kenny's local papers, had proclaimed its disappointment at the lack of any Connacht person in the Cosgrave senior cabinet. The paper noted that all the power lay in the east of the country, while Cosgrave succeeded in winning the election through gains in the west – such as the two out of three in Mayo West.

It is clear that Cosgrave sought to plug that 'country gap' somewhat when announcing the junior team, which included Henry Kenny, some days later. Dick Barry was joined by fellow Corkman, Michael Pat Murphy of Labour, and Michael Begley of Fine Gael from Kerry South, along with John Bruton from Meath. There were only two Dublin TDs, John Kelly and Frank Cluskey, among the seven junior appointments.

But while Henry Kenny was finally getting on with politics, his family were rapidly growing up.

****

In September 1963, Enda Kenny began secondary school in St Gerald's de La Salle on Chapel Street in Castlebar. "I recall cycling in the three miles that first day. I recall the noise, the sea of new faces, the long room on right-hand side and the desk, second from the top where I first sat in class," he wrote in another evocative memoir, this time for a magazine to mark his old school's centenary in 2009.

"I see the raised wooden platform on which a table stood at the foot of the class. I see that blackboard where the new words began to appear: Liber, Mensa, Silva, Geometry, Algebra, Trigonometry, Long John Silver and Mairtin O Direain. It's where the Wind In The Willows came alive when read by participating students until someone missed their cue and the strap was brought down on hands ready to be pulled back in an instant," he continued.

St Gerald's was named for the eighth-century English-born monk who had founded Mayo Abbey. The de La Salle brothers set up a primary school in Castlebar in 1888 and opened a secondary in 1909.

Enda Kenny and his brothers were following in their father's footsteps. It was a typically tough and rigorous school regime. Like so many others, he was taken by the move of Fianna Fail radical Education Minister, Donogh O'Malley, who announced free secondary education in autumn 1966.

"It seems like prehistory now, nobody had anything, but O'Malley's free education created a stimulus and career for most. Corporal punishment – yes, and plenty of it; sexual abuse – no and never heard of it," Kenny wrote.

The six-mile round-trip cycle was done in all weathers six days a week as there was also school on Saturday mornings, to be followed by handball games in the ball alley near St Mary's Hospital.

Not all the teachers were given to corporal punishment. Eamonn 'The Bull' Nally was remarkable and helped the young Kenny get a taste for Latin and Roman history.

"He carried a cane he never used and had the mastery of planting imagery in your mind. No need for projectors or DVDs when he said there was no truth in the rumour that Hannibal told his soldiers behind the whins to put out the Woodbines before the Romans marched into his trap at Cannae and Lake Trasimere in central Italy," Kenny recalled.

The geography teacher, Brother Paul, used the window pole kept for raising and lowering the sash windows for unsuccessful attempts to explain Mercator's mapping projections. He urged the pupils to imagine the window pole was a beam of light which would project shadows on a flat surface.

"How we ever found Djarkarta or Dar es Salaam I'll never know," Kenny remembered.

The more dynamic Brother Vincent appears to have had more success with science. "Brother Vincent from Roscommon soloed all the fields of Ireland with the stick of chalk while teaching science, compression, Boyle's Law and CO_2 emissions long before climate change became an issue."

Like millions across the world, Enda Kenny can remember exactly where he was when news came of the murder of one of his lifetime political heroes, John F Kennedy, in November 1963. He was sitting on the Flatley dryer in St Gerald's learning the Scalae Primae. For readers not versed in that element of prehistory, he was sitting on a clothes dryer widely used in institutions of that time and learning from the universal school Latin primer of that era. Soon the whole school was praying for the fallen US President.

He was also in class when news came through of Bobby Kennedy's assassination, and it was there he learnt of Patrick Nevin from Brize near Claremorris being killed in action with American forces in Vietnam. Years later, on a visit to Washington, that day came back into focus as Kenny found Patrick Nevin's name on that famous Vietnam monument in the US capital.

****

After leaving secondary school in June 1968, Enda Kenny wanted to go and study for a BA at University College Galway.

But with one brother just ahead of him in the education queue and a sister and brother behind, training at St Patrick's Teachers' Training College, Drumcondra, proved the less expensive option, with the real prospect of a job immediately after a two-year course. Like his father, Henry, he was to become a primary school teacher, then a school principal and then a politician.

He spent two happy years at St Pat's, an all-male college which more resembled a senior boarding school than a third-level college at that time. The students lived on the campus, with accommodation divided into houses headed by a prefect.

They ate together in a dining hall, or refectory, with individual permanent seats allocated to each student. Enda Kenny shared a table with, among others, Micheal Kitt from near Ballinasloe, Co Galway, appointed Leas Ceann Comhairle in March 2011 and a long-time Fianna Fail TD. Micheal Kitt's father, Michael F Kitt, was a TD at the time and died at the age of 60, in late 1974, just 10 months ahead of Enda Kenny's father. Like Enda Kenny, the young schoolteacher Micheal Kitt won the resultant by-election, in March 1975, just eight months ahead of Enda Kenny's election to the Dail.

Micheal Kitt would, instead of Enda Kenny, now be deemed Father of the Dail or longest-serving TD, but for broken service due to election defeats in 1977 and 2002. On each occasion he served a stint in the Seanad and regained his Dail seat in subsequent elections.

Another future Oireachtas member who was a classmate of Enda Kenny's in St Pat's was Ned O'Sullivan of Listowel, who has been a Fianna Fail Senator since 2007.

The college also at that time had a large number of future GAA high achievers as players and mentors.

The most notable of these was John O'Keeffe of Tralee, who would go on to win seven All-Ireland football medals with Kerry. The list is completed by Eamon O'Donoghue of Kildare, who distinguished himself as a player and mentor; Mattie Murphy of Galway, who successfully trained Galway underage hurling teams; and Murt Connor of Offaly, who starred in their 1971 All-Ireland ground-breaking football win.

His period there overlapped with that of Sean Kelly, the future GAA president and cousin of Kenny's wife-to-be Fionnuala, who was in the class a year behind him. The college is remembered as a happy place and Enda Kenny is recalled as staying in line with the relatively strict regime. There was a 10.30pm curfew, varied by a few late passes each term.

It is clear that he knuckled down to study and won a gold medal for educational psychology in the final examinations in summer of 1970. He hit the ground running in the job market, doing relief teaching for some weeks in Skerries, Co Dublin, before the July primary school holidays that year.

From there it was back to Mayo to teach: first in Carrowken-nedy, near Westport, a short commute from his parents' home, where he had returned to live. As well as teaching, he remained very active in sport, turning out for the Castlebar rugby team as well as his local Islandeady GAA club. He was also prominent in an initiative organised by his union, the INTO, to promote teachers' fitness courses.

He liked teaching and in 1974 was among an increasing number of younger teachers of that era to be appointed a school principal. He took over at Knockrooskey school, also close to Westport, from another teacher-politician Owen Hughes, a well-known Gaelic scholar who had served for many years on Mayo County Council and stood for the Dail as a Clann na Poblachta candidate.

In a very short time Kenny had made great headway in his chosen profession of teaching. He had also signed on to do a part-time BA course in University College Galway – but fate would intervene to ensure he would not complete that course.

****

Gaelic football was a huge feature of daily life. While at second-ary school, there were games each Wednesday at McHale Park in Castlebar or away games in places such as Ballinrobe, Claremorris and Ballinafad. "Sometimes when the bus was to return home somebody had let the air out of a tyre, which meant much merri-ment at the time," he later wrote.

The home club of Islandeady was the centre of much of the ac-tion. The club had been founded as far back as 1904 but struggled for long periods to stay in existence against the scourges of emi-gration and scarcity of transport, which made it difficult to fulfill fixtures.

In May 1950 Henry Kenny, as a football legend and principal teacher recently arrived in the parish, was among the locals who answered the call to help revive the club. Others who helped out included the late Peter Solan, who had the distinction of being the only Islandeady man to win an All-Ireland, having played on the 1950 victorious Mayo team.

As the four Kenny boys grew up it was taken as read that they would don the green and white of Islandeady. But by 1973 an-other crisis of doubt about numbers and commitment had struck and some members felt it was time to wind things up.

Others, including the Kennys, favoured giving it one last go. This view carried the day at a decisive AGM and a successful in-ternal parish league followed. With Enda Kenny, now a qualified teacher and serving as club secretary, they entered a team in the 1974 Mayo Junior Football championship and, after a very tough campaign, won it out.

Enda Kenny lined out at right half back in the key games and also helped lead training. The semi-final against Hollymount was a controversial match which had to be abandoned three minutes from time due to a player fracas which led to a pitch invasion. The

Mayo County Board awarded the game to Islandeady, who had been leading at the time, and they then went on to defeat Bohola in the junior county final.

Off the field, the club was also blooming. In April 1974 a planning application for a new community centre at Islandeady GAA Grounds in Kinaseer was filed to Mayo County Council by 'E Kenny secretary' on behalf of the club. The following September the club organised a two-week GAA festival with dancing to big name bands like Gerry and The Ohio and Doc Carroll and The Nightrunners.

Suddenly, a club facing extinction just months previously was now upgraded to intermediate level. Again, they fared very well and made the county intermediate final, on September 14, 1975, against Ballinrobe. That game was recorded as a very fractious affair with a lot of off-the-ball incidents.

The Connaught Telegraph reporter deplored a "blatant lack of sportmanship" by the winning Islandeady team, who took from their victory by the way they played the game. "Had the Ballinrobe players retaliated more than they in fact did, then the game could have developed into a real punch-up," the paper recorded. It added that, even before the ball was thrown in for the second half, a Ballinrobe player was stretched on the ground.

But the reporter also made a point of exonerating Enda Kenny and his brother Kieran by name and noting that they played a sporting game. The *Western People* reported that Islandeady used "punch and crunch tactics".

In any event, Islandeady won out by 1-7 to Ballinrobe's 0-8. The decisive score was a deflected own goal by a luckless Ballinrobe defender. There followed sporadic newspaper reports of a proposed objection by Ballinrobe.

But next mention of the winning Islandeady team is an advertisement for a 'Victory Running Buffet' fixed for the Welcome Inn Hotel Castlebar on January 19, 1976, which promised 'Dancing til 2am to The Hillsiders'. Tickets, at IR£1.50 each, were available from one Enda Kenny, among others.

Islandeady went on to be upgraded to senior level but, while they reached some divisional finals, they did not prosper as seniors.

Enda Kenny – though one local report calls him 'Andy' Kenny – emerges from match reports as a competent solid defender who played a sporting game. But all GAA supporters know that junior and intermediate club football are not for the faint-hearted, as brawn can frequently exceed the amount of brain deployed.

Carrying the family name of a football legend can be a heavy load for a young player. But Enda Kenny insists that his father did not press his four sons in any way to emulate his deeds – in football or politics.

"It never was a case of our father applying pressure on us to play football or get involved in politics. When you are growing up in a political household you see things going on and it sort of assimilates into you," he recalled.

Many match reports of the time pick out Kieran Kenny, the youngest of the four brothers, as a very promising player who, like his father, could dominate midfield and prove to be a very threatening forward. He wore the Mayo county senior colours with distinction and marked Dermot Earley in a Connacht Final against Roscommon in July 1979. On this and other occasions he was picked out as having huge potential – but injury curtailed his promising career.

Yet all of these sporting achievements by the Kenny boys of Islandeady were tinged with great sadness: Henry Kenny was very seriously ill and it became increasingly clear that he would not recover. The evening of the intermediate county football victory the boys went to tell the news to their father, who, it turned out, had just 11 days to live.

****

In fact, Henry Kenny organised his own 'wake' at Leinster House before the Dail summer recess in 1975. He had frankly realised he could not win his battle against cancer and it was most unlikely he would return in the autumn.

"I remember that morning when he left for the Dail. I said to myself: 'This is going to be his last trip.' It was the end of June or early July in 1975. I remember it was a beautiful summer morning. He had failed physically at that stage. And that was going to be his last trip to the Dail and he knew that. Everybody else up there knew that as well," Enda Kenny recalled in a book, Dail Stars, by journalist Conor McMorrow, published in 2010.

Cross-party cudgels were put down and humanity prevailed. "I suppose it was one of those occasions when the collegiality from whatever party was stronger then than it is now," Enda Kenny reflected in an interview on Kerry Radio in July 2011.

At the close of business Henry Kenny asked colleagues from all parties whose acquaintance he had made across two decades to come to the Dail bar for a drink. By rule all Dail bars stop serving one hour after the close of sitting of either the Dail or Seanad, whichever happens to be latest.

But on this occasion Henry Kenny's group tarried well into the night inside the members' bar, a restricted area, open only to current and former TDs and Senators. Dail folklore now has it that they stayed until breakfast time. But others present insist that this is an exaggeration.

"It was the height of summer and it was very probably bright when they were going home. But it did not last until breakfast," one of those present recalled.

Clare Fianna Fail TD and noted traditional musician Dr Bill Loughnane got his fiddle out of the boot of his car and regaled the company with some tunes. Dr Loughnane was well known for organising weekly music sessions in the Dail visitors' bar – something which would attract damning publicity these days.

Soon others took a hand. Henry Kenny's long-time Mayo political rival, Sean Flanagan of Fianna Fail, took Loughnane's fiddle and played some tunes including a memorable rendition of An Chuilfhionn. The company included Dun Laoghaire Fine Gael

TD Percy Dockrell, who added to the merriment by theatrically 'refuelling the fiddler', holding Loughnane's pint while he drank and continued to play without missing a note.

Enda Kenny brushes aside any suggestions of mawkishness associated with the occasion. "He would not have called it his own wake. He would have called it recognition of moving on from here and saying goodbye to his role as an elected representative with his colleagues who were also elected representatives.

"He knew it was his last trip and they made a night of it," he summed up.

Even heavily discounting Irish people's tendency to exaggerate the virtues of the dead, it remains clear that Henry Kenny was the most popular politician of his generation at Leinster House. A senior Dail staff member recalled that socially the two great popular figures of that time were Brian Lenihan Senior of Fianna Fail and Henry Kenny of Fine Gael.

"And of the two – when you think of it across all parties – Henry Kenny was the more popular. There was a genuine buzz when he came into company, he had charisma and he was very bright. His command of language and quickness of wit made him a delight," the staff member recalled.

It was a far less pressurised era, with far less media coverage from journalists, who were part of the club atmosphere, and Leinster House was a much more sociable place with a more marked tolerance for drink. Enda Kenny himself later recalled the mood of the 1970s and 1980s as he first came to know the place.

"You'd hear the Rose of Tralee on a Tuesday at six o'clock wafting out of the Dail bar," he said.

Taoiseach Liam Cosgrave visited Henry Kenny in his final weeks back in Mayo. The Taoiseach asked him if he had any pet projects he would like to see done in the area. Henry Kenny identified two which he had worked on for many years: the Robe-Mask Drainage Scheme and the development of Ballyglass Pier at Broadhaven Bay.

Each project was at varying stages of development, but funding was copper-fastened by this final conversation with the Taoiseach and the works were duly completed. However, as we will see later, the Ballyglass Pier issue was to be the subject of a nasty Fianna Fail-Fine Gael row before it was opened, almost two years after Henry Kenny's death.

****

Henry Kenny died on Thursday, September 25, 1975, in Swinford Hospital, at the relatively early age of 62.

Despite the forewarning of his prolonged illness, Henry's death came as a great shock to the family.

"Well, you see, you don't believe that your father is going to die. You don't talk about what is going to happen after he dies. You don't bring these things up. Like any other family in the country, you know things are going to happen yet you don't believe them. And then when it happens you say, 'Why didn't I say that or ask that?' It's the same for everybody,'" Enda Kenny recalled years later.

The area was treated to a chieftain's funeral from start to finish. As Henry Kenny's body was removed from the hospital that Friday afternoon, there were honour guards drawn from Castlebar Mitchels GAA Club, with whom he had starred, and Islandeady GAA Club, which he had helped revive and his sons sustain. Behind them stood members of Mayo County Council.

At the Church of Our Lady of the Holy Rosary in Castlebar, virtually the entire Cabinet awaited the arrival of the hearse. The tributes were entirely predictable but contained one notable comment from Fianna Fail's Micheal O Morain, known as someone who revelled in very robust political jousting.

"I do not recollect a single instance of rancour between us," Mr O Morain said.

Henry Kenny was buried next day at the scenic cemetery overlooking Bilberry Lake, in the parish he had made his home 27 years earlier. The Taoiseach, Liam Cosgrave, walked behind the hearse along with Finance Minister Richie Ryan, Minister for Lands Tom Fitzpatrick, Jim Tully, Local Government Minister also representing Labour, Mark Clinton, the Agriculture Minister, Justice Minister Pat Cooney and Tom O'Donnell, Gaeltacht Minister.

There were TDs and Senators from every party and every corner of the country. GAA secretary general Sean O Siochain was there with a host of players and administrators from all over the country, including Sean Purcell of Galway. The stalwarts of the 1936 Mayo side included Paddy Moclair, Tommy Hoban, Tommy Regan, John Munnelly and Paddy Quinn.

The heightened emotion of the occasion is now recalled as being summed up by the sight of veteran Fianna Fail Dublin TD Dick Gogan weeping unashamedly outside the church in Castlebar.

Gogan was a 1916 Rising veteran who had been a stretcher-bearer for James Connolly in the GPO and, as a founder member of Fianna Fail, a party diehard. But he was first elected to the Dail in 1954, the same year as Henry Kenny, with whom he had a strong personal friendship.

The Catholic Archbishop of Tuam, Dr Joseph Cunnane, presided and the Church of Ireland Bishop of Killala and Achonry, Dr JC Duggan, also attended.

But even amidst this grief and solemnity, thoughts were already beginning to turn inevitably towards a by-election.

It was not lost on some in the attendance that the brothers Henry Kenny Junior and Enda were most prominent and visible in the funeral proceedings. For some of the Fine Gael Dail veterans the mantle would more likely pass to Enda, who appeared the better option – but it was by no means a foregone conclusion.

Two nights after the funeral, Fianna Fail Castlebar town councillor Dick Morrin publicly castigated RTE for rushing into by-election speculation on radio. Cllr Morrin said Henry Kenny's remains were still lying in Swinford Hopital mortuary as that Friday's lunchtime news ran a discussion on the inevitable by-election and likely political consequences for a government living on the slenderest majority.

The councillor had phoned his protest to RTE and now got the Council's backing to write to the national broadcaster expressing their collective dismay.

In due course the councillors got a reply from RTE executive Rory O'Connor acknowledging their upset but noting that the radio item was based on a national newspaper article published that same morning. Cllr Martin Hopkins angrily argued that national newspapers did not receive licence-payer funding – but RTE did.

But by then all political talk had moved on to the by-election question.

****

Liam Cosgrave let it be known to the family and the party locally that he wanted a Kenny to stand in the by-election – it was the only way they could win. The only question now was: which one?

The two youngest ones were not likely candidates. Maria was studying physical education at the National College for Physical Education in Limerick, while her brother Kieran was pursuing a similar course in Belfast.

The eldest brother, John, was working in a bank in Dublin and unlikely to return. So it was back to the two most remarked upon at the funeral, Henry, then aged 27, and Enda, 24.

Henry was by then teaching in Co Sligo. Enda was teaching in Knockrooskey near Westport and living at his parents' home in Derrycoosh.

Enda, being available locally, had taken up a lot of the constituency work as his father's illness worsened. But some long-time Fine Gael supporters, especially locally, felt Henry was the better candidate.

Like all the Kennys, Henry had worked 'in the family firm' of politics from childhood. He also had the benefit of being called Henry Kenny.

The pressures of life choices were compounded by grief at the loss of their father. Both Henry and Enda were brought to meet the Taoiseach in Dublin, further evidence that the choice was not a foregone conclusion.

From the Kenny family side it was made clear to the Fine Gael leader that a Kenny would only stand if the issue of who was getting the late Henry Kenny's job as Parliamentary Secretary was clarified. In simple terms, this post could not go to the other Fine Gael TD in Mayo West, Myles Staunton.

Myles Staunton was from a well-known Westport merchant family who had set up a seaweed factory in nearby Newport. He had polled almost 4,000 votes in his first unsuccessful Dail election in 1969, when it was widely reported he had the unheard-of back-up of 15 paid canvassers working for him.

In the recent February 1973 general election, as already noted, Staunton eclipsed Henry Kenny and headed the poll. People with much slighter vote-pulling track records had got government office and, to cap it all, Staunton had the money, education and family connections which made him look like Fine Gael officer material.

But the Kenny family and Castlebar Fine Gael put the kibosh on Staunton's promotion prospects. Cosgrave needed a by-election win – and to get that he needed the Kenny name on the ballot paper.

So, on the evening of September 30, 1975, before the campaign ever kicked off and a mere three days after Henry Kenny was buried, Liam Cosgrave made an announcement. He moved Kerry South TD Michael Begley from the Department of Local Government to Henry Kenny's old job in charge of the Office of Public Works and promoted the maverick Oliver J Flanagan of Laois-Offaly to the junior government ranks.

The decision to promote Oliver J required no justification whatever: he had 32 years' Dail service, previous government experience and the Fine Gael vote in Laois-Offaly needed shoring up. But against that, there was now no government representative at all anywhere west of the Shannon, and Mayo, which had helped elect Cosgrave as Taoiseach in February 1973, was again snubbed by the Coalition.

The wisdom of this contemporary assessment by commentator John Healy in the *Western People* on October 11, 1975 is worth recalling. "Liam Cosgrave paid Kenny his own tribute. I am not talking about the statement which he issues when he heard of Henry's death: I am talking about the way he marked the Kenny family as the first family of Mayo in the Fine Gael hierarchy," Healy wrote.

Healy followed with a quick-fire piece of spot-on realpolitik analysis: "Liam's first priority is to win a vital seat in West Mayo. How does he do that? He does it by having a Kenny on the Fine Gael ticket. How does he ensure a Kenny will go? Does he ensure it by making Myles Staunton a Junior Minister? He does not. On the contrary. If Myles Staunton was elevated now it would be tantamount to saying the Stauntons were the first Fine Gael family in Mayo, supplanting the Kennys."

Healy was totally right about all that. He had grounds when he further ventured that once Staunton's appointment was blocked, Cosgrave dare not elevate another western TD. But in a very short time Healy would be proved seriously wrong about his claim that the West, and Mayo in particular, would be mollified over the loss of a junior minister by the creation of a new semi-state, the Western Development Board.

On the question of which Kenny would stand, Henry Kenny Junior explained the story to political writer Tom Kelly of *The Connaught Telegraph* in October 2000. Henry was speaking at a time of internal strife in the local Fine Gael organisation in Mayo and just three months from Enda Kenny shocking his Dail colleagues by declaring publicly that he wanted to be their party leader.

"The occasion was a very sad and emotive one. Pressure came on us very shortly after our father's death. I was older than Enda by about four years," said Henry.

"We were brought up to Dublin to meet the-then Taoiseach, Liam Cosgrave. I was the kind of person who passed the ball, even though long-time supporters said to me I should have been the candidate because I carried the name Henry Kenny.

"But, basically, I was not interested. I had worked politically for Dad for many years and was involved in election campaigns going back to the Sixties. But I was not keen to go forward and I have never regretted that decision.

"Enda went forward and got elected. He was very young and there was a fair amount of pressure on him to perform as our father did," Henry Kenny reflected.

But Henry also promised his younger brother practical support into the future. "I always told Enda I would provide a back-up to him as long as he was in national politics. I am glad to do that."

Indeed Henry Kenny Junior has provided considerable local back-up for his kid brother for the last 37 years and is a long-time member of Mayo County Council. He has also acknowledged himself that this has sometimes carried the risk of local party division, with others feeling on occasion that they have been deprived of opportunities to shine.

****

Enda Kenny had hired a substitute teacher for the school in Knockrooskey well in advance of the Fine Gael selection convention, which was a mere formality. In fact, as we will see, his teaching job would be held open for another 29 years – along with an entitlement to pension-scheme membership and the right to a small portion of the salary.

Liam Cosgrave himself presided at the selection on Sunday evening October 19, 1975, and had six government ministers by his side. There was Tom Fitzpatrick, Minister for Lands, who would also become director of elections for the upcoming by-election, Finance Minister Richie Ryan, Gaeltacht Minister Tom O'Donnell, Defence Minister Paddy Donegan, Justice Minister Pat Cooney and Education Minister Dick Burke.

Also present were Parliamentary Secretaries – or junior ministers as they were later called – Michael Begley of Kerry South and Dick Barry of Cork North East, who had been Henry Kenny's closest friend at Leinster House. Both he and Begley were to play a major role in the forthcoming campaign.

It was little over three weeks since his father's death, but the presence of such political heavyweights and up to 1,000 delegates was extremely impressive to Enda Kenny. Already he had set the campaign tone of gently alluding to his father while stressing that he did not expect automatic votes.

"The convention was a magnificent display of enthusiasm and a vote of appreciation for the services of my father. However, I am not relying on a sympathy vote – I am going to stand on my own two feet in this election," he told reporters that evening.

He also insisted on upholding his father's track record of clean and fair campaigning. "I want this to be a clean campaign. Personally, I am not going to engage in any form of bitterness during the election," he said.

Former Taoiseach and Fianna Fail leader Jack Lynch came to Castlebar for his party's selection convention the following evening. Like Fine Gael's gathering, the outcome was a foregone conclusion as all the politicking had been done well in advance. The advertising agencies in Dublin already had the candidates' photographs and had been working on the election literature for days.

Castlebar Fianna Fail had first signalled that they favoured their long-standing champion, Micheal O Morain. Lynch had required O Morain to resign as Justice Minister during the 1970 IRA Arms controversy due to his problems with alcohol abuse. He had then lost his Dail seat in the 1973 election and there was a feeling that he was not the person for this contest.

Local newspapers commented that Cllr Padraig Flynn was

absent from the local Fianna Fail meeting which seemed to favour O Morain. It was clear to many locals that Mr Flynn – who would dominate Irish politics and indeed fuel political satire for three later decades – had calculated that this one was not winnable.

Publicly, Flynn pleaded pressure of work and lack of time. "It would not be fair to my party, to my family or myself," he explained later. The-then Fianna Fail press officer, Frank Dunlop, later noted in his 2004 memoir, Yes, Taoiseach, that Flynn turned down the chance to stand because it was not likely to go his way.

"He thought it would be better if he didn't have failure on his report card," Dunlop wrote.

Fianna Fail chose Michael Joe McGreal, a 28-year-old county councillor, auctioneer and furniture-store owner. He came from Breaffy on the edge of Castlebar and reputedly had a network of cousins across the county – by one account he had 88 cousins around Westport alone. But he now lived in Balla, just across the constituency line in Mayo East, a fact which already delighted the Kenny camp as useful campaign ammunition.

The pair were joined on the ticket by Independent Basil Morahan from Louisburgh, who was a secondary-school teacher in Westport. He would add much colour to proceedings, without impacting upon the overall outcome.

Fianna Fail opened their election headquarters in Chapel Street, Castlebar. Fine Gael were nearby in Spencer Street.

The battle lines were drawn and the voters of Mayo West prepared to be engaged and entertained in equal parts.

CHAPTER 3

An Election from Prehistory

The Fianna Fail director of elections, Gerry Collins, took the microphone at the party's final rally at the top of Main Street in Castlebar.

"There are maggots and faggots and insects crawling out from the Coalition woodwork at the moment. But we have the pesticide to kill them," he bawled at the enthusiastic crowd, to loud cheers. Collins, a TD for Limerick West, was a former minister and heavyweight organiser famed for his prowess at speeches 'off the back of the lorry'.

Yet the consensus was that this by-election campaign, which gave the political world the future Taoiseach Enda Kenny, had less of the usual personalised and visceral nastiness expected in the mid-1970s. It was "conducted in a rare atmosphere of political graciousness," *The Irish Press* leader writer concluded with days to go to the election. The *Irish Independent* took a similar line on polling day itself, November 12, 1975.

But *The Mayo News* had a more earthy view from its Westport base. "The 'clean campaign' was kept for the large centres. But in rural areas, where the voter does not mind a rabble-rousing speech, the politicians delivered the goods," it noted.

Even that assessment appears to have only been true up to a point. *The Connaught Telegraph* gave the campaign "a relatively clean" rating but lamented that tempers did boil over, especially in the final days.

Enda Kenny – who had insisted on a clean campaign from start to finish in line with his late father's lifetime practice – to this day retains many vivid memories.

One iconic moment was when he and the Taoiseach, Liam Cosgrave, arrived at the edge of Ballinrobe just as darkness fell. They walked into the town flanked by men holding hay forks aloft on which they had mounted and lit petrol-soaked sods of turf.

"It was like a scene from an election back in the 1930s or 1940s. It's a kind of prehistory now," he recalled many years later.

Some of the Dublin commentators were quite sniffy about the political drama in Mayo West. But it was replete with the kind of theatre which characterised Irish politics in the raw at that time.

There were also many local bread-and-butter themes which mirrored the country's national economic problems: inflation running at 20 per cent, well over 100,000 people out of work and constant worries about petrol prices. Tight Dail arithmetic gave Mayo West a national dimension.

And, added to all of this, the campaign was played out in parallel with the dramatic kidnapping of Dutch industrialist Tiede Herrema by renegade IRA members. The kidnap conclusion, with the culprits' surrender and no loss of life after a 17-day siege in Monasterevin, Co Kildare, had a big impact on the by-election outcome.

In autumn 1975, Gerry Collins was some 15 years away from his statesman-cum-world-peace-crusader period as Gerard Collins, Minister for Foreign Affairs and President of the EU Council of General Affairs. *The Connaught Telegraph*, lamenting his comments, also decried the remarks of veteran local FF bruiser, Micheal O Morain, at that final rally.

"The remarks of Mr O Morain in the Herrema kidnapping, while being greeted with enthusiasm at the rally, were generally considered unnecessary and an unfortunate return to political speeches from an age rapidly being forgotten," the paper commented. It did not, however, report Mr O Morain's comments – which would appear lost to posterity.

Banish any inference that Fine Gael were behind the door in any of this. On the final campaign weekend, posters bearing the legend 'Keep Your TD In Castlebar' appeared in the early morning all across the county town.

This was a reference to the Fianna Fail 'import' Michael Joe McGreal, living in Balla, just over the constituency frontier in Mayo East. The move left the Castlebar Rugby Club second row little time or a local media outlet to again point out all his multiple personal and family connections with Castlebar.

There were reports, too, of a nasty Fine Gael-Fianna Fail confrontation at an after-Mass meeting at Parke on the final Sunday of campaigning. On the platform, Dublin Fianna Fail TD Ben Briscoe publicly decried the amount of Fine Gael election literature printed in the capital, in contrast to his party's leaflets printed in Mayo.

This drew a strong response from local Fine Gael heavyweight Cllr Frank Durcan. "I challenge you to come over here and prove me wrong. You come over here to me," Durcan called out.

By this stage, Briscoe had managed to retrieve some of Enda Kenny's literature, which clearly showed it was printed by Dorset Press, Hume Street, Dublin.

"All I want is 30 seconds to explain this to you. Mr Durcan, you are afraid to give me that time?" Ben Briscoe could be heard calling out.

Durcan had other ideas, and, more to the point, he had a microphone which he refused to hand over. "Briscoe is not an Irish name and you won't find it round this area. We don't want foreigners running our country," he said.

Eventually, an enraged Briscoe successfully managed to get a right of reply. He said he was an Irishman born and bred, that his father, Robert Briscoe, had risked his life fighting for Irish freedom, and he resented references to his Jewish faith.

Cllr Durcan later said that some of the Fine Gael print work was done in Dublin but 90 per cent of their election literature was the work of Mayo printers. *The Connaught Telegraph* speculated that behind it all lay the nasty business of rivals pulling down election posters. Fianna Fail told the paper that an estimated 10,000 of their total 15,000 posters had been pulled down, while Fine Gael estimated that half their posters had suffered the same fate.

It was not all political blood and guts – there was also fire.

Jackie Healy-Rae, a man who would not stride the national political stage for another 22 years, travelled all the way from Kilgarvan in Kerry South to work for Fianna Fail. His role, orchestrating torchlight processions, igniting tar barrels and providing other impromptu conflagrations, had begun in by-elections like that of 1967 and 1968 in West and East Limerick, which saw first Gerry Collins and then Des O'Malley elected.

Healy-Rae was clearly a big hit with the Mayo Fianna Fail troops – or maybe they just wanted to make sure he would return home. "There are sure to be fireworks in the Welcome Inn tomorrow night as Fianna Fail hold a send-off party for their fires expert, Jackie Healy-Rae from Kerry," one newspaper report from polling day said.

The local people were bemused by many of the quintessential city politicians who had descended upon the provinces. In a piece of Castlebar folklore which lives on, one Dublin TD is recorded as the man who hanged the farmer's donkey.

The story goes that the politician arrived in the farmer's yard to collect him for canvassing and was asked to tie up the donkey while the farmer changed clothes. The gormless city man used a slip knot and when the farmer returned much later that evening the poor animal was found dead from asphyxiation. The identity of both farmer and politician vary with the telling.

Former Fianna Fail TD and Senator from Belmullet, Joe Lenehan, clearly enjoyed expanding on his explanation of why he was crossing the party line and backing Fine Gael and Enda Kenny.

"There is nothing I could do only support Enda Kenny. I knew his father, Henry, for 30 years. In fact we shared accommodation together in Dublin for 10 years during my time in the Oireachtas," he told reporters.

"Actually, I would not be in the world at all were it not for an aunt of the late Henry Kenny, a Mrs Minch from Castlebar, who delivered me at birth," Lenehan continued. That same midwife delivered Charlie Haughey, Micheal O Morain and Henry Kenny.

"So if this woman has nothing to answer for – who has?" Lenehan asked, rhetorically.

Lenehan was now an Independent county councillor who declared he was finished with politics and "didn't give a damn for anyone at this stage". He was publicly coy about his reputed ability to sway 2,000 votes in the Bangor-Erris nexus for Enda Kenny. "Really, it is a waste of time preaching politics down our way. The people there are so used to fake promises being made that they now take no notice of them.

"All it does is bring business to the pubs," added Lenehan, who ran a pub in Belmullet.

On balance, Lenehan was calling it for Kenny. In fact he would later presciently predict for *The Mayo News* that Kenny would have 3,000-plus votes to spare. For now he appeared happy to add to Fianna Fail's woes about the rumour that their candidate was 'imported' from Balla in Mayo East. He said the people in Erris knew Kenny's home well – they passed it travelling to and from Castlebar.

"People in Erris don't know where Balla is. Some of them think it is in Africa," he ventured.

The Independent candidate, Basil Morahan, was not impressed by the by-election's potential to boost pub trade. He wrote an open letter to the other two candidates urging them not to buy drink in an attempt to buy votes. Furthermore he wanted all drink advertisements banned from RTE.

To that end, the 44-year-old teacher said he had refused to pay his television licence for two consecutive years. He had lodged the payments instead to a joint bank account in his own name and that of the Minister for Posts and Telegraphs. However the licence stance did not stop him availing of a free election broadcast on radio and television, which even opponents agreed he used to very good effect.

Morahan described himself as "dependent Independent". As well as being against alcohol, he also decried the huge dependence on social welfare by the people in the region. Being anti-drink and anti-dole was certainly aiming at a small political niche market.

The Independent candidate would have been even less impressed if he had heard a by-election anecdote Enda Kenny told many years later. After speaking from an election-rally platform late one night he was complimented by Liam Cosgrave, who had stood with him.

Then the Taoiseach pressed some money into the candidate's hand and said: "Now go and buy them drink!"

Padraig Flynn made his presence felt at the hustings, despite passing on the Fianna Fail nomination. Unsurprisingly, he needed no amplification when addressing the all-important impromptu after-Mass meetings. He had the name of often being better than his competitors at gauging Mass finishing times, a skill indispensable to a rural election campaign in which the maximum of churches needed to be covered.

One Sunday, outside second Mass in Parke, he was installed ahead of Fine Gael TD, Pat Joe Reynolds and Enda Kenny's younger brother, Kieran, when the pair arrived.

But the self-styled 'Pee' Flynn, Messiah from the West, was not ahead in all the campaign tussles. After Mass at Straide he unleashed his best invective in denouncing the state of the local roads. Fine Gael's Cllr Gerry McEvoy managed to get his loud riposte heard and, better again, reported.

"You showed little concern for the people who use them when you did not turn up to the meeting held here a few months ago," Cllr McEvoy reproved Flynn.

****

"You know the Achill man's grace after meals? 'Thanks for the next – we're sure of this.'"

Those words came from the inimitable John Healy, writing in the *Western People* ahead of the by-election. He was not belittling any of his fellow county people's struggle for economic survival – merely trenchantly arguing that they should extract a high price for their votes, given the huge depopulation and economic stagnation.

Taoiseach Liam Cosgrave and his lieutenants were keen not to be seen coming with empty hands hanging. And Fianna Fail were ready to go toe to toe on issues of farming, local development and investment. Auction politics was the name of the game all through this campaign.

On the first Sunday of campaigning, Liam Cosgrave appeared at Masses in Kilmaine and Shrule, and said Mayo farmers could soon expect to gain IR£10 million from EEC disadvantaged-area schemes. These were the first windfalls of European Economic Community membership, which formally started in January 1973, a month before Fine Gael and Labour took office. The Taoiseach also lost very little time in announcing the establishment of the Western Development Commission to help address the economic and social problems of the western seaboard.

This announcement apparently rattled Fianna Fail, as party leader and former Taoiseach Jack Lynch took the offensive, playing on voter cynicism based on past false promises. For Lynch this was just a new layer of bureaucracy with no details of its budget, but with all the potential to hamper the work of the existing agencies working in Mayo: the IDA, Gaeltarra Eireann and Roinn na Gaeltachta.

Cosgrave was unfazed by these criticisms, saying that the Western Development Commission was proof that his government would explore all efforts to develop the West. In a further echo of the abiding importance of land issues in Mayo, he reminded voters that a section of the Land Commission would soon move to Castlebar, bringing 160 jobs to the town.

Finance Minister Richie Ryan brushed aside suggestions that all this was blatant vote-buying, arguing it was planned anyway. "It is in one way the Government's final tribute to Henry Kenny," he told the *Western People* newspaper.

Tom O'Donnell from Limerick East had been an unexpected choice as Gaeltacht Minister in June 1973 and had brushed up his Irish with encouragement from Henry Kenny. O'Donnell had also by now spent a lot of time in Mayo's three Gaeltacht regions: Iorrais, Acaill and Tuar Mhic Eadaigh.

O'Donnell had good credibility with many west Mayo people and had worked especially on Achill, linking successful emigrants in Britain and USA with island development schemes. He had also helped set up a lamb-fattening station on the island, which became a model for two more in Galway and Kerry. The Fine Gael director of elections, Minister for Lands Tom Fitzpatrick, decided to harness this goodwill by putting O'Donnell in charge of the western half of the constituency. In the post-election analyses this was deemed a master stroke by all commentators.

The Gaeltacht Minister also showed a great sense of political timing as he pledged to push for an RTE studio to be opened in Castlebar, managing to rope Fianna Fail TD Denis Gallagher of Achill into a meeting on the issue. In several speeches he argued that Fianna Fail had only paid lip service to western development as Mayo lost 20 per cent of its population to emigration during the previous 15 years of Fianna Fail governments.

As well as campaigning, O'Donnell gave frequent lifts from college in Limerick to the candidate's sister, Maria. She was helping her mother, Ethna who, despite her tragic loss, had thrown herself into the campaign from the start and canvassed in every corner of the constituency, including Clare Island.

The EEC's Regional Commissioner, George Thomson, visited west Mayo in mid-October. When his car was involved in a minor accident on a bad back road, locals took it as the best illustration of their case for grant aid. The new and minuscule Brussels regional fund was run by just 37 staff dealing with applications from nine EEC member states and was a pale shadow of the heady EU structural fund billions which would emerge for

Ireland in the 1990s.

But there was an announcement of some IR£9 million in Brussels funding for Ireland on October 16. These included seven Mayo projects, which got a total of almost IR£1 million in grants. Two days later at the convention which crowned Enda Kenny as Fine Gael by-election candidate, Liam Cosgrave pushed home the point.

"Indeed Mayo has received the largest single grant allocation of any county," he said.

Fianna Fail's election advertisements in all the local newspapers were a foretaste of the lavish promises which won them a landslide in the general election in June 1977.

The opposition party promised the abolition of all rates on people's houses, a IR£25 calf subsidy which was in vogue in Italy but ignored by the-then Fine Gael-Labour government and a kickstart to the building sector by, among other things, a doubling of housing grants.

On the campaign trail they concentrated on accusing the government of woeful financial mismanagement. Fianna Fail finance spokesman George Colley talked about "suicidal rates of borrowing" which could hit IR£300 million by the year's end. Even adjusting for years of cumulative inflation, that amount nowadays seems more reminiscent of the petty-cash account.

Fianna Fail continued to play on voters' doubts about the efficacy of the National Coalition in government. Their slogan was 'Vote No 1 McGreal – And Speed The Return Of Good Government'. But they lacked access to the wherewithal to bribe the voters, nor had they access to these new EEC funds.

Two weeks after the election it emerged that farm-grant claims for the area were being given priority. The *Sunday Independent* agriculture correspondent, Aengus Fanning, reported that "tens of thousands of pounds in EEC disadvantaged area grants" arrived in the post to West Mayo farmers in early November. Some of the cheques were for sums as high as IR£300.

Fianna Fail director of elections Gerry Collins just could not muster the energy to protest too much. "I don't want to seem to be making excuses for our defeat. But the massive inflow of government money into the area must have had a big influence on the vote," he commented.

****

Castlebar Fianna Fail stalwart Micheal O Morain had infamously labelled the Labour Party as "political queers from Trinity College and Telefis Eireann".

Many people west of the Shannon found O Morain's language objectionable – but the assessment did have resonance. Some Labour big names did indeed have a TCD and/or Donnybrook background and their mantra that "the 70s will be Socialist" was problematic. In 1975, the realpolitik was that Fine Gael people viewed Labour support as a very mixed blessing on the stump in provincial Ireland.

Labour did not field a candidate in this Mayo West by-election. But locally the small Labour organisation came out strongly for Enda Kenny as the National Coalition candidate.

Despite this, much was made earlier in the campaign of the absence of their heavy hitters from the Enda Kenny canvass. After all, the two parties were part of the National Coalition Government elected on a common platform in February 1973.

For some in Fine Gael, Labour intellectual Conor Cruise O'Brien, the Minister for Posts and Telegraphs, could have stayed away altogether. 'The Cruiser' gave an interview in October 1975 to *The Word,* a widely read magazine published by the Catholic Divine Word Missionaries, which criss-crossed most of the Fine Gael-Labour fault-lines, best avoided at election time.

Cruise O'Brien felt divorce was a necessary evil where marriage had irretrievably broken down. The 1922 Free State Constitution had not banned divorce as the 1937 Constitution had. A new constitution would reverse that situation.

He felt the influence of celibate clergy was bad for education, society and the clergy themselves. Elements of Catholic bishops' statements on the sanctity of human life had been oppressive to women. But he praised the work of many Irish missionaries abroad who he found "more broad-minded".

Yet, as often happens in politics where unlikely friendships emerge, Conor Cruise O'Brien had been quite friendly with the Mayo West candidate's late father, Henry. Years later, Enda Kenny would recall that soon after Cruise O'Brien was first elected to the Dail in June 1969, he began to talk to the Mayo man with 15 years' experience at Leinster House and enjoyed Kenny senior's street wisdom.

"In many cases, rural TDs would be wiser to the world than a lot of academics in the first place," Enda Kenny recalled.

But from the Kenny camp point of view, the timing of The Cruiser's comments offset potential harm. The national news agenda was dominated by the Herrema manhunt and subsequent siege lasting a total of 35 days.

Fianna Fail people, who would have enjoyed maximising Fine Gael local embarrassment at 'The Cruiser' and 'Godless Labour', had their own problems. Fianna Fail's Michael O'Kennedy was embarrassing his leader, Jack Lynch, by pushing for a party policy to call on Britain to declare their intention to withdraw from Northern Ireland.

This allowed campaign terrier and Finance Minister Richie Ryan to say at a meeting in Achill that there was no difference between Fianna Fail and Sinn Fein. In Northern Ireland, SDLP leader Gerry Fitt expressed his dismay. Fianna Fail looked in disarray and party leader Jack Lynch's authority was, not for the first or last time, seriously challenged.

The Labour big names did arrive in numbers in Mayo for the final 10 days of the campaign and coverage across all local media revealed no evidence of Fine Gael-Labour strains for that period.

Labour leader Brendan Corish was well received on visits to the various towns and was applauded on the platform at Fine Gael rallies. The Cruiser's notoriety and personable streak proved an asset, with local papers recording that he was a big hit on visits to several local bars.

Labour party historian John Horgan writes in his book Labour: The Price of Power, of Conor Cruise O'Brien arriving in a Mayo bar and cutting a rather eccentric figure. He describes The Cruiser as "wearing a white linen suit and looking for the world, as one observer put it, like a tea planter with amnesia".

The irony of it all, amid the continuing grief at his father's loss, was not lost on Enda Kenny. But he clearly appreciated the presence of the Labour big names. "I remember Dr Conor Cruise O'Brien advising people to vote for 'young Kenny' and also saying they must put down the IRA," he recalled.

"I was still grieving, as he [my father] was still only dead a few weeks. It was one of the last of the old-style by-elections as the entire Labour Party were down canvassing for Fine Gael. You had Brendan Corish, Justin Keating, Conor Cruise O'Brien, Michael O'Leary and Frank Cluskey. They were all down canvassing and it was a hilarious by-election when you look back on it – as all by-elections are," he remembered.

As the contest built, each morning at a Castlebar filling station there was a queue of State cars refuelling for the day's campaign ahead. All the big names of Leinster House were there.

In the evening, journalists held court in various local bars, mainly The Cobweb and round the corner in the Imperial Hotel, which had the distinction of being the place where Michael Davitt's Land League was founded in 1879.

Journalists and politicians mingled, exchanging gossip and lore – some of which was even fit for print.

Labour's tale of woe west of the Shannon was neatly encapsulated by the Kenny by-election.

A week after the count, at their 1975 annual conference in Dun Laoghaire, Joe Connolly, then chairman of Dublin County Council, drew a mixed reaction when he criticised the party's failure to put up a candidate in Mayo West.

Mr Connolly's insistence that the party must contest all future elections was supported by the radical politician Dr Noel Browne. "Are we going to become in future an organisation which is going to spend its time in coalition with Fine Gael or Fianna Fail?" the maverick former Health Minister asked.

The audience heckler who said, "You should know – you were in them all," got loud laughter and applause. There was also applause from conference delegates at mention of the Enda Kenny win.

On the eve of polling, *The Irish Times* had reported an eye-catching little story about Labour's Justin Keating, a former Telifis Eireann presenter, outside Mass in Newport on the final campaign Sunday, speaking into a loudhailer held by arch-conservative Fine Gael TD Oliver J Flanagan.

"Would you give a kick in the pants to the Government that brought a happy ending to the [Herrema] kidnapping?" Keating asked the crowd.

****

At 6.50 am on Tuesday, October 21, 1975, four armed detectives charged up the garden path of 1410 St Evan's Park in Monasterevin, Co Kildare, and kicked in the door. Just as candidates Kenny and McGreal were preparing for 20 hard days on the Mayo West stump, the nation's interest dramatically switched elsewhere.

The 18-day manhunt for Dutch industrialist Tiede Herrema was over, but a tense and grinding 17-day siege of the house's upper storey had begun. Herrema was boss of the Ferenka factory in Limerick, which at the time employed 1,200 people. The international spotlight was on Ireland, and the wider implications for the future of inward investment and jobs added to the immediate fears for Dr Herrema's life.

There had been pressure on government to quietly manage some sort of deal, with contacts involving clergy and union leaders during the manhunt with his captors, renegade IRA members Eddie Gallagher and Marian Coyle. The pair, who were promptly disowned by the IRA, began by seeking the release of three IRA prisoners, including British aristocrat turned IRA woman Rose Dugdale, the mother of Gallagher's son, and two others, Kevin Mallon and James Hyland.

The government's own statement of the time acknowledged the inherent difficulty while stressing there would be no negotiation and no prisoner releases. "The position we adopt is a simple one politically, although from an emotional and psychological point of view, when a man's life is at stake, it is difficult," it said.

As things dragged on, the kidnappers' demands changed to safe conduct away from the siege and a large ransom.

But the government utterly refused to concede an inch and many of their hardest-hitting statements were made while campaigning in this Mayo West by-election.

On November 2, Taoiseach Liam Cosgrave condemned the men of violence and made it clear that the Monasterevin stand-off could only end with unconditional surrender by Gallagher and Coyle. "They have robbed our banks and post offices, shot at and assaulted our security forces, hijacked vehicles, attacked trains and destroyed property. They have intimidated the innocent in their effort to undermine the free functioning of our courts," the Taoiseach said.

Labour's Conor Cruise O'Brien, who made a career of denouncing the IRA, echoed Cosgrave's comments while speaking at campaign meetings in Breaffy and Belcarra.

This not-an-inch stance seemed further justified by a spate of republican murders of rival factions in Northern Ireland around that time. For much of the siege Dr Herrema had a gun to his head and the nation was hanging on every report from the hordes of reporters from all over the world camped out at the scene.

But both the outcome and its timing could not have been more fortunate for Enda Kenny's Dail election hopes. Just after 9pm on Friday night, November 8, 1975, Gallagher and Coyle surrendered and Herrema emerged looking fit and well, having stood up magnificently to his terrifying ordeal.

With days to polling, the weekend papers were full of good news for the government. One garda had his finger shot off in an incident during the prolonged siege. Otherwise nobody was harmed.

Controversy about a supposed sentencing deal for the captors continued for years afterwards. The security authorities' response was that there was no deal – and since any such talk had been done at the point of a gun, it was therefore irrelevant. Gallagher was later sentenced to 20 years in prison and Coyle to 15 years.

Two nights after the happy outcome, Justice Minister Pat Cooney was hailed as a hero as he was introduced to the crowd at the final Kenny election rally in Castlebar. *The Mayo News*, in a masterful piece of understatement, noted that the siege outcome did Fine Gael and Enda Kenny no harm at all.

****

It says everything about the inexact nonsense that so often comprises political prediction that sometimes the bookmakers are the most reliable source of information.

Thus, in early November 1975, as polling day drew closer, both Fine Gael and Fianna Fail predicted that their man would squeak home in a very close contest. All such predictions carried a serious health warning.

More interestingly, the bookies' odds of 4/6 money-on suggested a narrow Enda Kenny win – compared to 5/4 odds on a win by Fianna Fail's Michael Joe McGreal. Those odds would not interest too many sporting Mayo folk.

The spread bets offered something to tempt the more dedicated punter with a political nose. Kenny to win by 500 votes or more was 6/4; by 500-1,000 votes was 2/1; a 1,000 or more win was 3/1; with a win by a margin of over 2,000 votes was 7/1.

Comparable odds were being offered on a spread for the Fianna Fail man. But a McGreal win of 2,000 or more votes rated odds of 10/1. Journalist Martin Curry in *The Mayo News* reported brisk trade at the bookmakers.

But, predictably, the politicians were as quickly spinning the betting data to seek advantage. Wealthy Dublin publican and Fine Gael TD Paddy Belton told the *Irish Independent* sports and political writer Raymond 'Congo' Smith that he had put IR£5,000 at even money on Enda Kenny to hold the seat. Belton had a smaller, undisclosed wager at 6/1 – down from 7/1 – that the winning margin would be over 2,000 votes.

"I find the reaction to young Kenny so good on the canvass that I am convinced he will hold the seat for the National Coalition," party grandee Belton insisted.

Not all the betting was of the high-roller variety. Cork South West Labour TD Michael Pat Murphy had IR£20 at even money with Fianna Fail's Des O'Malley from Limerick East. One local unnamed local man was quoted as saying acerbically that big betters didn't usually discuss their business in public.

There was a lot of Fine Gael huff and puff about Fianna Fail stalwarts in Westport being challenged to put their money where their boastful mouths were. Fine Gael Senator John Blennerhassett from Tralee was reported to have left £500 at the reception of a Westport Hotel with a challenge to the local Fianna Fail lads to "cover it".

Some versions of the story suggest they did rise to the challenge. But mercifully polling day was at hand.

On Wednesday, November 12, voters went to the 163 polling stations across Mayo West. That night the ballot boxes were taken to Castlebar Military Barracks and put with the boxes already in from Clare and Innishturk islands, where polling had been done some days earlier.

Enda Kenny's older brother, Henry, had been on Clare Island with two other campaigners on the eve of voting there. They hired a van and driver for IR£10 for a day's canvassing. The van retained its vivid red paint and Royal Mail logo from a previous life in London, and only half its gears worked under protest, but it did the job.

That evening they adjourned to one of the two island pubs and positioned themselves at the opposite end of the bar from the Fianna Fail group, who included Padraig Faulkner from Louth, Noel Davern from Tipperary and local politician Martin J O'Toole.

The islanders got an evening's free entertainment calling for speeches from both groups to help them decide how to vote the following day.

Before the counting even began there was a sense of a generation change in public life. Whatever the outcome the Dail – still peopled with some 1916 Rising and War of Independence veterans – would get a deputy born in the latter half of the century.

Newspapers in autumn 1975 also reflected this trend of change. That October the local papers all gave big coverage to a function in the Central Hotel, Westport, saluting Paddy Burke, who was retiring after 50 years in public life.

The man from Muckla, Kilmeenagh, Co Mayo, a place with which he retained strong links, had done all his political work in Dublin Fianna Fail. Now he was passing the baton to his son Raphael Burke, better known as Ray, a name people would hear much more of in the future.

The news reports were also filled with reminiscences arising from the funeral of Eamon de Valera at the start of September 1975. News of the prolonged illness and impending death of Franco in Spain also loomed large.

From the start of this Mayo West by-election campaign, the back-room people on both sides were acutely aware that 4,000 new voters aged between 18 and 21 years had been added to the register of electors. The voting age had been lowered in a referendum passed in December 1972.

Some Dublin commentators might have been dismissive about the contest from the outset. But, by its close, it had achieved national significance as the government's future was at risk.

In the final campaign week, Fine Gael Tipperary North TD Tom Dunne was involved in a serious car crash which left him out of politics for several months and unavailable for Dail votes. He was driving to canvass in Mayo West when his car collided with a cattle lorry near Ballaghaderreen in Co Roscommon and he spent the rest of the campaign in Roscommon Hospital.

The Fine Gael-Labour Government had begun life with a majority of one in June 1973. This had been extended to two when Fine Gael had a surprise win in a by-election in Monaghan, arising from the election of Fianna Fail's Erskine Childers as President the following November.

By now, if Enda Kenny could not win back his late father's seat and Tom Dunne remained too injured to attend the Dail, the coalition would be entirely dependent on the casting vote of Ceann Comhairle Sean Treacy and the goodwill of two Independent TDs, Joe Sheridan and Neil Blaney.

****

Even before all the boxes were opened at the Castlebar Military Barracks, the Fine Gael stalwarts were smiling from ear to ear. By noon Fianna Fail campaign director Gerry Collins had seen enough to openly concede that Enda Kenny would be the new TD for Mayo West.

Fine Gael boasted that the simple arithmetic showed this as a 10 per cent vote gain on Fianna Fail compared with the June 1973 general election. They left arguments about the invalidity of comparisons between general elections and by-elections for the mathematics professors.

The big function room at the Travellers' Friend Hotel was booked for a monster celebration on December 11. Cllr Frank Durcan talked about the possibility of annihilating Fianna Fail next time out.

By lunchtime the post-mortems and political lessons to be extrapolated were well ventilated around Castlebar and beyond. It was agreed that Fine Gael had worked the simple by-election winning formula of the time to great effect: you pick a close relative bearing the same surname as the deceased deputy and give the campaign absolutely everything your party has – and a bit more.

We were still almost a decade away from Irish voters systematically using by-elections to send an angry message to government.

Of seven by-elections during the 1973-77 Dail term, the Fine Gael-Labour Government held all their seats and actually gained one at the expense of Fianna Fail in opposition. By contrast, no governing party was to win a by-election between July 1982 and October 2011.

Martin Curry in *The Mayo News* pithily identified three reasons for Enda Kenny's clearcut win: 1) The Henry Kenny sympathy factor; 2) A successful and timely outcome in the Herrema kidnap, vindicating the government's hardline response; 3) Gaeltacht Minister Tom O'Donnell's huge impact in the western part of the constituency.

It was an assessment shared by other analysts nationally.

The showing of Independent Basil Morahan allowed him to emerge with dignity from the contest. Some Fianna Failers at the count centre quietly took up a jingle about Morahan which went 'Planted by Fine Gael/ To harm McGreal'. There was no second count to test that conspiracy theory – but the tally men suggested it was nonsense.

But even amid this game of Fine Gael happy families, the source of future tensions might be discerned.

Journalist Donal Foley, in the popular Saturday Column of *The Irish Times* later that month wrote glowingly about local strategist Cllr Frank Durcan, who was described as the real brains behind the Mayo West win "even though he knew he was burying his own Dail seat hopes for a long time to come".

The comment ultimately presaged, though years ahead of time, one of Mayo's most bitter and long-running political feuds: Kenny versus Durcan.

Away from Mayo, it was good news indeed for Taoiseach Liam Cosgrave. His majority was not reduced to the knife-edge minimum. And, despite his government dishing out the harshest fiscal medicine, they were evidently motoring well beyond the half-way mark in their term.

"I see no reason to doubt the capacity of the Coalition to last its full term," the Taoiseach said, with his standard economy of expression.

It was trouble for Fianna Fail leader Jack Lynch, however, all the time weakened by having lost the 1973 general election. "Even the most ardent supporter must now admit something has gone wrong," the Fianna Fail-friendly *Irish Press* editorialised the next day.

But Lynch was also looking at the longer game. "We are not for burning yet. Or, as Sean MacEntee once put it, we will not allow anyone to dance on our coffin for a long while yet," he told reporters.

****

It was just after 4.15 in the afternoon when Enda Kenny finally arrived at the count centre in Castlebar Military Barracks.

The full extent of his victory was now abundantly clear and the returning officer, Bernard Daly, had told the Fine Gael team he was ready to announce a final result and declare their man elected. Predictions of a cliffhanger count with recounts into the evening were well wide of the mark.

Enthusiastic Kenny supporters descended upon their hero just as he arrived and carried him on their shoulders into the count centre. There was wild cheering and impromptu bursts of The West's Awake.

Eight out of 10 Mayo West voters had turned out, and, of almost 30,000 votes cast, Kenny got a total of 15,584 – nicely over the quota in the first count for a very clear-cut victory.

Fine Gael had taken 53 per cent of the vote. Punters brave enough to take the bookies' 7/1 odds on a Kenny winning margin of 2,000 votes or more went home very happy indeed.

Fianna Fail's Michael Joe McGreal got 12,448, a very decent

vote, but well off the required pace. The Independent, Basil Morahan, who had started as something of a joke candidate, got a creditable 1,481 votes.

McGreal personified graciousness in defeat. "I knew Enda Kenny's father well, he was a good friend of mine. And if I were not a candidate, I honestly feel I would have put a Number 1 in the box for Enda," he said.

The Fianna Fail man, who was aged 28 to Kenny's 24 years, felt the two of them had brought something new to Mayo politics: two young candidates who had delivered a good, clean campaign.

Morahan, who had spent the earlier part of the day in his classrooms at CBS in Westport, was also gracious, admitting that since he had faced two huge party machines he would have been happy with half the vote he got.

But the Independent man could not resist also striking a sour note. He did not think it was such a clean campaign – though he acknowledged that neither Kenny nor McGreal, nor any elected politician, had been involved in the personalised attacks on him. Other party people who abused him were still party members, and not called to account by their leaders.

The hour, however, belonged to the victor. But, just seven weeks after Henry Kenny's death, this was clearly also a time of very mixed emotions for Enda Kenny, his mother, Ethna, his three brothers and his sister. "This is a vote of appreciation for my father, Henry Kenny, and an endorsement of government policy for the past two-and-a-half years," Enda Kenny said modestly.

As he had done throughout the by-election campaign, he tried to strike a balance between highlighting his father's legacy and being his own person. "I can't be Henry Kenny – I can only be myself," he told one reporter, while again echoing his father's well-worn message that he would do his best to serve all constituents, irrespective of party allegiance.

Thirty-five years later, as he reflected on that campaign, Enda Kenny could afford to be far more forthright in admitting his late father's name made him a TD.

"Over 15,000 people did not vote for me. They didn't know who I was except that I was Henry Kenny's son. They gave me the vote for the work he had done as a deputy over the years. It wasn't in respect of me as a novice, it was in respect of his legacy. I learned lessons from him – and one of them was to treat everyone the same," he recalled in 2010.

But from now on Enda Kenny was on his own, launched into the world of national and local politics – and would be judged on his own merits. The Monday after his Dail by-election win he was co-opted to his late father's seat on Mayo County Council. That piece of politics was done quietly and swiftly, in sharp contrast to the long and noisy Dail campaign.

Cllr Frank Durcan, with whom Enda Kenny would have a major acrimonious dispute some years later, proposed and Cllr Eamon Carey seconded. No councillor dissented.

Next day, Tuesday, November 18, 1975, he arrived at Leinster House with a large and happy band of supporters. Their green and red banner had The West's Awake! upon it and an even more angelic photo of their hero appended; the green and red of Mayo was proudly disported.

Taoiseach Liam Cosgrave and government chief whip John Kelly greeted them at the door of Leinster House. The supporters watched in rapture from the public gallery. The Clerk of the Dail matter-of-factly read the by-election result into the Dail record. Then the newest and youngest deputy was formally introduced to the Ceann Comhairle, Sean Treacy, before taking his back-bench seat beside Mayo West party colleague, Myles Staunton.

The Irish Times reported loud and enthusiastic applause from the government benches but noted that only John Callanan, from neighbouring Galway, clapped on the Fianna Fail side. The Fianna Fail-friendly *Irish Press* reported loud applause all round.

As a TD Enda Kenny's gross salary was to be IR£5,403 per year. He had begun his journey towards Government Buildings and the job of Taoiseach. That journey would take over 35 years to complete.

PART 2

Slow Burner Or Underachiever?

CHAPTER 4

'Purports To Be A TD'

Enda Kenny waited one year before making his first major speech in the chamber of Dail Eireann.

Indeed, for most of his early career he rarely spoke in the Dail and when he did it was, by his own admission, mainly to get his name in the local newspapers.

His preoccupation is best summed up by one short sentence which appeared in his local newspaper, *The Connaught Telegraph*, on July 7, 1976, just nine months after he became a TD.

Framed in a little box headlined 'STOP SIGN', that sentence read: "Following representations by Mr Enda Kenny TD a stop sign has been erected at Irwin's pub, Keelogues."

Kenny first entered the Dail on the afternoon of November 18, 1975, and made his maiden speech on November 10, 1976, on a measure reducing ESB charges to speed the completion of rural electrification.

The Dail record shows that his contributions were scarce during that parliament's lifetime, which ended on May 25, 1977, when Taoiseach Liam Cosgrave called what turned out to be a disastrous election.

Kenny survived the drubbing voters across the country gave his party and was re-elected for Mayo West on June 16, 1977.

But he did not rush into things after the Dail resumed on July 5. While he asked questions and contributed in passing to some debates, he made his first substantive speech in that Dail on

February 23, 1978.

Enda Kenny began that long and rambling 1978 speech by praising another future Taoiseach and future direct adversary, Bertie Ahern, who had spoken just before him. "I compliment the previous speaker on his fine delivery. I do not know whether this is his maiden speech but I congratulate him on it," Kenny said.

It was not, in fact, Bertie Ahern's first speech in the Dail. Ahern had been first elected for Dublin Fingal in the June 1977 election and made his first speech on October 26, 1977, on legislation establishing direct elections to the European Parliament. Once Charlie Haughey was elected Taoiseach in December 1979, Ahern began his slow but steady career climb.

Kenny's maiden speech in November 1976 began: "My first statement in this historic Chamber will be somewhat brief and to the point." He kept that promise: his contribution covered just one-and-a-half A4 pages, and the message was practical and addressed to his local constituency.

The legislation concerned – the Electricity Supply Amendment Bill – was a very good piece of law which had its origins in the Mayo by-election campaign in which Kenny was elected. It aimed to make the rural electrification scheme, begun 25 years earlier, finally reach remote western areas where farmers and householders were discouraged by huge cabling costs.

This law capped householders' electricity installation costs at IR£700, which could be paid off over several years. Any costs above IR£700 would be paid by the State.

Kenny noted that the measure was inspired by the Tranport and Power Minister, Peter Barry, who had gone canvassing in Bellacorick in west Mayo the previous autumn and found it without an electricity supply.

The Mayo West deputy also managed to mention several other places in his constituency.

Kenny had chosen to follow in his father's footsteps and become chiefly a local broker for the people. To borrow the words of veteran former West Cork Fine Gael TD PJ Sheehan, used to describe his own approach, Kenny was "an advocator" – he was not "a legislator".

Enda Kenny, the personable son of popular deceased local deputy Henry Kenny, was successfully digging in for the long haul as the Fine Gael TD for Mayo West. The question of aiming for higher office was for the future.

****

His second electoral outing, in June 1977, was all a long way away from his father cadging lifts while out canvassing in the mid-1950s. Mayo politics was becoming seriously professional.

Mayo West Fine Gael boasted 500 cars at their disposal on polling day for Enda Kenny's second election outing. There were up to 1,200 party workers co-ordinated from a house on Rathbawn Road in Castlebar, which had been recently bought as a permanent Fine Gael constituency headquarters.

Frank Durcan, his future sworn local rival, had taken three weeks away from the day job to ensure everything would go smoothly as he directed the campaign to re-elect Kenny and Myles Staunton of Westport. He said they could match Fianna Fail for turnout and he was putting the bright side out on the prospect of holding Fine Gael's two out of three seats.

In Dublin and across the country, Liam Cosgrave and Brendan Corish were publicly bullish about the prospects of their Fine Gael-Labour coalition getting another term. Newspaper, radio and television journalists could not see any other outcome – the government would be re-elected.

As it turned out, they were all horribly wrong. Fianna Fail skated home in the biggest landslide election win in Irish political history – a scale of reversed fortunes which would not be repeated until February 2011, when incoming Taoiseach Enda Kenny actually topped that 1977 outcome amid vastly different circumstances.

It took until late into the campaign for the outgoing coalition's stark reality to percolate down to Mayo and other parts west. Taoiseach Liam Cosgrave had surprised everyone, not least his own organisation, by calling a snap election on May 25, 1977, and fixing polling for June 16, nine months ahead of the Dail term's natural end.

At 10am on Saturday, June 4 – 10 days into the campaign – Fine Gael and Labour kingpins gathered to hear the results of their first opinion poll: Fianna Fail, 59 per cent; Fine Gael, 25 per cent, and Labour, 10 per cent. Garret FitzGerald was later quoted as asking grimly but rhetorically: "Can we un-dissolve the Dail?"

The overall outcome shocked everyone bar Fianna Fail strategists such as the late Seamus Brennan, then the party's general secretary. Fianna Fail gained 16 seats, taking them to 84 TDs; Fine Gael lost 11 seats, bringing them to 43; Labour dropped two to 17.

Cosgrave and his allies had badly miscalculated, based on the buoyancy of winning by-elections such as Enda Kenny's during their term. His campaign emphasis on economic stability and law and order against the IRA threats could not match Fianna Fail pledges to abolish domestic rates and car tax, amongst other very lavish giveaways. These bought voters' favour for Jack Lynch and Fianna Fail but they were also to start a debt spiral, bringing the country to the verge of bankruptcy within years.

Fine Gael-Labour had also wrongly counted on the so-called 'Tullymander' – a blatant gerrymander or unfair constituency redraw – named after Local Government Minister Jim Tully of Labour. Tully was reversing another constituency stitch-up attempted, with few successes, by his Fianna Fail predecessor Kevin Boland in 1969.

One good lasting outcome of all this was the handing over of constituency boundary divisions to an independent commission for the future. The combination of public reaction to two dubious constituency mapping jobs and a huge Dail majority led incoming Taoiseach Jack Lynch to feel generous enough to actually deliver an election promise and do this. In time this commission would make changes in Mayo which Kenny would have to deal with.

But the 1977 outcome was a Mayo West triumph for Enda Kenny, who topped the poll there with 29 per cent of the vote, and it set him up as a big vote-getter in his own right. He had clearly benefitted from the enormous publicity a by-election brings any successful candidate, but he had also done his local work well over the previous 18 months.

In the final campaign days, local feedback and word from Dublin headquarters led to a big Fine Gael push to bolster Kenny's vote over that of Staunton.

Myles Staunton of Westport lost his Dail seat and after that did not pose a big threat to Kenny's Fine Gael supremacy in the constituency. Staunton was first elected in 1973 ahead of Henry Kenny, and was tipped as someone with future government potential, but blocked for promotion after the 1975 by-election by the Kennys and Castlebar Fine Gael.

Staunton, who died in June 2011 aged 75, would serve in the Seanad in the late 1970s and again in the 1980s and was deemed unlucky not to take a European Parliament seat for Fine Gael in Connacht-Ulster in 1979. But he stood just once more for the Dail in June 1989, when, ironically, transfers from his 3,500 votes helped Enda Kenny get elected in a very difficult contest.

****

Garret FitzGerald did not rate Enda Kenny at all and gave him very little promotion during his decade at the helm of Fine Gael.

In Garret's voluminous memoirs, Enda Kenny gets one glancing reference and his father is not mentioned at all. Even close to the end of his life in May 2011, the long-time elder hero of Fine Gael is known to have had doubts about the man who followed in his own footsteps as party leader and eventually Taoiseach.

Garret certainly favoured and encouraged young people, and had first encountered two party stars, John Bruton and Alan

Dukes, as students at UCD. People he favoured had to come across as urbane and serious; young Enda Kenny was just too flippant and folksy.

From Enda Kenny and other Fine Gael TDs' point of view, Garret FitzGerald as party leader was an immediate consequence of the June 1977 general election meltdown. Liam Cosgrave, who had taken a fatherly interest in "young Kenny", the candidate who held Mayo West for him 18 months earlier, did not hang about.

One week after the election, at the very first Fine Gael parliamentary-party meeting to review the election reverse, Cosgrave announced that he was quitting as leader at the young political age of 57 years. The party's TDs and Senators unanimously chose Garret FitzGerald as leader on July 1, 1977.

Garret would take the party to new heights of popular support in the early 1980s and leave them at a low ebb when he departed in March 1987. But for the vast bulk of that period, Enda Kenny remained in the shadows as Garret FitzGerald served briefly as Taoiseach from June 1981 until March 1982, and again at greater length from December 1982 until March 1987.

The only semblance of promotion for Enda Kenny came in February 1986 – more than 10 years after his first election as TD – when he was made Junior Minister for Youth Affairs in what was generally perceived as a botched reshuffle by Garret FitzGerald.

But even his first promotion came as much out of a perceived threat in Mayo West from the newly formed Progressive Democrats. It was all clearly not quite how Enda Kenny and Castlebar Fine Gael stalwarts had foreseen things in the autumn of 1975 around the time of the by-election. When they blocked Myles Staunton's promotion, they expected Liam Cosgrave would be elected for at least one more term as Taoiseach and that Enda Kenny would be on his team.

But Enda Kenny successfully and quickly adjusted to backbench life. Pretty soon after first entering Dail Eireann, a nice pattern of working and living emerged for him.

He still lived at home with his widowed mother in Derrycoosh, some three miles from Castlebar, and played football with the local Islandeady side. Monday was for County Council business. Then, early on Tuesday morning, he set off for Dublin and Leinster House and returned about teatime on Thursday.

In the Dail, as we will see, the days were spent dealing with constituency correspondence and tabling questions about matters of local interest. Like his father before him, questions involved the local concerns: automation of Castlebar telephone exchange, the development of the local hospital, the future of the bacon factory and the state of local roads.

In Mayo politics he managed to avoid controversy and stand back from local polemics. When necessary, he was quite a clever self-publicist and played the local papers with skill by having the name of being available to journalists and always being friendly and polite.

The net result was that he was very frequently mentioned in low-key ways and registered his presence right across the constituency. "You had to hand it to him – he was good if you were a local reporter. Just a really nice fellow – simple as that," one veteran who reported local events in the 1970s and 1980s recalled.

At Leinster House Enda Kenny had absolutely no enemies in any party. Like his father, he moved easily with colleagues, irrespective of party membership. He managed to comfortably occupy that 'GAA political-free space' which transcends party boundaries, helped by his father's iconic football status and his own solid local club record.

He was a non-drinker when he first came to Leinster House. But that changed soon afterwards. "Nobody remembers Enda Kenny the teetotaller," one colleague said simply.

In Garret's Fine Gael he had the junior job of parliamentary party secretary, which mainly involved note-taking at the weekly TDs' and Senators' meetings. These are remembered as tense enough occasions chaired by Kilkenny veteran TD Kieran Crotty, who was no fan of Garret's.

"These meetings were at times stressful occasions for Garret," a

FG senior politician recalled.

Enda took copious notes, wrote them up and there were never any complaints about accuracy. But once that was done, he was up and out about the town with his pals on those Tuesday and Wednesday nights.

"He was a bit of a wild man and didn't bother to hide it. He enjoyed himself and he did not seem unduly bothered about what Garret thought of him. The party often concluded in some late-night haunt on Leeson Street in the very late hours. A lot of drink was taken on occasions," one contemporary commented.

Others in the company on those occasions included the late David Molony from Thurles, who had first come into Leinster House as a Senator in July 1977 and who was just months older than Kenny. On occasion they were joined by Maurice Manning, at various stages a TD and Senator as well as an accomplished academic, and by Waterford TD Austin Deasy, among others.

Deasy's political career had been enhanced by a Seanad nomination from Liam Cosgrave in 1973 and he was returned as a TD in 1977. Though Kenny was 15 years younger than Deasy, the two remained good friends for many years until the relationship cooled.

Most people agree they strongly disagreed about John Bruton's leadership of the party. Kenny was a loyal Bruton supporter but Deasy believed for a long period that the party needed a new leader.

Soon after Austin Deasy was succeeded in Waterford by his son, John, in May 2002, Enda Kenny was elected Fine Gael leader. John Deasy made Kenny's first team as Justice spokesman but soon quarrelled with his boss. He was sacked in 2004 for smoking in the Leinster House members' bar, days after the workplace smoking ban came into effect, and has remained one of Fine Gael's permanent awkward squad ever since.

There were some great excursions around the country in days when a more lax view was taken of drink-driving. Tales of these have lost nothing in the telling and retelling over the years. In one escapade, Maurice Manning drove to Castlebar to link up with Enda Kenny over a summer weekend.

Some say their ultimate plan was to go to the Rose of Tralee Festival. But in reality they had it in mind to head for West Cork. They eventually made it to Connemara, where they hooked up with Pat Lindsay, a great sociable colleague of Kenny's late father, who was living there in not-so-quiet retirement.

Days later, they still clung to the fiction of heading to the far south-west and they hit the road again. This time they made it to Lisdoonvarna in West Clare, and met Fine Gael politician and hotelier Jim White. This is where, some days after that, the excursion ended with an eventual return to Castlebar for Kenny and to Dublin for Manning.

Yet, despite a love of partying, Enda Kenny still set great store on his physical fitness.

In 1979 he was among a host of celebrities – including showband members, singing priests and politicians – who competed in the RTE Superstars to choose a candidate for a similar international competition.

The Irish contest was won outright by Kerry footballer Pat Spillane, who would win a total of eight All-Irelands and nine All-Star awards over a very accomplished career.

But Kenny distinguished himself in the 100-yard dash, in an apparent dead heat with the late Dublin Fianna Fail TD Liam Lawlor, who had played hurling with Dublin and Leinster and would later find notoriety for various other reasons. It took the RTE video footage to untangle the pair – and the winner by a whisker was Enda Kenny.

Leinster House of the 1970s and into the 1980s was a friendly and clubbable place, and Enda Kenny had picked up the local political skills from his late father to make things work on the ground. But beneath the veneer of civility, the politics of Mayo West remained very keenly contested between Fianna Fail and Fine Gael.

Fianna Fail had been rocked back on their tracks by Fine Gael's two-out-of-three win in February 1973. Fianna Fail were determined there would be no repeat and, after the arrival of Padraig Flynn restored their two seats in June 1977, a rather nasty incident occurred which showed just how bloody-minded things could get.

Immediately after the general election, while Fine Gael-Labour continued as a caretaker government, it was decided to formally open the IR£500,000 Ballyglass Pier in West Mayo and steal some last-minute glory for Fine Gael. After all, this had been one of the late Henry Kenny's pet lifetime projects and a special request from his sickbed to Taoiseach Liam Cosgrave had secured final funding for the works in autumn 1975.

When Michael Begley, the Kerry South Fine Gael man who replaced Henry Kenny as Junior Minister for Public Works, arrived to cut the tape, all but one of the Fianna Fail representatives boycotted proceedings. Fianna Fail TDs Denis Gallagher and Padraig Flynn and their party colleague, Mayo County Council chairman MJ O'Toole, refused to even talk about it.

But Fianna Fail's director of elections, Cllr Dick Morrin, had this to say: "It was another example of a discredited government running State cars into the ground to claim for posterity that they brought about this development," he said.

The Fianna Fail man acknowledged that the late Henry Kenny had made the project happen. But he found the opening ceremony had been organised with "indecent haste" to claim glory for Fine Gael.

Enda Kenny was at the opening of his father's beloved project and at a follow-up social function in the Travellers' Friend Hotel in Castlebar. But he remained tight-lipped and stayed far away from the controversy.

****

Over the years, when he felt he was in safe social company, Enda Kenny has enjoyed mimicking the extraordinary clownish

A seven-year-old Enda Kenny (right) in a photo at Cornanool National School with his two brothers Henry (10, centre) and five-year-old Kieran

Enda Kenny as a young TD in 1977

Henry Kenny, father of Enda Kenny, and *(below)* Enda with his wife Fionnuala and his mother Eithne in 1996, his 21st year in the Dail

The Taoiseach's father Henry playing football and *(inset)* Enda Kenny's grandfather James McGinley

Enda Kenny with Jack Lynch and *(below)* after his election in 1975, with Frank Durcan, Taoiseach Liam Cosgrave and John O'Donnell

The Islandeady team that won the Pete McDonnell Cup on December 29, 1974; Enda Kenny is kneeling in the front row, third from left, and *(below)* the team in 1971 with Enda Kenny in the back row, fourth from left

Enda Kenny on July 2, 2011, with his son Ferdia, after crossing the finishing line in Killarney at the annual Ring of Kerry charity cycle

Enda Kenny pictured with Rory McIlroy at the 2011 Irish Open Pro-Am in Killarney, Co Kerry

bombast of Padraig Flynn.

That June 1977 general election gave Padraig Flynn of Fianna Fail to the nation when he was elected TD for the first time, taking the third seat with 4,000 first preferences fewer than Enda Kenny. Denis Gallagher of Achill had come in second for Fianna Fail and was appointed Gaeltacht Minister by Jack Lynch.

The usually flamboyant Flynn was surprisingly matter-of-fact on the day of the 1977 count at the cramped Pavilion Ballroom in Westport and confined himself to thanking the local organisation and his running mate, Tim Quinn of Erris, whose transfers saw him home.

A few days later, Flynn treated his pupils at St Patrick's Primary School in Castlebar to lemonade and crisps as a farewell to the day job. His election had meant that all three Mayo West TDs were now former teachers.

But flamboyant Flynn was on display in all his glory on his arrival at Leinster House when the new Dail convened on July 5. The tale is best told by Frank Dunlop, then the government press secretary, and who into the future would be, like Padraig Flynn, a notorious tribunal witness and among the few to serve a jail term for his actions.

Dunlop recalls how he was with the newly crowned king of Irish politics, Taoiseach Jack Lynch, watching the drove of new Fianna Fail TDs arrive to great fanfare on that first day.

"There was a particular hullabaloo as a man in a white suit and polka-dot shirt was shouldered to the front door. 'Who in the name of God is that?' asked an incredulous Lynch. 'That', I said, 'is the one and only Padraig Flynn from Mayo,'" Dunlop told Jack Lynch.

'Pee' Flynn's sign-off in his speech at the count centre at his second election win in May 1981 was more typical of the man. "Flynn loves you all," he unashamedly told the crowd.

Dunlop's other point in telling the Dail arrival anecdote is that Lynch should have known Flynn – who had already been befriended by Lynch's foe Charlie Haughey. Lynch would soon find out how many other new backbenchers Haughey had got on side in his successful plot to become Fianna Fail leader and Taoiseach within 18 months.

The Kenny-Flynn Mayo dynamic, which lasted 15 years, is very interesting. Both Kenny and Flynn are Castlebar natives from well-known local families, and both are past pupils of St Gerald's de la Salle school, though Flynn is almost 12 years the elder.

Being in different parties meant they were always rivals rather than political enemies. But there was enough voter crossover in the constituency's main population centre, and some people within local Fine Gael often felt Kenny should have done more to challenge Flynn head-on.

"He never took Flynn on – he accepted him as part of the land-scape," a veteran Mayo Fine Gael activist said. But others concede that Flynn's huge presence within Mayo Fianna Fail helped Kenny in outlying areas.

"The 'non-Flynn Fianna Fail people' were receptive to Kenny: it helped create a favourable impression," another source noted. This was clearly demonstrated in a difficult general election for Kenny in June 1989, when transfers from a dissident former Fianna Fail candidate, Paraic Cosgrove, helped him home.

Viewed over time, Kenny was the better vote-getter – though largely because in many elections he did not have an established heavy-hitter candidate on the ticket with him. Across seven general elections, from 1977 to 1992, Flynn polled significantly more than Kenny on just one occasion.

While Flynn had 600 votes more than Kenny in the June 1989 general election, it was in November 1992 that Flynn, on 9,629 votes, had 50 per cent more than Kenny in the first count. That election is also hugely about the arrival of Kenny's Fine Gael constituency rival, Michael Ring, a constant competitor for the following 20 years.

For many years Kenny was accused of having a "one-seat men-tality" and aversion to risking his own seat to overturn Fianna Fail's two-to-one advantage. An analysis by Sean Donnelly, an expert on Irish election statistics, looked at nine general elections in Mayo West, from 1969 to 1992. Henry Kenny stood in the first two of these and his son Enda in the following seven, while Michael Ring first stood for Fine Gael in 1992, the last election examined.

Donnelly's analysis found that Fianna Fail, with an average 53 per cent, were 10 per cent ahead of Fine Gael's average. Fine Gael deprived Fianna Fail of the second seat just once over that time, in 1973, when Fianna Fail went one percentage point ahead. In that election Henry Kenny's rival, Myles Staunton, topped the poll.

Reversing Fianna Fail's two-one advantage would have taken considerable co-operation, trust and some risk for Mayo West Fine Gael. The situation changed dramatically after the 1992 general election, when the independent constituency redraw merged Mayo West and Mayo East, each with three seats, into a unitary five-seat constituency covering all of Mayo. There would follow some furious internal party struggles.

For a long time Flynn proved far shrewder than Kenny and was more successful in getting political promotion, though his hand was strengthened by Fianna Fail getting and keeping the two Dail seats. Flynn also clinically switched to the right side when it counted. Even before he was elected a TD, he backed Charlie Haughey in his successful conspiracies against Jack Lynch; later he threw in his lot with Albert Reynolds and helped oust Haughey.

Flynn was appointed a junior minister in March 1980, having to wait three months after Charlie Haughey's election as Taoiseach for legislation to expand the junior ranks from 10 to 15. He was a senior minister in all subsequent Fianna Fail-led governments.

Two years before Kenny finally got full ministerial rank, in December 1994, Flynn was ensconced in the lucrative and prestigious post of EU Commissioner in Brussels, and he still remains the longest-serving Irish nominee in that position.

But there is another crucial difference between these two Castlebar politicians. The Mahon Tribunal findings were scathing about Padraig Flynn, causing him the most profoundly serious reputational damage.

In March 2012, the Mahon Tribunal ruled that when Flynn was a government minister in the summer of 1989 he had "wrongly and corruptly" solicited a IR£50,000 donation for Fianna Fail from a property developer. The Tribunal said Flynn subsequently used this money for his own benefit, and dismissed as incredible and untrue Flynn's own explanations about money in overseas bank accounts.

No allegation of corruption – even to the smallest degree – has ever been made against Enda Kenny.

It is also possible to invoke a certain hare-and-tortoise analogy when comparing the Kenny and Flynn political trajectories. By autumn 2012, both Flynn and his daughter, Beverley, who succeeded to the 'Flynnasty', had gone from public life.

And Enda Kenny was Taoiseach.

****

If you ever wondered what a TD does all day at Leinster House, read Enda Kenny's account of it all. What emerges is rather banal.

Speaking about Dail reform in February 1983, he gave a very honest and frank view of his work as a country TD. He said TDs came to Leinster House with varying degrees of ambition – but once elected they all shared the desire to get re-elected.

He remembered a fellow TD putting a small transistor radio to his ear while walking through the Dail lobby to vote. "He said he hoped to hear on the 6.30 news what was going on in the Dail," Kenny said.

Then, in his eighth year as a member of Dail Eireann, he frankly conceded that he and his colleagues often had no idea what they were voting for. There were dozen of votes – and it was not always possible to keep up with the detail of all of them.

He also quite openly said that for a rural TD to stay in business it was vital, above all else, to be seen in the local papers as going about their constituents' concerns.

"One of the reasons for a rural Deputy speaking at all in the House is that he has the opportunity of sending details of his contributions to local papers, thereby keeping his name before the people he represents. This enables constituents to read what their Deputy has been advocating," he told the Dail.

For the rest, it was largely a question of getting those letters about everyday bread-and-butter issues out to the potential voters.

"We might ask what the ordinary backbencher does in relation to his membership of Dail Eireann. He comes here every Tuesday morning with a briefcase full of correspondence. This correspondence relates to such items as medical cards, dentures, hip replacement operations, land division, blocked drains, potholes in the roads and so on," he told the Dail.

"During the three days he spends here, the Deputy writes about these various matters to the people on the Front Bench and receives an acknowledgment, which he then passes to the relevant person at home. He will say that he had a letter from his TD but that the potholes, for instance, are still in the road."

"The Deputy gets in touch with the county manager, who says there is no money to carry out the work concerned. In turn, the case is put to the Minister for Finance through the Department of the Environment but the potholes remain in the road," he continued.

It was a very plain-speaking outline of the old dichotomy for TDs. Do the big-picture national thing and lose your Dail seat? Or stay local and pursue constituents' everyday demands and keep that Dail seat? And if you have chosen the local survival route – how do you cut a national dash and show you are ministerial material?

To illustrate his arguments, Enda Kenny cited the case of former

Labour TD Justin Keating, who had been Industry Minister in the Fine Gael-Labour 1973-77 Coalition, and had campaigned strongly in the by-election which saw Kenny enter public life.

"I have much respect for a former minister, Mr Justin Keating. I spent many hours listening to him speak here. One of the reasons for his not being returned here was his concentration on his ministerial duties.

"This meant that he was not available to answer the everyday whim and call concerning all the little problems in his constituency. Deputies are between two minds: whether to try to become effective legislators or to give a social service second to none," Kenny argued.

That February 1983 debate was presided over by John Bruton, who, as well as being Minister for Industry and Energy at that time, was also given the title Leader of the House and had special responsibility for Dail reform. Bruton had been blamed for causing the fall of FitzGerald's first government in late January 1982 over his proposed VAT levy on children's shoes.

He could not be Finance Minister again in FitzGerald's second government and was given charge of Dail reform as a sop to make his cabinet posting look more impressive. But that evening Bruton, clearly enjoying himself, offered a remedy for the potholes.

"Fill them up with Tayto," the future Fine Gael leader and Taoiseach quipped.

Kenny conceded his frustration at the Dublin Independent TD, the late Tony Gregory, getting so much media attention for simply not wearing a tie in the Dail.

"I suppose that if somebody were to arrive in a tracksuit he, too, would be given attention by the media," he remarked, quite correctly.

But Kenny also let the cat out of the bag about some of the showbiz attached to Dail business. "If a Deputy wishes to be put out of the House, he will probably talk to the Chair beforehand and tell him that he intended to create a racket and wished to be thrown out," he confessed.

That would play well in the newspapers and impress many constituents that he was fighting the good fight for them. But it undermined the Dail's role as national law-maker.

"That is the kind of procedure that we have had for a long time so that one's role as an effective legislator has been diminished by the antics of the House," he commented.

Kenny noted that tabling Dail questions on a particular issue to the relevant minister was a good option for an ordinary TD. The replies were, however, framed by civil servants and the Minister's aim was to give the least possible information to the opposition deputies.

But he then let slip another political trick of the trade. "If he is a good minister, he will have phoned the government deputy telling him his opposition colleague has asked a question and he will tell him the answer he is giving," Kenny added. The government TD would be sworn to secrecy about the source of his information but free to use it as he wished.

Minister Bruton reacted to this piece of honesty-in-dishonesty with a home truth of his own.

"Deputy Kenny will not get any more phone calls," he commented.

"Telephone calls are welcome," Kenny replied, signalling that while he was blowing the gaff on the game, he was still prepared to play along with it.

He said it was time to modernise Dail procedures and John Bruton, with his knowledge of international parliamentary best practice, was well fixed to do this.

Lengthy and repetitive Dail debates after the Budget, spread over several weeks, were no good. Kenny felt it would be better to have such debates before the Budget was framed – another bright idea which would sink totally without trace.

Kenny also believed that there was too much time-wasting correspondence being shunted about and things had become too bureaucratic.

Broadcasting Dail debates would help inform the public but

some handicap system would have to be worked out to ensure good media performers did not get more than their share of the limelight.

All in all, it was a good speech with a dangerously honest and accurate description of daily political life in Ireland as it was then, and largely remains to this day.

But Enda Kenny had another interesting matter to deal with in that speech. He wanted to give a good political kicking to journalist and commentator Vincent Browne. He had been waiting in the long grass for Browne for over a year.

****

The Vincent Browne versus Enda Kenny row has lasted 30 years, culminating in Kenny's refusal to appear on Browne's television programme in the run-up to the 2011 general election and the 2012 EU Fiscal Treaty Referendum.

"I will not participate on any programme that Vincent Browne has anything to do with," Enda Kenny said emphatically in February 2011.

Like the old theme tune says: 'It started on the Late Late Show', presented by Gay Byrne.

On Saturday evening, January 16, 1982, the pair were among a large number of guests involved in a political discussion on RTE's Late Late Show which had huge viewing figures. The very bruising debate lasted over 70 minutes, excluding two commercial breaks, and resulted in the phone switchboard being jammed with calls.

The state of Ireland then has depressing echoes of the situation in 2012. The country was broke and runaway government borrowing was making things worse; unemployment was high and would have been higher had it not been for emigration. Inflation was above 20 per cent.

If all that was not bad enough, unbeknownst to most people that evening, Garret FitzGerald's Fine Gael-Labour government would fall just 11 days later over that ill-starred John Bruton Budget and its planned VAT levy on children's shoes. That collapse would bring the second of three elections in the politically chaotic 18 months between May 1981 and November 1982.

Perhaps there was a clue in the item on Part One of that evening's Late Late Show: writer Anthony Burgess discussing James Joyce's influences on A Clockwork Orange, his book which had became notorious across the globe after the controversial movie version by Stanley Kubrick. A comic musical interlude from the duo Musical Therapy appears to have been no help in calming things for the political discussion which filled the remainder of the programme.

Vincent Browne, known more recently for his late-night robust discussion show on TV3, was then a well-known print journalist. He had successfully launched *Magill* current-affairs magazine and was trying to take over the *Sunday Tribune* newspaper with, as things turned out, financial backing from Ryanair founder Tony Ryan.

Browne's ability to irritate politicians was as good then as now, and was heightened by politicians' knowledge that he had been a Fine Gael activist at UCD in the 1960s. In fact, for a time he edited a Fine Gael newspaper, *The Citizen*, as one of his early jobs in journalism.

Speculation about Browne and Fine Gael would recur more than 10 years later. In the spring of 1994, as Browne was between jobs after losing the editorship of the *Sunday Tribune*, there was again speculation that he would stand for Fine Gael in European Parliament elections in Dublin. All of the main parties at that time were seeking big-name parachute candidates and the reports concerning Browne and Fine Gael caused considerable tensions inside the party.

This ended when Fine Gael Dublin director of elections Richard Bruton issued a statement saying Vincent Browne would not be seeking a Euro nomination due to "personal and career reasons". It is also worth noting in that regard that ministers in two

Fine Gael-led governments and one Fianna Fail administration had authorised taps on Vincent Browne's telephone.

But back in the early 1980s, many politicians found Browne's new style of full-on-attack journalism difficult and they liked to say he was a "disappointed politician". During the course of tough exchanges on this particular Late Late Show, Fianna Fail's Flor Crowley, who was seated close to Enda Kenny, took that tack.

"Hell hath no fury like a rejected politician – which Vincent Browne is," Crowley said. Browne dismissed this and other attacks as "simply a diversionary tactic".

Appropriately enough, the programme producers gave Browne a soapbox as he issued a blistering four-minute tirade against reckless and irresponsible politicians who had brought the country to the brink of ruin through rampant borrowing to fund false election promises. The economic journalist Paul Tansey and economist Sean Barrett were in the audience to offer guidance on facts and figures.

There was a very wide selection of politicians present, spanning all parties plus town and country. They were seated in both the audience and the panellists' space, which added further verve to proceedings.

There were many characters who loomed large across several generations of Irish public life.

Fianna Fail had Bertie Ahern of Dublin Central; Paddy Power and Charlie McCreevy of Kildare; Jim Gibbons from Carlow-Kilkenny; Eileen Lemass of Dublin West, and Flor Crowley from Cork South West.

Fine Gael had Nora Owen, Dublin North; Tom Enright, Laois-Offaly; Richie Ryan, Dublin South West; Sean Barrett, Dun Laoghaire; Brendan Griffin of Tipperary South; Michael Noonan, Limerick East and Enda Kenny of Mayo West.

Labour had Ruairi Quinn of Dublin South East and John Ryan of Tipperary North. Jim Kemmy of the short-lived Democratic Socialist Party from Limerick East was also there.

A curious feature of the programme was that Bertie Ahern did not utter a single word and he was not called upon to do so. The future Taoiseach, looking very serious but somehow hidden-in-plain-view, remained seated beside Labour's Ruairi Quinn, who made frequent and long contributions from the second row of the audience.

Given that huge cast of politicians, it is not surprising that it took beyond the half-way mark before Enda Kenny got a chance to speak.

But he gave Browne both barrels, accusing him of "verbal butchery", of calling politicians "all sorts of hoodlums" and of fuelling public cynicism with his destructive journalism.

Kenny said he had quite some time ago invited Browne to come and tour his constituency with him. "He refused to accept that challenge in order to acquaint himself with the challenges we face as practical politicians."

As TD for Mayo West, Kenny returned to a tricky local and national issue referred to earlier in discussions: his own government colleagues' failure to finance Knock Airport, on his own doorstep. Kenny had suffered politically on this issue and would again.

"It wasn't the first unpopular decision we had to take and it probably won't be the last one," Kenny told the Late Late Show studio and home audience.

"The traditional role of coalition governments is to clean up after Fianna Fail governments. It may well be the case again. I don't know," Kenny added.

He said there was an urgent need to reform the Dail and make it a more effective law-maker and public-spending watchdog.

Browne replied that he had no need to visit a rural constituency with Kenny – he came from one himself. "That point hardly suffices," Browne said dismissively.

There followed some rather personalised barracking of Browne by Fianna Fail's Flor Crowley. Then Browne said he would respond to both Kenny and Crowley together.

"Since these people were last elected by the electorate, Enda Kenny has not spoken in a single debate in that active time. And he is now representing himself as a serious politician concerned about these issues. Well, the public can judge for themselves," Browne remarked.

He added that Crowley had spoken a handful of times, urging more spending on constituency projects but never saying where the funding would come from.

Host Gay Byrne then extended Kenny a right of reply.

"I have already said the role of the TD is very much diminished because it really is pointless, in many cases, speaking on Bills that are going through the system – because the Bill is drafted in advance before we ever see it," Kenny argued.

Kenny said a TD's Dail contributions were rarely listened to and the only reason for speaking in the Dail was to relay a message to the constituents via the local newspapers. The only other use for TDs' Dail speeches was to allow people like Vincent Browne to count their frequency and size.

"But you don't speak at all. You don't speak at all!" Browne boomed back.

****

It was a very unpleasant experience for Enda Kenny, to be humiliated on prime-time television by Vincent Browne. But he kept his counsel and, probably because Browne was by now a rival publisher, there was a very limited take-up in the newspapers beyond some passing references.

The item was given the-then ritual 'Ballymagash' denunciation at a meeting of Westport Urban District Council a fortnight later, where Browne was dubbed "a pup" and Gay Byrne accused of being an unfair chairman.

Even Fianna Fail members joined local upcoming Fine Gael town councillor Michael Ring – a future tough internal Mayo Kenny rival – in defending Enda Kenny.

Locally, the view was that Browne did not really count on the western seaboard as his publications' sales were largely based around the greater Dublin area. Kenny's pride was hurt, but his local political standing was unharmed and he and his political allies kept their own counsel.

One local Castlebar journalist, Sean Rice, writing in *The Connacht Tribune*, saw the Fianna Fail backing on Westport Urban District Council for Kenny as very helpful since there was a general election campaign in full flight by then. The writer concluded that, after seven years, while some of the youthful gloss was inevitably fading from Enda Kenny, he was still a strong vote-getter.

That prediction was totally correct. Kenny proved to be a poll-topper in both the February and November 1982 general elections in Mayo West, with a quarter of the first-preference vote on each occasion. Gratifyingly for him and the local Fine Gael support, he was nicely ahead of Fianna Fail's two standard bearers, Denis Gallagher and Padraig Flynn, and he coped with the consequences of his party's rebuff to the Knock Airport project.

But Enda Kenny had not forgotten the Late Late Show attack by Vincent Browne. Kenny's final message in that Dail reform debate – 13 months after the RTE show – clearly shows that.

"I remember having the doubtful fortune of appearing on a well-known television programme where a well-known journalist said of me: 'This guy purports to be a Deputy, but he did not even speak in that Dail.' That Dail only lasted for a short time, but the journalist was right: I did not speak in this fashion in the chamber during that Dail.

"I thank the journalist for pointing this out in his own way. Indeed, I go further and remind him of my invitation to a week of travel around a rural constituency to see how TDs live and operate, which challenge has not yet been accepted.

"If he wants to accept it and give a full report in that well-run magazine and all the publicity which he wants, I will pay him royalties."

Thus Kenny concluded – for the moment – in his ongoing tussles with Vincent Browne.

****

Charlie Haughey, Garret FitzGerald's nemesis, always liked Enda Kenny. He saw him as a decent young man who never posed the slightest threat.

Haughey enjoyed playing the Mayo card occasionally, citing family and personal links there among his claim to a host of counties, which also included Dublin, Derry and Kerry. In fact Haughey was born in Castlebar in 1925 and his family lived there until he was four years old.

But this link was enough for him to receive Mayoman of the Year in 1978 from the influential Mayo Association in Dublin. Through the late 1970s and 1980s Padraig Flynn revelled in welcoming 'The Boss' to Mayo, shamelessly declaring him as one of their own.

Enda Kenny's grand-aunt, a Mrs Minch from Castlebar, delivered Charlie Haughey as well as Enda's father, Henry Kenny. Haughey was first elected to the Dail in 1957, three years after Henry Kenny's arrival, and the pair always enjoyed a cordial but casual friendliness.

But Haughey really got on good terms with Enda Kenny when they were both working on Taoiseach Garret FitzGerald's New Ireland Forum, which brought nationalists from all over the island together in efforts to break the logjam in the continuing violence and strife in Northern Ireland.

Enda Kenny was one of the seven Fine Gael delegates to the Forum – one of the first signs of any kind of preferment from Garret. Its sessions ran from May 1983 to February 1984, and Charlie Haughey took to giving Enda Kenny a lift in the State car he had as former Taoiseach when they were dashing from Dail sittings at Leinster House to forum sessions in Dublin Castle.

The good relations with Haughey were extremely useful to Enda Kenny. Some time later, a west of Ireland Fianna Fail TD complained to Haughey about potential confidentiality breaches associated with his press officer, Fionnuala O'Kelly, who was dating Enda Kenny of Fine Gael.

"But Haughey deployed his best vernacular to tell him precisely where to go," a Leinster House official of the period recalled. That attitude helped the couple continue a relationship which would result in their marriage in January 1992.

The New Ireland Forum's operations were the cause of Garret FitzGerald's rather glancing memoir reference to Enda Kenny. On page 488 of his 1992 autobiography, All In A Life, Garret recalls that his party delegation felt in March 1984 that Fianna Fail were getting too much of their own way in shaping the final draft report.

"Ivan Yates said our 'bottom line' had now been reached, and Enda Kenny told me that Fianna Fail now viewed me with contempt," FitzGerald wrote. Unsurprisingly, he felt that Fianna Fail could be overcome by SDLP support for Fine Gael's and Labour's view of the world and was eventually proved correct.

Enda Kenny enjoyed working on the Northern Ireland issue and struck up a good social relationship with many of the participants, especially those in the SDLP, which was then the biggest nationalist party in the North. In January 1985 Kenny was among a group who travelled to the USA, to Warrentown in Virginia, for an important seminar on the North.

It was remarkable for the presence of Northern Unionists, most notably Ian Paisley's deputy leader, Peter Robinson, and resulted in some frank personal discussions on potential ways forward. Charlie Haughey had officially snubbed the event because he disapproved of the Irish-American organiser's criticisms of Fianna Fail.

Fianna Fail's Des O'Malley and Mary Harney attended 'in a private capacity' – a move which was later seen as highly symbolic when the breakaway Progressive Democrats were launched late that same year. But those among the Fine Gael group remember the great rapport between Enda Kenny and SDLP politician Seamus Mallon.

"The pair spent a lot of time socialising together and hit it off.

Mallon dubbed Enda Kenny 'Young Lochinvar' – the dashing cavalier celebrated in Walter Scott's epic poem," one veteran politician recalled. The poem is out of fashion these days – but it tells the breathless tale of daring Young Lochinvar stopping a church marriage ceremony and rescuing his true love from an arranged match.

After a decade in politics, Enda Kenny was an established TD – but promotion was slow in coming. Against that, he was having fun, and his relationship with his girlfriend, Fionnuala O'Kelly, was becoming more serious.

CHAPTER 5

Love Across Enemy Lines

In June 1981, Padraig Flynn predictably named Pope John Paul II as the person he would most like to meet. But Enda Kenny picked "my future wife" as top of his wish list.

These little revelations came in election-time newspaper pen pictures which were a mix of the banal, the twee and the pious. Pee Flynn's favourite food was Black Magic chocolates, Enda Kenny's was steak; Flynn was most influenced by Eamon de Valera, Kenny by his own father, Henry; each of them had an ambition to serve the people of Mayo to the fullest extent.

But one way or another Enda Kenny, now aged 30 and beginning to be cited on magazine 'eligible bachelor' lists, was about to meet his future life partner. The way he has since told it, retold it, told it again, and then retold it again, he was unexpectedly struck by Cupid's arrow in the most unlikely place: the chamber of Dail Eireann.

"I was in the Dail chamber one day, doing my constitutional duty, standing up and speaking about something or other, and I saw this apparition on the press gallery, dressed in blue with long chestnut hair, and I said to myself: 'Jesus, who is she?'

"I was in a considerable state of anxiety for some time afterwards – and here we are," Enda Kenny said more than 25 years later, going from dramatic love at first sight to fast-forward into long-time marriage.

The "apparition" was Fionnuala O'Kelly, a newly appointed

Fianna Fail press officer, and soon to be a valued adviser to Charlie Haughey. Some six years later she would be appointed head of the-then Government Information Service.

Enda Kenny had fallen for one of the 'enemy'. But it would take the two of them 10 more years to make it to the altar after an on-off courtship which they believed was largely clandestine.

"Of course, I thought it was a great secret. But it was the worst-kept secret in the country at the time," Fionnuala O'Kelly recalled in an engaging joint interview she and Enda Kenny gave to radio presenter Matt Cooper in January 2007.

In the summer of 1990, nine years after starting with Fianna Fail, she decided to take a job as RTE head of public relations and she went to Taoiseach Charlie Haughey to tell him.

"Is this anything to do with young Kenny?" she recalled Charlie Haughey asking her.

"And he did say to me: 'Well, you needn't go, you know. You can marry him and stay here.' I have to say, he was very good to me," she recalled.

So, what did Fine Gael think of one of their TDs dating one of the 'other crowd'?

"Well, love works in strange ways," Enda Kenny dodged.

If our romantic drama were set in more recent times, Enda Kenny might have been spared an 'enemy thunderbolt', at least inside the Dail chamber of love. For many years now, press officers are not allowed on the Dail gallery – it is restricted to accredited journalists only.

****

Fionnuala O'Kelly, who is almost six years younger than her husband, grew up on Blackheath Avenue in the prosperous and confident Dublin suburb of Clontarf. Her mother was Eileen O'Hanrahan, a Dubliner who worked as a civil servant until forced to resign on marriage – according to the regulation in force at that time.

Eileen O'Hanrahan was one of four children, two of whom entered the religious life. Her sister, Breda, became a nun with the St Louis order, while her brother Patrick Joseph became a Redemptorist missionary priest in Brazil, later ordained bishop, and known in family circles as Bishop Joseph.

As Bishop Patricio Jose Hanrahan he distinguished himself in defending poor local farmers in their agitation for land reforms in the vast Brazilian diocese of Santissima Conceicao do Araguaia. He fended off Vatican criticisms of his priests' so-called 'political work' and was famously described by Pope John Paul II as "the Irishman who is more Brazilian than the Brazilians themselves".

He died in contentious circumstances in Brazil in May 1993, with his body later exhumed to test unproven suspicions he might have been poisoned. Colleagues remember him as an able and very courageous man. The suspicions remain unproven.

The youngest member of the O'Hanrahan family was Stiofan B, known to the family as Breandan, who was a lecturer in Irish at St Patrick's Teacher Training College in Drumcondra. One Enda Kenny, the future husband of his niece, was among his students in the years 1968-70.

Fionnuala's father, Sean, was also a civil servant from the townland of Knockataggle, in Kilcummin parish just five miles from Killarney, and where his brother had continued to run the family farm. Sean Kelly, as he was known in Kerry, maintained strong links with his original home. Echoing the Henry Kenny story, in his younger days he sometimes took the late-night mail train out of Dublin to go back to Kerry and play football with his local club, cycling the final 40-mile leg of the journey from Mallow.

In Dublin he played Gaelic football with the Civil Service club, where teammates included future Fianna Fail Taoiseach Jack Lynch. He got a late call-up to the Kerry senior team and figured in their 1953 All-Ireland win, and again lined out in the 1954 final, which they lost.

Sean Kelly was very successful in his job and rose to be Secretary of the Department of Posts and Telegraphs, based in the

GPO. Eventually, he led the Department break-up, with the creation in 1984 of two semi-state firms, An Post and Telecom Eireann, and then took early retirement. He never owned a car and either cycled or walked each day between home and work, a round trip of almost seven miles.

Fionnuala was the third in a family of seven, five girls and two boys. All were part of the link with Kerry, enjoying long summer holidays in a house retained by their father at Knockataggle. Here they played with their seven first cousins and later joined in saving turf, haymaking and other farm work.

Over the years there has been some banter between the Kerry branch of the family, known as Kelly, and the Dublin branch, which preferred O'Kelly. In fact, Fionnuala O'Kelly's father was a man of at least three names: Sean Kelly in Kerry and on the football fields; Sean O Ceallaigh as a senior civil servant; and finally Sean O'Kelly in everyday and family life around Dublin.

It is also notable that her mother preferred O'Hanrahan, while her uncle Bishop Joseph was always known as Hanrahan and her other uncle, Stiofan B or Breandan, always used the Gaelic form, O Hannrachain. Perhaps the best way of describing this variable issue of names is to note that on his daughter's wedding certificate he is recorded as 'Sean O'Kelly'. She is recorded as marrying 'James Enda Martin Kenny'.

One of the Kerry cousins was young Sean Kelly, the future GAA president and ultimately a Fine Gael member of the European Parliament. They have all maintained the Kerry connection. Fionnuala's younger brother, Brian, went as a boarder to St Brendan's College, Killarney, and when Sean Kelly went to do teacher training in Dublin he was a frequent visitor to Blackheath Avenue, Clontarf.

When the young bachelor Sean Kelly got around to building his own house in Killarney, Fionnuala chose the fitted kitchen for him. "She did a good job, too, because when I got married a few years afterwards, Juliette thought the kitchen was class," Sean Kelly recalled in his 2007 memoir, Rule 42 And All That.

As we have already noted, Fionnuala and her own family now holiday at their father's Kerry home each summer. Friends often refer to her as a "Dublin Kerrywoman" and the Taoiseach has made inroads into Kerry social life.

****

She answered an anonymous newspaper advertisement in the summer of 1981, placed by a "national organisation" based in the Dublin 2 area. Fionnuala O'Kelly was fresh from college, with an MA in French and a diploma in European studies.

The advertisement turned out to be for Fianna Fail, who were seeking a press officer. Though she was aged 25, it was her first real job and, by her own version of events, she knew nothing much about party politics.

"I'd never even met a politician at that point. But from the first day I went there, I loved it. Whatever about the weaknesses of politicians, by and large they are fun people, and Leinster House had a kind of college-campus atmosphere," she recalled for *The Irish Times* in 2009.

It is probable that she knew more of politics than she admits, perhaps even to herself. In April 2007 she said her father, as eventually the most senior civil servant in the Department of Posts and Telegraphs, had dealt personally with ministers from Fianna Fail, Fine Gael and Labour.

"He liked and respected some more than others. But we were a kind of neutral house, politically," she told TV3.

Clearly Fionnuala learned very quickly, and was soon working closely with some of the gurus in the trade, notably PJ Mara, Charlie Haughey's press officer, and then Charlie himself, who happened to be one of her family's local Dublin North Central TDs.

By any standards her debut in the engine room of Ireland's biggest political organisation was a complete baptism of fire as the country was broke and in huge political turmoil. In the year after she joined Fianna Fail, there were two quick-fire general elections, one of which Charlie Haughey won and unseated Fine Gael-Labour; in the other, Garret FitzGerald ousted Haughey as Taoiseach. She also served through the June 1985 local elections, the February 1987 general election and the June 1989 general election campaign.

During her term at the Fianna Fail press wheel there was also a referendum on divorce in June 1986 and another on the EU Single Market in May 1987. On both these issues Haughey adopted an obstructive stance, only belatedly coming on board for the EU issue after winning power in February 1987, and allowing Fianna Fail to unofficially sabotage Garret FitzGerald's efforts to bring in divorce.

But what really characterised the politics early in that period were the three vicious internal heaves against Haughey's leadership of Fianna Fail: in February 1982, Des O'Malley made a half-hearted attempt; in October 1982, Charlie McCreevy mounted a challenge, and in February 1983, a large group of anti-Haugheyites had another go.

Haughey saw off all of these challenges and confounded media pundits who predicted his defeat – but at the cost of utterly poisonous relations within a very riven party.

Fionnuala O'Kelly also served through the split in Fianna Fail which saw Des O'Malley and Mary Harney form the Progressive Democrats in December 1985. And she was close to the smoke-filled rooms when her boss cut a coalition deal with his old foe O'Malley in July 1989, breaking Fianna Fail's core value of never sharing power in government.

That Fianna Fail-Progressive Democrat coalition saw her continue in Government Buildings as head of the Government Information Service. PJ Mara continued as government press secretary along with Stephen O'Byrnes, who was the Progressive Democrats nominee to the press service. Her move to a public relations job with RTE in July 1990 came after Charlie Haughey's very successful 1990 EU presidency.

"In nine years she saw as much raw, gut politics close up as many a veteran politician would see in a lifetime. Those lessons she learned were invaluable when it came to helping her husband, especially helping him to fend off a leadership heave years later," one former colleague summed up.

The recurring strife within Fianna Fail, which often became naked hatred and then open warfare, did sometimes take a toll on her.

One friend recalls Enda risking a diplomatic incident one particularly fraught evening by arriving Sir Galahad-like at the Fianna Fail press office to whisk her off and help her try to forget it all for a short while.

Political journalists of that era remember Fionnuala O'Kelly as shrewd, efficient and good-humoured. "She didn't preach the party line but managed to keep the bright side out when her boss was embroiled in controversies," one political writer recalled.

"The key thing about her was that she kept channels of communication open between Fianna Fail and the media at times when relations were very bad indeed on both sides. She usually got you the reaction or the line in good time," the writer added.

Her good looks, glamour and easy manner were a big help in dealing with the largely male group of journalists, politicians and officials. Charlie Haughey certainly had an eye for a good-looking woman but he also appreciated that she was street-smart and had natural political nous.

Another journalist of that era recalls that Haughey made his high regard for her quite plain.

"I remember at one Ogra Fianna Fail function in Malahide, Charlie grudgingly and morosely presided at a lunch for the press, whom he detested. There was no alcohol on the table and Charlie kept sipping tea. Suddenly, he turned very pointedly to Fionnuala and said: 'Would you like a glass of wine, Fionnuala?'

"She said: 'Ah no, boss, I'm staying off it at the moment.' There was no tension whatever – there was clear mutual regard," the journalist recalled.

Another veteran journalist recalled her carefully setting up a standing ovation for Haughey after he addressed another Ogra Fianna Fail conference. "It's good for his ego," she joked afterwards, when some journalists teased her about it.

PJ Mara, as Haughey's key press advisor, did all the heavy lifting in media handling through the confrontation years. But Fionnuala was relied upon as sound back-up and trusted with considerable access. It is very hard to find anyone from that era with something bad to say about her.

"The key thing about her was that she was smart, efficient and well able to express herself on paper and orally. She was trusted and popular with the party front bench and the generality of the parliamentary party," another senior colleague recalled.

In the middle of the 1980s, PJ Mara spent a lot of time and effort trying to reshape Haughey's media profile, with some considerable success. Party insiders believe that Fionnuala O'Kelly's presence and involvement were a help.

She has many times spoken in public of Haughey's professional and personal kindness and she joined her husband, who was by then Fine Gael leader, at her old boss's burial in St Fintan's Cemetery in Sutton in June 2006. "I was genuinely very fond of him and of his family," she later recalled.

Her husband likes to point out that she was among the few to stand up to Charlie Haughey, who could be infamously irascible at work.

Former Fianna Fail general secretary Pat Farrell once summed up how he sought to deal with Haughey. "I always said to myself: be focused, be brief, be gone."

But Enda Kenny has on a couple of occasions told how Fionnuala O'Kelly once threw a file at Haughey after one of his celebrated outbursts – and eventually got an apology from him, a very rare occurrence.

To this day, Kenny likes to highlight his wife's Haughey and Fianna Fail link, partly out of mischief, but also to play it as an advantage.

Accompanied by journalists on the canvass trail in Meath in April 2007 he expressed his delight when a woman told him the dog she was walking was named Charlie.

"Well, now I want you to meet the original Charlie's angel," he said, pointing over to his wife.

He could not resist a jocose reference even on the day he was finally elected Taoiseach, March 9, 2011. In a generous Dail speech, Fianna Fail leader Micheal Martin added a warm note of personal congratulation to Fionnuala O'Kelly, as a former Fianna Fail press officer. "Were she still with Fianna Fail, it might be in a much stronger position today," the new Taoiseach replied, less than graciously.

In that joint radio interview with Matt Cooper in January 2007, she faced questions about Charlie Haughey's controversial money dealings and how she now viewed her old employers, Fianna Fail. Some of the party back-room people felt Cooper was pushing into subjects which were not agreed in advance. But the interview was just weeks after publication of the Moriarty Tribunal Report, which contained very damning findings against Haughey.

"On a professional and personal level, Charlie Haughey was very good to me and, as I say, was very good about my relationship with Enda. But I have to say I was also appalled when I read the reports of the Moriarty Tribunal," she said.

"My function was the press and I dealt with that. It wasn't my place to go beyond that. I did have my suspicions and I did ask people about the source of his wealth. They said: 'Oh well, he did very good land deals in the Sixties and Seventies.' I suppose I was very young and very naive," she continued.

"I think there are lessons to be learned. There are people whose responsibility it was to ensure these things didn't happen and I think they fell down as well. This was the culture at the time and an awful lot of people fell down in their job," Fionnuala argued.

But she insisted that she could not comment on Fianna Fail after Haughey and would not be drawn on questions of whether she thought there was still corruption in the organisation. "I'm out of Fianna Fail more than 16 years," she replied.

Her remedy for avoiding future corruption and skulduggery came as no surprise. "The one thing I will say is that if Enda Kenny is Taoiseach nothing like that will ever happen."

****

Enda Kenny tells of his first sighting of his future wife as a tale of 'coup de foudre', or thunderbolt. Fionnuala O'Kelly's version is only fractionally less dramatic.

She remembers giving out Fianna Fail news releases on the Dail press gallery and glancing down at Enda Kenny, who was speaking. "He winked up at me. I was mortified ... I nearly fell out over the gallery, so I did," she recalled in another joint interview, this time in April 2007 with journalist Ursula Halligan on TV3.

By then she knew well who he was, as she had spent her early months at Leinster House rechecking the politicians she encountered against their photographs and short profiles in the political bible, Nealon's Guide. But despite the mutual impact, it took them several months to finally get together, though they did exchange a few occasional sociable words.

She recalls another conversation with her future husband, in late January 1982, just after the government dramatically fell over Fine Gael-Labour Budget plans to tax children's shoes. "He said: 'If I hold my seat I'm going to ask you out when I come back.' But he took his time about it – it took him about another three months," Fionnuala O'Kelly recalled.

By her own account the fateful evening was May 26, 1982, and she was very down after a by-election count which had gone disastrously wrong for Fianna Fail. Her boss Charlie Haughey had barely won a general election in February 1982, and, in efforts to boost his slim Dail majority, persuaded the Dublin West Fine Gael TD and former European Commissioner, Dick Burke, to return to Brussels as Ireland's Commissioner.

110

Haughey had to win the resultant by-election but Fine Gael won against the odds, with Liam Skelly defeating Eileen Lemass. Fionnuala O'Kelly had been involved in the campaign, and after the result that evening she was heading out the Leinster House back gate intent on going straight home to bed.

But she bumped into Maurice Manning, a Fine Gael TD and UCD lecturer whom she had known from her time studying at Belfield. He persuaded her to join a group of his party colleagues drinking in O'Donoghue's pub on nearby Merrion Row.

The group included Ivan Yates and his future wife, Deirdre, Sean Barrett and Enda Kenny. She remembered later that the latter managed to make her laugh, cheered her up, and soon they were going on regular dates.

After going out together for quite some time – secretly, as they thought – they separated for a period.

"It was off for a while and I was seeing other people, and I found myself thinking, 'They're not half as funny or interesting,'" she recalled.

But the need for discretion and secrecy did add spice early on. "It was almost like an affair, except no-one else was involved," she added.

In 1987 another young Fine Gael politician, Senator Gerry Reynolds from Co Leitrim, started going out with Fionnuala O'Kelly's Fianna Fail press office colleague and friend, Sinead Gorby. "Now the two couples were ducking and diving and meeting in secret. It was comedy. They were seen together by other politicians and journalists from time to time but it helped that the media was far less likely to write about such things in those times," a friend recalled.

Both Enda Kenny and Fionnuala O'Kelly concede that, looking back now, few people – if anyone – were really fooled. Everybody more or less averted their eyes and played along, once they were not flaunting their relationship too publicly.

"I think the media has changed now. But in those days – you know, we're talking about the Eighties – the journalists and everybody knew," Fionnuala reflected. In retrospect also, she felt the seriousness of the relationship just crept up on her.

"I certainly never thought that it would ever go anywhere. I mean, it was a little bit of boldness, a little bit of fun. And all of a sudden you realise it's gone beyond that," she summed up.

Socially, life in Dublin in the mid- to late 1980s was good fun for young people in reasonably well-paid jobs. Enda Kenny's pattern of returning to Mayo each Thursday slipped. He frequently did not return until Friday or early Saturday and there were lots of snatched breaks and holidays, sometimes built around political events.

But the strain of being from different sides of the political divide did begin to take a real toll. From 1987 onwards, as Fianna Fail were back in government, Fionnuala O'Kelly, as head of the Government Information Service, was increasingly privy to secrets to which your average Fianna Fail politician did not get access. Things were starting to get tricky.

Friends believe the pair might have married sooner but Fionnuala's mother became ill and in November 1990 she died in Beaumont Hospital in Dublin. After the funeral Fionnuala decided to delay the wedding until after her mother's first anniversary had passed.

But by now she was ensconced in the public-relations office of RTE on a reputed salary of IR£30,000 per year, while Enda Kenny was a bit behind that on a backbench TD's annual salary of almost IR£28,000. They could ease up on the pretence of not going out together.

He proposed to her in the summer of 1990, a short while after she took up the RTE job. They both recall that they were on Inisheer, the most westerly of the Aran Islands, where his grandfather James McGinley had once served as an assistant lighthouse keeper.

"I went down on one knee with the Atlantic washing up and surf breaking around us and asked her to be my wife. And then I was down that aisle like the hammers of hell," he recalled almost

20 years later – again indulging his mixture of drama and fast-forward in recounting their courtship.

On Thursday evening, December 19, 1991, the Dail adjourned for the Christmas break with goodwill messages from the Ceann Comhairle and all the party leaders. Fine Gael leader John Bruton added his own jolly note by wishing Mayo West deputy Enda Kenny well in his forthcoming wedding to former Fianna Fail press officer Fionnuala O'Kelly.

"It is a match which will find favour on both sides of the House," he told deputies. What started in the Dail chamber was now a matter of Dail record.

****

The wedding was on January 3, 1992, more than 10 years after their eyes first met across the Dail chamber. It was front-page news, as the handsome photographs were deemed by editors just the thing to banish early-January blues.

The tales of clandestine love in the corridors of power were dusted down and lost nothing in the telling. As he waited for his bride in St Mary's Church on Haddington Road in Dublin, just 10 minutes' walk from Leinster House, Enda Kenny sportingly played along with the 'secret love' theme.

"At last I will be proud to take her anywhere with me," he told reporters. Sure enough, he had written the headline for the next day's *Irish Independent*.

He also delighted in telling everyone it was an All-Ireland wedding, with his parents, from Mayo and Donegal, taking in Connacht and Ulster, and her parents, from Kerry and Dublin, roping in Munster and Leinster. That fed a headline for *The Irish Press*.

The headache of what could have been an endless guest list was avoided by keeping it to just 25 invitees, largely members of family and a few very close friends. A long-time family friend, Fr Tom Shannon from Ballinrobe, officiated and Fionnuala's father gave his daughter away.

Enda's mother, Ethna, led the Kenny clan along with brothers John, Henry and Kieran, who acted as best man, and sister Maria. Fionnuala's sister Breda was bridesmaid and her other sisters, Maria and Noreen, were joined by brothers Brian and Michael. Her youngest sister, Niamh, was otherwise engaged as she had given birth to her first baby on Christmas Day.

The bride avoided a grand entrance by being a trifling four minutes late. She wore a beautiful lace and chiffon dress in ivory with a design of roses picked out in peach and carried a bouquet of pink and white roses. The groom wore a dark suit with a slight mauve tinge and a matching mauve patterned tie.

The spilling winter rain mattered not at all. They all adjourned around the corner to Le Coq Hardi restaurant on Pembroke Road for a meal and a small party.

Le Coq Hardi would later have the dubious distinction of featuring in two Tribunal reports on political corruption and was notoriously much patronised by Fionnuala's old boss, Charlie Haughey. Some years later it emerged that Haughey and his mistress, the gossip columnist Terry Keane, splurged a total of IR£15,084.44 there in 1991 alone, all paid for by five cheques drawn on the taxpayer-funded Leader's Allowance – with all five countersigned by Bertie Ahern.

Later again, that same posh Dublin 4 eatery was cited in the Mahon Tribunal report which showed it was the venue for a meeting of the "4 x 2 Club" ahead of an important Dublin County Council rezoning decision in December 1992. The '4' were a quartet of Fine Gael women politicians, Olivia Mitchell, Mary Elliot, Therese Ridge and Anne Devitt, and the '2' were developer Owen O'Callaghan and his lobbyist, Frank Dunlop.

But that was all for the future. For the moment Enda Kenny and his new wife, Fionnuala O'Kelly, went on a week-long honeymoon touring undisclosed locations in Ireland – and then went back to work.

****

The newly married couple first lived in her small townhouse at 72 Baggot Lane, a very short distance from where they married and held their wedding reception. Fionnuala O'Kelly had bought this place, 10 minutes' walk from her work at Leinster House, in the summer of 1986, five years after she started with Fianna Fail.

By the autumn of 1995, the couple had two infant children, one aged almost three years, and the other 15 months. They sold Baggot Lane and moved on to a more spacious house at 38 Seafort Avenue in Sandymount, about halfway between her work in RTE and his at Leinster House.

In June 1992, a delighted Fionnuala O'Kelly told friends that she was expecting her first child. On October 22, Aoibheann Kenny, weighing seven pounds and 14 ounces and just a few hours old, briefly stopped proceedings at Dail Eireann.

Leas Ceann Comhairle Jim Tunney formally sought the indulgence of the house to bring the good news that Deputy Enda Kenny's wife had given birth to a baby girl at nearby Holles Street Maternity Hospital.

Justice Minister Padraig Flynn, Kenny's Fianna Fail constituency rival – who had been leading a fraught referendum debate on the right to travel arising from the notorious 'X Case' abortion controversy – wanted to be first to offer congratulations.

Some good-humoured banter followed, as TDs welcomed a lightening of topic. Fine Gael TD Nora Owen proposed Padraig Flynn as the child's godfather.

"I am not convinced that this will be a Number One vote for Padraig Flynn. But one never knows," Mr Flynn joked.

In any event, it was the start of big changes in the Kenny-O'Kelly household – and not just involving moving house. In due course Fionnuala O'Kelly returned to work as head of public relations in RTE.

Almost two years later, on July 12, 1994, their son Ferdia was born and on October 7, 1996, their youngest son, Naoise, came into the world. The couple had hired a full-time childminder and

Fionnuala's father, Sean, took an active childcare role.

Though himself the father of seven children, Sean O'Kelly had never changed a nappy – but he learned as a grandfather. "It was a case of needs must. Men in those days just didn't change nappies," she said of her father's literal hands-off/hands-on role change over the two generations.

Despite the childcare back-up, the stresses were beginning to show. Enda Kenny and his wife had to register a strong presence in his Mayo constituency, juggle two jobs with irregular hours and demands, and sustain some semblance of a family life with three young children. The real crunch came as the eldest, Aoibheann, approached school-going age.

The commute by train to and from Castlebar at weekends was the major issue. They had to be seen in Mayo to ensure the muttered accusations that he was becoming "an absentee TD" did not take root. They knew that rivals outside Fine Gael – and within it – would not be slow to exploit such an opportunity and a general election was inevitable some time in 1997.

Fionnuala O'Kelly explained that it was a challenge with one child and tougher again with two. "But when the third came along and you've only got two arms to carry them on to a train ... it just became impossible."

Things were compounded by Enda Kenny finally getting promotion in politics.

An extraordinary turn of events in December 1994 had led to the collapse of the Fianna Fail-Labour coalition and the formation, without an election, of the Rainbow Government under John Bruton.

Enda Kenny became Minister for Tourism and Trade, a job which involved a huge amount of overseas travel and lengthy absences from home. He was at a trade conference in Pittsburgh, USA, when their third child was born and only got back two days after the birth. In Fionnuala O'Kelly's own words, something had to give.

When her maternity leave for the third child, Naoise, ended

early in 1997, Fionnuala O'Kelly formally took a year's leave of absence from the RTE publicity department. The family moved their home to Mayo and she never returned to the job; 16 years in a professional role at the forefront of Irish media and politics were at an end.

It was a tough decision – she had been tipped as a high-flyer. After years at the top in politics and government followed by a senior post in RTE, big and lucrative opportunities in the world of Dublin public relations had appeared well signposted for Fionnuala's future.

Soon afterwards, in June 1997, after the Rainbow Coalition narrowly lost to Bertie Ahern's rejuvenated Fianna Fail, Enda Kenny returned to the opposition benches. "Some people felt at that time that she had sacrificed a better future than Enda ever had in front of him," one friend said, rather matter-of-factly.

It was five years away from Enda Kenny declaring his intention to lead Fine Gael and his bid to become Taoiseach. In 1997 there was not the faintest hint of such ambition.

Other friends believe that Fionnuala O'Kelly was happier at Leinster House than at RTE. But her RTE years, 1990 to 1996, were also a time when children and family life intervened and began to take precedence: she had three periods of maternity leave.

"Within RTE, her appointment at the time was seen as politically clever and as an attempt to improve the often extremely fraught relations between the station and Haughey's Fianna Fail. She had, after all, come directly from Haughey's office, so to speak. But she is not remembered as ever being 'political' and she was popular with colleagues in day-to-day matters," one senior RTE staffer of that era recalled.

There is always a push-pull relationship between the public-service broadcaster and government. But relations were very poor indeed at many times during the Haughey era as his RTE-obsessed lieutenant, Ray Burke, kept responsibility for communications over five years, even as he moved across three government departments.

Newspaper reports indicate that Fionnuala O'Kelly took her role as defender of the station seriously and she wrote frequently to the newspaper letters-to-editor pages, taking critics to task in great detail. But in the overall scheme, her period in RTE was a time when show business rather than politics and current affairs held sway at Montrose.

In early 1994, she was also called upon to publicly smooth things over following some public tensions between two big RTE personalities, the outgoing Late Late Show host, Gay Byrne, and his successor, Pat Kenny. Fionnuala O'Kelly told the *Irish Independent* that there was no evidence to suggest Gay Byrne "has a sell-by date".

It was the era of Ireland's dominance of the Eurovision Song Contest, with an unprecedented three-in-a-row wins beginning in 1992, and another in 1996. This brought a recurring logistics and publicity nightmare as hosting the Contest compounded the station's funding woes. As she departed in early 1997, the station was preparing to host its fourth Eurovision in five years.

A dozen years after opting to abandon the professional world for family life, Fionnuala O'Kelly publicly admitted the difficulties associated with the decision.

"If my mother had still been alive, I don't know if I could have done it," she said in an *Irish Times* interview. She was a woman who had to give up her job and made such sacrifices to put the seven of us through education. And there was guilt – I felt I was letting womankind down."

****

The Kenny family home in Castlebar is on the edge of a golf course. It is a comfortable, lived-in, two-storey house which has been decorated to Fionnuala O'Kelly's taste, honed by her taking a course in interior design.

Her Kerry family background helped her adjust to provincial life – though she has conceded it was not easy at first. Involvement with the local school committee and other local activities helped break the ice socially.

But for quite some time she missed not having an inside track on the running story of the day. During her time at Leinster House and RTE, friends would often ring her to ask what the "real story" was – but in Mayo that just stopped dead.

"All of a sudden I had to wait for him to come home – and he's just no good at gossip," she recalled ruefully.

When the children were smaller, Fionnuala missed the sociability of work and the lack of adult conversation at times. The children did most of their growing up in the decade after her husband was elected Fine Gael leader in June 2002. This involved considerable absence from home and left the bulk of day-to-day parenting duties to their mother.

By autumn 2012, their eldest daughter, Aoibheann, has completed her first year at college; their second child, Ferdia, had sat his Leaving Certificate; and their youngest, Naoise, is in the final years of secondary school.

Their father has tried to compensate for considerable absence over the years by ensuring he spoke to them by phone morning and evening and trying, where possible, to keep Sunday free for family activities. He also tries to ensure that there are special family treats, such as trips to big matches. Summer holidays in Kerry are also mainly family occasions, with reading of Irish newspapers banned for the duration.

But public life puts a big strain on family life. Both Enda Kenny and Fionnuala O'Kelly agree the absences and planned compensations cast him as 'fun Daddy' – leaving her the primary role of 'laying down the law'. Both agreed, and totally lived up to, a pledge to keep their children out of the limelight.

She says he occasionally tries to do things about the house, with not very good results. Cooking is not his forte, she told Newstalk's Henry McKean in February 2011.

"Cinderised sausages are about the height of his cuisine," she remarked.

****

In autumn 2010 – weeks after Enda Kenny had totally stymied a plot by the majority of his key Fine Gael lieutenants to ditch him as leader – Fionnuala O'Kelly spelled out her feelings to a friend.

"We have just put much too much into all of this to give up now," she said.

The comment again raises the oft-discussed issue: how much is Enda Kenny's wife the real power behind the throne? Has she been a major factor – perhaps *the* factor – in propelling him into Government Buildings as Taoiseach?

It is no surprise that she publicly and peremptorily brushes aside any such suggestion.

"The role I play is that I let him be out there. I make sure that he doesn't have to worry about us and that he could concentrate on what he is doing," she told TV3 in April 2007.

Around that time, she even took over his one constant home chore of grass-cutting to ease the pressure on her husband.

But, as a former back-room PR person, does she not advise on presentation and image?

Fionnuala insists that she does this only in a very general way.

Certainly, she is responsible for his clothes. "He has no interest in what he puts on. I tell him what to put on. It's as simple as that. I choose his clothes and tell him what to wear because he doesn't have any interest in that," she told Newstalk before the 2011 general election.

In late 2006, Enda Kenny generated some attention by appearing with a markedly different hairstyle. Was this his wife's doing?

No. It was simply a case of a different hairdresser on duty in the shop offering a different style. "A young woman came in and said: 'I'd like to do it differently.' As far as he is concerned, he couldn't give two hoots what his hair is like," she recalled, apparently bemused by the attention given to the topic.

Enda Kenny concurred. "The important thing is that it's my own and it's growing and there isn't any colour in it," he said, a little proudly.

His wife supported this. "I have grey for the two of us and there's plenty of colouring in mine," she added.

Fionnuala O'Kelly insists there is no time for her to get involved in interview preparations or post-mortems and she is loath to use their limited time together in this way. "I'm a perfectionist by nature and by nature I'm very critical. Sometimes I have to bite my tongue," she said on TV3.

But does she not assess his big media occasions and weed out flaws?

"I tend not to. I try to keep as far away from it as possible, for two reasons. Firstly, because I see so little of him, and if he comes in on a Sunday night and we have three or four hours together, he needs to get a break and the last thing he needs is somebody barracking him. Secondly, I tend to be very negative, and if he stood on his head it wouldn't make me happy," she told Matt Cooper in January 2007.

So what does Enda Kenny think of his wife's involvement in his media work?

"Let's put it this way. She doesn't suffer fools gladly. And in respect of any media performance, she doesn't suffer fools gladly – as would be right and proper," he said.

But the Taoiseach also insisted that there is no time for detailed input by his wife into interview preparation. In general, her advice on media presentation is always just about the big picture and the overall image and message put across.

"She would say as a former communicator – have your message very clear and keep it simple," he summed up.

Since the foundation of the State, the wives of Irish political leaders were occasionally seen but never heard. Older generations may recall photographs of the wives of Taoisigh – Sinead Bean de Valera, Eileen Lemass, Vera Cosgrave, Mairin Lynch, and Maureen Haughey – but their voices were seldom recorded.

Fionnuala O'Kelly might be seen as an exception here. In November 2006 she delivered a strong speech to a lunch of 400 Fine Gael women supporters in Dublin. She warned of the danger of Ireland becoming a "one-party state" if Fianna Fail were elected for a third consecutive term in the upcoming general election.

"It is really a question of people needing an alternative. It is an inevitable consequence of people being in government too long that they become arrogant," she said. Her words were given added weight as a former Fianna Fail press person and potential Taoiseach's wife.

In the six months that followed – the run-up to the general election of May 2007 – the Irish public got to see much more of Fionnuala O'Kelly. Three joint interviews followed: on January 2, 2007, with Matt Cooper on Today FM radio; on April 1, 2007, on TV3 with Ursula Halligan, and, that same month, a joint video of the couple was posted on YouTube.

At the close of his Fine Gael Ard Fheis speech on March 31, 2007, broadcast live on television, Fionnuala O'Kelly was the only one to join her husband on the podium. The traditional mobbing of the leader by the grinning front-bench members was cast aside.

Fine Gael strategists agree that bringing Fionnuala O'Kelly into the picture was a considered and deliberate strategy with which she agreed. "It was an attempt, simply first off, to raise his profile and make him better known. It was also about softening and humanising his image and revealing another side of his personality," one back-room person told this writer.

What no strategist will ever privately, let alone publicly, admit is that Enda Kenny, husband and family man, also contrasted with his rival, Taoiseach Bertie Ahern. At that stage, Mr Ahern and partner Celia Larkin had gone their separate ways after years together; Bertie Ahern had separated from his wife, Miriam, in 1986.

But beyond these programmed media forays, Enda Kenny's wife has been very sparing in her public utterances. At election time she is seen on the canvass trail – but she is not involved in the local Mayo constituency organisation and does nothing of the day-to-day politics her late mother-in-law, Ethna Kenny, busied herself with for many years.

As we have seen, the three joint media performances in early 2007 contained a huge element of their beguiling tale of 'love across enemy lines', with endearing snippets of how long it took them to get together and marry.

It is clear they prepared and co-ordinated carefully and they very probably took media advice for these performances. But there is enough freshness and spontaneity to make them credible.

Enda Kenny is adamant when he says that his wife has facilitated his political work to the highest possible degree. He rightly insists that, without her understanding of how politics works and the huge time demands associated with it, he could not succeed.

But for many close to Kenny and Fine Gael, Fionnuala O'Kelly is far more than the person who keeps the home fires burning and facilitates her husband's round-the-clock political involvement.

For many friends and associates, Enda Kenny's relationship with her has seen him transform himself from a happy-go-lucky backbench TD with the potential to perhaps be a middle-ranking government minister. With her help and encouragement, he has over time changed his attitude and sharpened his focus to become party leader and Taoiseach.

"Fionnuala is, without doubt, his best political adviser – not in routine or everyday matters. She has a long-term view and she understands the game of politics," one friend summed up.

CHAPTER 6

Party Wars & Woes

The sensible ones had ducked into TJ Gibbons's pub to take shelter and perhaps fortify themselves against the bitter February wind.

From 6pm onwards a crowd, which would eventually swell to over 400 people, began to congregate at the bridge near Shrule. It happened to be Valentine's Night: February 14, 1986.

But politics rather than romance was the focus for this crowd awaiting the return to Mayo of their newly promoted local hero, Enda Kenny. After 10 years and three months in Dail Eireann, and just weeks short of his 35th birthday, he had finally achieved junior government office as Minister of State for Youth Affairs attached to both the Departments of Education and Labour.

On the Galway side of the bridge, the new Junior Minister left the BMW car driven from Dublin by Fine Gael Senator Patrick Durcan of Westport. Once he had walked across to the Mayo side, Enda Kenny was greeted, amid loud cheering, by Michael Raftery, the most senior of the local Fine Gael councillors.

There among the throng were his mother, Ethna, sister, Maria, and Maureen Kenny, the wife of his brother, Henry. It was a family moment to treasure as almost 13 years earlier, the late Henry Kenny senior had a similar triumphant Mayo homecoming after being appointed a junior minister.

A little over 24 hours before this welcome party began assembling, Taoiseach Garret FitzGerald had told Enda Kenny of his new appointment. "I felt then as I did at my First Communion – but the Taoiseach told me it was Confirmation," he quipped to reporters when asked for his reaction.

Enda Kenny's junior appointment was one of the few positive stories at local level from this cabinet reshuffle by FitzGerald. Nationally, it was another publicity disaster heaped upon a woefully unpopular government grappling with a broken economy, high unemployment and emigration. FitzGerald was left looking even more inept and weak.

It had been vital that the Taoiseach reshape his team to give it a fresher, softer image, as a general election was expected any day and was, at the very most, 20 months off.

But FitzGerald's cabinet reshuffle plans, which had been delayed on previous occasions, were thwarted by the well-publicised refusal of Barry Desmond of the Labour Party to move from his job as Health Minister.

Desmond had tabled cost-cutting measures which included extensive hospital closures, and his Labour colleagues totally supported his view that he could not be made a political scapegoat. In the end, the only fig leaf FitzGerald got was that Desmond ceded responsibility for the Social Welfare Department, which had until then been twinned with the Department of Health.

After two days of tense Fine Gael-Labour negotiations, the reshuffle was hastily announced in the Dail late on February 13 by FitzGerald, to much jeering from a jubilant Fianna Fail opposition. None of the senior government team was dropped, though everybody except Desmond moved portfolio.

Paddy O'Toole of neighbouring Mayo East, whom Garret FitzGerald had originally preferred over Kenny in November 1982, was moved sideways from his double portfolio, Fisheries and Forestry and the Gaeltacht, to be Minister for Defence and Gaeltacht Minister. O'Toole, described by Garret as "a gentle westerner and Gaelic speaker", had been appointed to cabinet as a reward for taking grief over the Fine Gael-Labour Coalition's refusal to fund the Knock Airport development in the heart of his constituency.

O'Toole's gain was Kenny's loss, as that seemed to fill Mayo's cabinet allocation. But Kenny had grounds for resenting not making the junior ranks from the start of Garret's second government, though he was not the only Fine Gael TD upset by FitzGerald's ministerial choices.

During his short-lived first coalition, from June 1981 to January 1982, FitzGerald appointed Professor Jim Dooge to the Senate specifically so he could make him Foreign Affairs Minister, using a little-known provision which allows Senators as well as TDs to serve in cabinet. This was justifiable as Dail numbers were extremely tight and Fianna Fail could not be relied upon to offer a voting pair when the Foreign Afffairs Minister was overseas.

But Dooge was not just a brilliant academic. He also had a track record as a Dublin County Councillor, an elected Senator representing the National University and a back-room party advisor.

Two other FitzGerald appointments were a bigger source of irritation to some TDs, especially those who had been on the Cosgrave conservative wing of the party and who were now out of favour. One was the appointment of Alan Dukes as Agriculture Minister on his first day in the Dail in June 1981, despite his qualifications as an economist and experience in Brussels with the Irish Farmers' Association and the European Commission.

The other was the appointment of Gemma Hussey as Education Minister in November 1982, after just 10 months in the Dail. Long-serving TDs with previous cabinet experience, such as Tom O'Donnell and Richie Ryan, felt insulted.

Other changes in this February 1986 reshuffle are worth noting here as they concern two future Fine Gael leaders, Alan Dukes and John Bruton, both of whom would influence Kenny's career in various ways and figure in it for a long time.

Alan Dukes moved from the intense fire of the Finance Department to the only slightly lower-heat frying pan of the Justice Department, later joking ironically that his boss, FitzGerald, felt he needed a "softer image". John Bruton returned to the job of Finance Minister, signalling an end to his period of penance for his ill-fated January 1982 Budget, which had proposed tax on children's shoes and was the trigger that toppled Garret's first government.

When all the junior announcements were made, Kenny's Fianna Fail Mayo rival, Padraig Flynn, took the first opportunity to cross the Dail chamber and give him a bone-crushing handshake.

As the Dail agenda moved on to the last item of business, concerning the closure of a tannery in Carrick-on-Suir, most senior government figures took the chance to beat a quick retreat from the Chamber. But the new Junior Minister sat where he was, to savour the moment.

"Good man, Enda. At least you stayed to face us," Fianna Fail's future leader and Taoiseach, Albert Reynolds, called out.

The carefully choreographed welcoming back to Mayo soil at Shrule was only the start of the local celebrations, with receptions and votes of congratulation all across the Mayo West constituency. St Patrick's Day was set aside for special celebrations in Enda Kenny's home parish of Islandeady, with bonfires and a formal welcome.

It was rounded off at the local Halfway House, where there was dancing to the music of the Hillsiders and a special guest appearance by the harpist Frankie Waldron. All of that for just IR£2 admission.

The local newspaper coverage was hugely positive, with the editorial writer of *The Connaught Telegraph* strongly stating that Kenny's promotion was long overdue.

"It will help soothe the pain his supporters felt in the past when his talents went without recognition," the editorial stated. But in a swift return to realpolitik, the same writer added that since Kenny was appointed to the Education Department, he must help deliver a planned Regional Technical College for Castlebar.

The celebrations as advertised and reported had the air of garnishing some very targeted political activity by local Fine Gael members. In the four weeks immediately after his promotion,

128

Kenny presided at a series of eight local meetings.

He and his supporters there – in common with political activists all across the country – were on constant campaign footing. By Christmas of that year, the writing was on the wall.

On January 20, 1987, the four Labour Ministers quit the coalition government because they could not agree Finance Minister John Bruton's Budget cutbacks planned for the coming year.

Polling was fixed for February 17 and a gruelling four-week campaign loomed.

Enda Kenny's first taste of government action had lasted just one year.

****

Ironically, Enda Kenny's first government job had more to do with Des O'Malley and the Progressive Democrats than with the belated recognition of his talents within Garret FitzGerald's Fine Gael.

It also had much to do with local Fine Gael wars in his Mayo West home turf: specifically, conflict with local dissidents Frank Durcan of Castlebar and, to a lesser extent, Martin Finn of Claremorris.

Cllr Frank Durcan, a successful Castlebar auctioneer and businessman, had been a very able Fine Gael organiser and was influential in launching Enda Kenny's career. He was also a formidable local vote-getter in his own right, being first elected to Castlebar Urban District Council in 1967 and to Mayo County Council in 1974 – several times chairman of these two councils.

He also had national political ambitions of his own, which he was unable to advance once Enda Kenny succeeded his late father, Henry Kenny, as the Castlebar-based Fine Gael TD in November 1975. The conventional party view was that there was no room for a second Fine Gael TD based in the Mayo county town.

A series of rows through the early 1980s left relations very frayed between Frank Durcan and his Fine Gael Council colleagues, and especially with Enda Kenny, leader of the party's Mayo County Council grouping. In February 1984 Frank Durcan stopped going to Fine Gael meetings and just before Christmas declared that he would contest the June 1985 local elections as an Independent – and was also looking forward to the next Dail election.

Frank Durcan said he had got no support from Fine Gael colleagues in his efforts to expose waste of taxpayers' money. It was not surprising that his call to bar teachers from membership of the Mayo County Vocational Education Committee (VEC), on the grounds that they could not be employers and employees at the same time, did not gain traction. Many senior Mayo politicians, including Enda Kenny, who had chaired the County VEC, were former teachers.

Frank Durcan was especially disillusioned by Fine Gael councillors combining with their Fianna Fail colleagues to stymie his efforts to have the full extent of Mayo County Council staff travel and subsistence expenses published. His call was ahead of its time in that pre-Freedom of Information Act era. But Durcan said Enda Kenny, Fine Gael Senator Jim Higgins from Ballyhaunis and the other Fine Gael councillors had dissociated themselves from that call for transparency on Council staff expenses.

Durcan was scathing about the Fine Gael local leadership – which meant Enda Kenny – for a total lack of discipline and a failure to follow through on agreed party decisions. "I cannot stay in a party which is achieving nothing ... there is now, in my view, no such thing as a Fine Gael party in West Mayo," he said.

Kenny and his local lieutenants avoided open conflict with Frank Durcan for long periods in the run-up to the June 1985 local elections. But Durcan was now a clear threat to Kenny as he had been extra careful to exempt ordinary Fine Gael members from his criticisms and insist he remained loyal to the party's founding principles.

Henry Kenny, Enda's older brother, who had passed on the opportunity to stand for the Dail when their father died in 1975, was mobilised to stand for the County Council. Henry joined Enda Kenny and Cllr Paddy Burke on the party ticket for the Castlebar area.

But that local election was a poll-topping triumph for Durcan in both the County Council and Castlebar Urban District Council contests. Henry Kenny got 640 votes – way off the pace for a County Council seat. Both Enda Kenny and Paddy Burke were elected, but with far fewer votes than Durcan.

Some of the Kennys' immediate embarrassment was spared by their absence from the Castlebar count centre as the results emerged. They had joined other family members to celebrate the wedding of Maria Kenny to Westport garage owner Tim Hastings.

With 2,053 council votes, Frank Durcan was increasingly being talked about as a Dail prospect in an upcoming election in which it would be hard to fly the colours of an exceptionally unpopular government.

And it was just at this time that the Progressive Democrats burst on to the national stage. The new party was launched in a blaze of publicity by Des O'Malley and Mary Harney in Dublin on Saturday, December 21, 1985.

Both founders had been expelled from Fianna Fail for various reasons – but essentially because of their long-running bitter conflict with the Fianna Fail leader, Charlie Haughey. The new party supported economically liberal policies, the lowering of crippling taxes, welfare reforms, separation of Church and State, and reform of contraception and divorce laws.

Once the exodus of anti-Haughey Fianna Fail people stopped, it became increasingly clear that the Progressive Democrats were likely to be fishing from the same pool as Fine Gael.

On January 23, 1986, the Progressive Democrats unveiled their new Connacht recruit, Bobby Molloy, the erstwhile Fianna Fail Galway West kingpin, at an emotionally charged rally in the Leisureland complex in Salthill. Cllr Frank Durcan of Castlebar was an invited guest among the 2,000 people crammed into the conference hall.

It was part of the Progressive Democrats' membership strategy to recruit likely established politicians in efforts to get a foothold in new terrain. At that stage things looked upbeat, with Harney in Dublin, O'Malley in Limerick, Pearse Wyse in Cork and Molloy in Galway.

Durcan was suitably enigmatic about it all, and after the Salthill rally admitted that the message from the Progressive Democrats podium addressed the issue of the day. "Politics is about jobs and if they continue along these lines it is possible I would become a member."

He was more noncommittal about his general election plans. "I might not run at all, and I could run as an Independent, or possibly even as a PD candidate," he told the *Western People,* in one of the finest ever examples of a politician's 'definite maybe' statement.

Durcan's threat was augmented by another dissident former Fine Gael politician, Martin Finn from neighbouring East Mayo, who was also flirting with the Progressive Democrats and made a show of travelling to the Salthill rally. Finn, a councillor from the Claremorris area, was even more colourful in his actions as a former Fine Gael TD and Senator, and had obliged Enda Kenny to lead moves to have him expelled from the party.

He had stood unsuccessfully on the same Fine Gael Dail election ticket as Enda Kenny's father in 1961 and 1965. But under reconfigured constituencies he became a TD for Mayo East from 1969 to 1977. After failing in the 1977 Dail election he was a nominated Senator for about six weeks before losing out in the subsequent Seanad elections.

In June 1984 Finn was outgoing Mayo County Council chairman when he switched his Council vote to Fianna Fail in that summer's round of internal elections. The net result was that he kept the Council chair for a total of three years – but, more importantly, he deprived his long-time Fine Gael colleagues of the chair and membership of a host of influential committees.

"You have in practice joined the Soldiers of Destiny," Enda Kenny told him publicly. Kenny added that whatever battles Fine Gael members had in private, they must support one another publicly.

Finn was unimpressed, saying he got no support from his Fine Gael Council colleagues in the Seanad elections in early 1983. "I could be a Senator now – only for them," he said.

Then Finn rubbed salt into the wounds after the June 1985 Council elections by using his balance-of-power vote to give the chairmanship to Fianna Fail, netting a host of committee memberships for himself and again depriving his old colleagues of political goodies. When Fine Gael cried foul, Fianna Fail councillors reminded them of their previous winner-takes-all attitude. High politics this was not – it was the fiercely competitive stuff encouraged by our electoral system and especially the multi-seat constituencies.

Neither Durcan nor Finn ever stood for the Progressive Democrats in Mayo. In fact Martin Finn, who died in March 1988 aged 70, never stood for the Dail again.

Frank Durcan stood for the Dail only once, as an Independent in June 1989, when he failed to get elected but polled almost as much as Kenny and clearly took a big share of his Castlebar vote. At time of writing he remains a vocal member of Castlebar Town Council and Mayo County Council, and periodically mounts scathing attacks on the Kennys.

But none of this could be guessed at in January-February 1986, when Garret FitzGerald felt it necessary to shore up the Mayo vote. More importantly, these local would-be Progressive Democrats noises fed into alarming opinion-poll returns for FitzGerald and his senior colleagues in Dublin. In February 1986 Fine Gael had just 23 per cent support and their Labour coalition colleagues were on a measly four per cent.

This combined government showing of 27 per cent contrasted sharply with Fianna Fail's 42 per cent rating. But most alarming of all, the upstart Progressive Democrats were on 25 per cent.

Clearly, thanks largely to the Progressive Democrats locally and nationally, the time had come for Garret FitzGerald to give 'no-longer-so-young Kenny' some preferment.

****

It is hard to grade performance in a junior job within a virtually bankrupt government which lasted just a year.

But Kenny's supporters have grounds for arguing that he did reasonably well and he certainly gained good profile in that period, February 1986 to January 1987, as Junior Minister for Youth Affairs. He was in tune with his main boss, Pat Cooney, who had taken over as Education Minister, and he got responsibility for school building, adult literacy and school transport.

Kenny took advantage of the publicity opportunities associated with being closer to the government action. In April 1986 he had the pleasure of opening a newly refurbished Sancta Maria College in his own constituency at Louisburgh. And at the tail end of the year he got to give out the good news of two new factories for Castlebar which could eventually, or so the announcement went, mean 135 new jobs.

He had an eye for a photo opportunity and was pictured in a desk in the classrooms at Knockrooskey School, where he had taught 11 years previously, for a back-to-school feature in the *Irish Independent* in September 1986. A month later he managed to have his share of the credit publicly acknowledged for securing a place of honour at Leinster House for a portrait of fellow countyman and Land League founder Michael Davitt.

He sat in with Education Minister Pat Cooney in an endless round of talks with teachers over pay. On November 20, 1986, he handled Dail Question Time, fielding questions on a variety of topics including rats in schools, school building funds, school uniforms and psychological services, all with competence and good humour.

But it was not all joyous photocalls: he had to bite the bullet on refused funding for an IR£300,000 cable-car link to the island of Innishbiggle, close to Achill, on his home patch. On a visit to the island with a grinning rival, Padraig Flynn of Fianna Fail, he had to say he really did not think the islanders would get any funding, and, according to local banter, thereby lost the only Fine Gael vote on Innisbiggle.

In March 1986 he did not have to travel beyond his own office to learn about rats in schools. The parents of children at Ballinadee school, near Bandon, Co Cork, brought him a six-minute colour video with all the details of furry long-tailed animals who shared their time between the 118-year-old school and the adjoining cemetery.

And when Dail questions were raised about a social employment scheme in Ranelagh, it fell to Kenny to respond – even though the project was located in Ruairi Quinn's Dublin South East constituency and he was the senior minister responsible.

It is a very safe bet that Enda Kenny would have been happier not to have been a member of government at all on May 30, 1986, when Knock Airport was formally opened – by the leader of Fianna Fail in opposition, Charlie Haughey.

The carefully crafted set of words on the plaque unveiled by Haughey summarise a mammoth political tale which, among other elements, includes two decades of grief for the Fine Gael party in Mayo.

It read: "The establishment of this international airport was authorised by An Taoiseach Charles J Haughey TD on 25 September, 1980, and was officially opened by him on 30 May 1986." The inscription does not say Haughey was Taoiseach when he opened it – or does it?

Mayo journalist Terry Reilly summed things up in his marvellous book On A Wing And A Prayer, which recounts the saga of Knock Airport's development: "As far as the airport board were concerned there was only one real Taoiseach!"

Enda Kenny was the only member of the Fine Gael-Labour Government to show his face at the new airport that day. But he did not attend the opening proper; "due to duties in Dublin" he did not arrive until late afternoon.

Haughey had the bulk of his Fianna Fail shadow cabinet on parade; the Catholic Church sent an archbishop and three bishops; the Church of Ireland sent a Bishop; the GAA sent their national president, and Bord Failte sent their director general. The government did not send anyone, though a local junior minister did drop by later in the day.

Haughey was Taoiseach when he backed the project the day it was first put to him in summer 1980 by the extraordinary phenomenon that was Monsignor James Horan, parish priest of Knock. Monsignor Horan had already fundraised and built a huge IR£1.8 million basilica at the scene where local people reported a vision of the Virgin Mary and other saints in 1879. He also received Pope John Paul II there in September 1979, the centenary of the first reports of such a vision.

By summer of 1981 the workers were on site at Barrnacuige, a place from where parts of all four of Ireland's provinces are said to be visible on the odd day it is not raining. But soon after that Garret FitzGerald was elected Taoiseach of a government which lasted seven months.

Supporters of Knock Airport were exultant for 10 months in 1982, when Haughey was back as Taoiseach. But FitzGerald was to head a long-stay Fine Gael-Labour government beginning in February 1982, and in December 1983 that cash-starved coalition pulled the plug on the funding, leaving an IR£3 million gap – an enormous sum at the time.

Kenny's Fine Gael colleagues in adjoining Mayo East, Paddy O'Toole and Senator Jim Higgins, took much of the flak since Knock was in their constituency. But Kenny could not avoid grief: this was a huge Mayo project and it also impacted on his role as a party leader on Mayo County Council, where his Fine Gael colleagues could not resist the pressure to defy the party whip.

Elsewhere, it was a battle of city versus country; traditionalists versus secularists; economically prudent versus expansionists. There were notable and sometimes vocal sceptics in Fianna Fail, including Des O'Malley, David Andrews and Sile de Valera.

But over time Haughey outwitted his Fine Gael and Labour rivals on this one. Kenny and his Mayo colleagues had to bite their lips as Labour Health Minister Barry Desmond delivered scathing criticisms of the Knock project and Transport Minister Jim Mitchell, of their own party, dismissed the site as a "foggy, boggy hill".

The controversy brought some other embarrassing moments for Enda Kenny, apart from appearing like a lost sheep at the opening. In November 1981, *The Sunday Press* reported that Paddy O'Toole, Gaeltacht Minister at the time, had strongly defended the airport project at a Fine Gael meeting but Kenny said little: "As secretary of the parliamentary party he was too busy taking notes," the newspaper noted.

Bertie Ahern was to use that same note-taking defence in explaining why he had not heard some scabrous comments at a Fianna Fail meeting which discussed a heave against Charlie Haughey. Another useful defence of 'not being home' was invoked by Kenny in the general election campaign of June 1981.

Knock Airport campaigners had no bother getting Fianna Fail candidates in Mayo, Sligo, Roscommon and Leitrim to sign a pledge of support. But Fine Gael's Paddy O'Toole flatly refused to put his name to it.

"His Mayo West colleague, Enda Kenny, was missed out by the action committee because he was on the canvass trail when they called," author Terry Reilly recalls.

In summer 1982, rumour abounded that military alliance NATO were eyeing this strategically placed runway. This rumour was immortalised by singer Christy Moore in the songlines: "Did NATO donate the dough, me boys? Did NATO donate the dough?" But Kenny actually put a question to Foreign Affairs Minister Gerry Collins, who treated him to a lecture on Irish neutrality.

In 1983, Kenny objected to petition signatures being collected outside churches on grounds that it was politicising an occasion of religious worship. But airport campaign member Stephen Tarpey hit back, saying political parties had no problem with financial collections at the same locations.

Monsignor James Horan died while on a pilgrimage to Lourdes on August 1, 1986, just weeks after the airport opening, apparently overcome by the great strain he had placed upon his health. Government representatives at his funeral got a distinctly cool reception.

Looking back on the issue in 2006, as Fine Gael leader in opposition, Enda Kenny frankly said he disagreed with the 1983 cabinet decision to cut Knock Airport funding – but as a backbencher he could not stop it. He said Fianna Fail had outmanoeuvred them.

Others in Fine Gael estimate that it took them up to the 1997 general election to get over the damage done to the party. They also acknowledge that help Kenny gave Knock Airport as Transport Minister in the period 1994-97 played a part in undoing the harm to the party in Mayo.

Away from the minefield that was Knock Airport, Kenny stood his ground in a row with the GAA over their campaign to have hurleys exempted from VAT. Firstly, he criticised the distribution of campaign leaflets at the Connacht Football Final.

"It is objectionable and beneath the tradition of the GAA to continue to campaign in this fashion," he said, in a statement which carried more weight given his own and his family's GAA pedigree. He pointed out that the government had met the GAA to hear their case on this issue and also had got little recognition for grants to the GAA totalling IR£100,000.

It is safe to conclude that, outside of Connacht's only hurling stronghold of east Galway, VAT on hurleys was not one of that province's burning sporting issues. But the government-GAA row went up a gear weeks later as the All-Ireland finals drew near.

Kenny joined former Galway football All-Ireland-winning

captain and Fine Gael TD, John Donnellan, in criticising the GAA decision to ban TDs from their VIP section on big match days at Croke Park as part of their VAT-free-hurley campaign. Kenny emphasised that he always paid his own way going to games.

"I see no reason why they should adopt tactics such as these," he said. Later he made it clear that he had attended the football final between Kerry and Tyrone – though seated elsewhere in the ground.

But time was running out. One of his later tasks was to launch an Irish-language pocket dictionary – a project which had echoes of his father's first ever Dail speech 30 years earlier on teaching the language.

"I wonder what the Irish for knife-edge is?" he quipped at the launch.

The phrase was not in the new dictionary – but it summed up the position of the government, which had just weeks left to survive.

****

The expected Fine Gael general election disaster of February 1987 saw Garret FitzGerald exit the party leadership as swiftly as his predecessor, Liam Cosgrave, had done after a similar result a decade earlier.

The election saw Charlie Haughey returning as Taoiseach without an overall majority and FitzGerald replaced as Fine Gael leader by Alan Dukes – whose elevation did nothing for Enda Kenny's national political career.

But the Fine Gael party was rapidly heading into the first of a series of bouts of bitter internal strife. Garret FitzGerald, with the aid of excellent back-room people like Peter Prendergast, had transformed Fine Gael and brought them to stellar heights.

At the November 1982 general election Fine Gael had 39 per cent of the vote and 70 Dail seats. But their period in government was afflicted by global recession, crippling debt, high unemployment and persistent emigration.

Partnership with Labour meant they were never empowered to make the required drastic spending cuts. Instead, the country had the worst of all worlds – with a lingering economic slump.

Alan Dukes inherited a party now reduced to 50 Dail seats which was caught in a pincer movement between Charlie Haughey's resurgent Fianna Fail and Des O'Malley's newly launched Progressive Democrats. The new party had 14 TDs – though none in Mayo – and were the focus of everybody's attention.

In contrast to Fine Gael's national fortunes, Enda Kenny fared extremely well in Mayo West in that February 1987 general election. He topped the poll on 7,410 votes, just 53 fewer than his 1982 performance.

Fianna Fail rivals Padraig Flynn and Denis Gallagher were not far behind, and all three were elected together on the second count. Kenny's victory motorcade toured Castlebar and champagne corks popped at a victory celebration in the Breaffy House Hotel.

It mirrored Kenny's campaign, which had a 'hang the recession' air to it, with reminders that Mayo farmers had got IR£14 million in EU headage payments the previous year. He continued to wear his ministerial hat to good effect throughout the campaign.

He was able to announce that plans for Mayo Regional Technical College were advancing for Castlebar and that his old school, St Gerald's, was on the Education Department's priority list for a gymnasium. He even managed to shrug off an attack by the third Fianna Fail candidate, Paraic Cosgrove, that he had a cheek to be saying "ye never had it so good".

In something of a publicity coup, he appeared in a front-page photograph on *The Connaught Telegraph* of February 11 – six days from polling – chairing an Organisation for Economic Co-operation and Development (OECD) seminar in Paris entitled Active Living for Handicapped Youth.

But all was not sweetness and light within the Mayo West Fine

Gael camp. Kenny's running mate, Senator Patrick Durcan of Westport – who had chauffeured the new Junior Minister back to Mayo a year earlier and polled a creditable 5,700 votes this time – was very annoyed indeed.

Patrick Durcan, an accomplished solicitor, said Enda Kenny had got sole canvass rights in Castlebar but was not to campaign in Westport and Erris to the west, while the southern portion of the constituency was open to both candidates. Durcan said he observed the agreement – but the same could not be said of Kenny.

He said between 800 and 1,000 personal letters from Kenny had been distributed in his Westport base and claimed the local Fine Gael organisers had run the campaign very much from the point of view of the Castlebar candidate.

"On the other hand, I did not send one letter to Castlebar seeking support," he said. Patrick Durcan added that he accepted the result but felt with a little co-operation they could have achieved the difficult task of winning a second seat.

"Realistically, it was very difficult to win a second seat. But we should be trying to, and given the proper approach by all concerned, with no one candidate trying to undermine another, I have no doubt that the two seats are winnable," Patrick Durcan told *The Mayo News*.

In November 2011 Patrick Durcan was appointed a District Court judge. But from the early 1990s onwards he worked as an organiser on every election campaign fought by Kenny's great Fine Gael rival, Michael Ring, and proved that it was possible to win many seats in Mayo.

In Dublin Enda Kenny had supported John Bruton in the party leadership vote which also saw Peter Barry stand in a three-way contest. Fine Gael succeeded in keeping the leadership election well-mannered, in contrast to the public blood-letting which had characterised Fianna Fail leadership battles throughout the first half of the 1980s.

"Dukes had been on the chicken-and-chips circuit for at least a year before. He was better organised than the others," one con-

141

temporary Fine Gael politician recalled.

Kenny continued in his role as secretary to the parliamentary party and was named on Dukes's first front bench in March 1987 – but only barely made the team as Gaeltacht Affairs spokesman. "He was one of the few Gaeilgeoiri in the parliamentary party at the time," a colleague said.

Things started well for Alan Dukes, then aged almost 42, with press coverage which noted that he was one of the most accomplished people of his generation in public life. He was generous to his opponents, appointing John Bruton deputy leader – but not Finance spokesman: that job went to Michael Noonan of Limerick. Peter Barry relinquished the deputy leadership he had held under FitzGerald, but was appointed Foreign Affairs spokesman.

Dukes even presented the RTE television novelty programme Saturday Live on April 13, 1987, just weeks after his election – and got positive reviews. His guests included entertainer Twink, sailor and entrepreneur Enda O'Coineen, radio journalist Marian Finucane and his own sister, Veronica. The programme had been designed with a huge potential to allow the guest presenter to bomb – but he did not.

However there was major resentment towards Dukes within Fine Gael from the start. Veteran party members like John Boland and Fergus O'Brien, both Dublin TDs, felt he was not experienced enough and had not paid his dues to the party, having only been a TD since 1981 and yet appointed a minister on his first day at Leinster House.

"You'd hear things like 'Dukes is six years in the party, and now he's leading – leading us,'" one party veteran recalled.

From the outset, Alan Dukes made it clear that he was not going to oppose Charlie Haughey's economic policies for opposition sake, amid the growing public realisation that tough economic decisions were inevitable. As time went on this irked Fine Gael TDs, since Haughey had promised voters he would avoid austerity, and, more importantly, he was vulnerable to opposition since he did not have an overall Dail majority.

On September 2, 1987, Alan Dukes outlined his policy in a speech to Tallaght Chamber of Commerce. Under the so-called 'Tallaght Strategy', Dukes pledged not to oppose the government when they were pursuing the right policies to correct the economy.

"Any other policy of opposition would amount simply to a cynical exploitation of short-term political opportunities for a political advantage which would inevitably prove to be equally short-lived. I will not play that game," Alan Dukes said.

It was a startling example of grown-up politics not seen before in Ireland and undoubtedly ahead of its time. But there were immediate grumbles within Fine Gael about lack of consultation before the speech.

****

In late April 1988, Enda Kenny strongly disagreed with his party leader, Alan Dukes, over his move to expel maverick Galway TD John Donnellan. It was a tricky time for Dukes as he had earlier seen an apparent solo run by Wexford deputy Ivan Yates, who called for closer links with the Progressive Democrats, and then Waterford TD Austin Deasy quit the front bench so he could have more freedom to speak his mind.

Donnellan's offences included a poor attendance record for Dail votes and discourteous treatment of the leader in his role as National Executive chairman. It had culminated in him publicly saying that Dukes cut a miserable figure as leader. "If it was raining soup Alan would have a fork in his hand," Donnellan said.

The Galwayman's family links with Enda Kenny's own family went back at least to the 1940s, when the Kennys lived in the Donnellans' home village of Dunmore. Henry Kenny played football for five years with the Dunmore club, with which the Donnellans had a long association.

John Donnellan's father, Mick, was first elected to the Dail in 1943 for Clann na Talmhan, the party he had actually founded, and was an established TD when Henry Kenny arrived at Leinster House in 1954. They were both former inter-county footballers: Mick Donnellan a star with Galway in the 1920s and early 1930s; Henry Kenny a Mayo star of the 1930s and into the 1940s.

John Donnellan is to this day remembered as captain in 1964 of the first of Galway's three-in-a-row All-Ireland football wins. Tragically, he received the cup without knowing his father had died during that final at Croke Park. He was recruited to Fine Gael and won the subsequent Dail by-election; he was popular with colleagues though regarded as a law unto himself.

In the dispute with Dukes, Kenny was among those seeking a lesser penalty for Donnellan. But Dukes easily got the necessary two-thirds majority to expel Donnellan and restore some of his own standing.

Enda Kenny never commented on his stance on the Donnellan vote. But he was dropped by Dukes when he announced a revamped front bench just months later, on August 31, 1988. Out, too, went Dukes critics John Boland and Fergus O'Brien, creating a neat conspiratorial rump.

Ivan Yates, despite a solo run on Progressive Democrats links, was retained on Dukes's first team. There is more than a suggestion that, while the Donnellan issue did not help Kenny's frontbench case, the old doubts about his application and interest in the job were also at play.

"Enda appeared pretty unfocused at that point. His marriage some years later definitely changed that," one colleague said.

Dinny McGinley, a native Irish speaker from Donegal South West, took on Kenny's job as Gaeltacht spokesman. Another Mayo rival for promotion, Dail newcomer Jim Higgins from Mayo East, took over the pivotal job of Chief Whip.

Fine Gael was now languishing in the opinion polls. Dukes was being upstaged in the Dail by Des O'Malley and the Progressive Democrats, who seemed able to get headlines while also backing Haughey's cutbacks.

144

Dick Spring of Labour, one of the shrewdest politicians of his generation, came to be associated in the public mind as leading the challenge to Haughey. Effectively, Spring was seen as leader of the opposition.

Alan Dukes's time as Fine Gael leader would prove very short indeed.

****

Few people wanted the general election Charlie Haughey called for June 15, 1989, after just 26 months in government. But Enda Kenny had his own very acute reasons for not wanting it.

When the local Mayo West Fine Gael organisation met to pick candidates on Friday, May 26, proceedings were delayed for two hours as they could not get a western running mate for Enda Kenny. Patrick Durcan of Westport, who had unsuccessfully stood four times previously and in February 1987 publicly criticised the local organisation's failure to enforce canvass territory agreements, insisted he was not available.

Kenny argued that, since Fianna Fail heavy-hitter Denis Gallagher of Achill was retiring, the two out of three for Fine Gael was now a real prospect. Patrick Durcan was unmoved. He said nobody should be surprised, as three months previously he had said he would not be standing in the next election due to family and work demands.

"The campaign organisers were well aware of my intentions months ago," he told *The Connaught Telegraph*.

The meeting was adjourned until the following Monday night, May 29, little over a fortnight away from polling day. Officially, the story was they were delaying to see who the Fianna Fail replacement candidate for Gallagher was, but in reality a weekend of frantic Fine Gael activity ensued.

On that Saturday night, Kenny's former director of elections and now long-time local foe, Cllr Frank Durcan of Castlebar, declared he was standing as an Independent.

Frank Durcan promptly stole a march by getting the endorsement of the Mayo anglers, who were part of a loud and effective campaign against a rod-licence fee.

The rod-licence row had bedevilled Haughey's government as the campaign opposing it swept the country. It was promptly dropped by the next administration.

Patrick Durcan of Westport insisted that the candidature of his cousin, Cllr Frank Durcan of Castlebar, had no bearing on his decision not to stand alongside Kenny. Those who knew the two Durcans appreciated the truth of that statement as they were not especially friendly.

But to some outside Fine Gael who liked their political conspiracies, this one looked rather like Kenny could be the meat in a 'Durcan and Durcan sandwich'. It could have fuelled a puckish verse or two from their namesake, the celebrated Mayo poet Paul Durcan.

There were some predictions that Frank Durcan's impact would be to end the 'Fianna Fail two, Fine Gael one' result which had persisted in the previous five elections, with Kenny being knocked off his poll-topping perch and Fianna Fail at risk of losing their second seat. But all these theories aside, the reality was that Kenny seriously needed a strong candidate as sweeper in the west of the constituency.

His dilemma was resolved by the surprise emergence of the man one local paper called Myles 'Lazarus' Staunton, at the resumed Fine Gael convention on that Monday night.

There was a great deal of irony here as the Westport-based businessman's government promotion prospects had been blocked by the Kenny family as the price of providing Taoiseach Liam Cosgrave with a by-election candidate in October 1975.

Myles Staunton, who died a revered Westport community figure in June 2011 aged 75, had announced he was quitting politics for business after being very disappointed at losing in the 1979 European Parliament elections.

Back in 1973, he had outpolled Kenny's father, making him a

real threat, and he was in later times a Senator.

The reasons for Staunton's June 1989 political resurrection are still a matter of speculation. No evidence of a deal emerged, but it is notable that he had enough party support to succeed in winning a Seanad seat after the Dail election concluded.

Towards the end of the campaign, a clearly frustrated Enda Kenny accused the media of underplaying, if not ignoring, Fine Gael's support for the anti-rod-licence campaign. His supporters resented the fact that the anglers had put the Kenny name after that of Frank Durcan on the list of candidates recommended for support.

Kenny, in common with other candidates, also supported a campaign to stop the 'Rape of the Reek' by opposing gold-mining plans for Ireland's holy mountain, Croagh Patrick, situated in his constituency. "One wonders what the official reaction would be if a company sought permission to mine on Fujiama, Japan's holy mountain, or Ayers Rock in Australia," he said.

Overall, this proved Enda Kenny's toughest campaign in his 14-year career thus far. Luckily for Kenny, Frank Durcan also ate into Fianna Fail candidate Padraig Flynn's Castlebar vote, helped by a backlash to the Fianna Fail government's rod-licence plans. In the end, it finished with a depleted Flynn heading the poll on almost 5,700 votes, Kenny on 5,385 and Fianna Fail's MJ O'Toole taking the third seat with 5,400 votes.

Kenny got 2,150 of Staunton's 3,573 votes in transfers, enough to take him over the quota in the second count. He was first home – but it was far from the usual poll-topping experience.

Frank Durcan polled a creditable 5,187. However it was not enough, and proved the high-water mark in his battle to overcome the Kenny machine in Dail elections.

Thanks to Myles 'Lazarus' Staunton, Kenny remained in business.

****

About 4pm on the evening of November 8, 1990, Alan Dukes was driving out the gate of Leinster House when the medium-sized brick that was his mobile phone sounded. It was the Fine Gael party chairman, Tom Enright, to tell him that dissident Fergus O'Brien had tabled a motion of no-confidence in him.

The end of Dukes's leadership was ugly, and centred on a very poor Fine Gael performance in the 1990 presidential election which saw Mary Robinson registering a historic win for a Labour-led grouping. It was a helter-skelter election, with Fianna Fail's candidate, Brian Lenihan, dramatically undone by giving two totally different accounts of phone calls he and colleagues made to the President's residence eight years earlier, in January 1982.

Lenihan, Haughey and others had tried unsuccessfully to contact President Patrick Hillery and persuade him not to dissolve the Dail but instead allow Fianna Fail a chance to form an alternative government without an election. Lenihan had first lied about the whole thing – then he was forced "on mature reflection" to admit it had happened.

There was a strong Mayo element to the contest, with Mary Robinson coming originally from Ballina and Padraig Flynn helping her to victory by way of a voter backlash to his very snide comments about her family life. On radio, Flynn said Mary Robinson had a new-found interest in her family – comments which won her votes.

But for Enda Kenny, the end result was a change from a second boss who did not rate him.

The June 1989 general election was a bigger struggle for Alan Dukes than it had been for Kenny. Fine Gael's gain of five seats was not enough and a proposed coalition pact with the Progressive Democrats went nowhere because they had lost eight TDs, bringing them down to six.

Eventually, the net result was a depleted Fianna Fail breaching a core value for the first time in their 63-year history and sharing cabinet seats in government. Haughey cut that deal against the very public advice of Padraig Flynn. To add to the irony, the deal was with Des O'Malley and the Progressive Democrats who, less than four years earlier, could not live inside Haughey's Fianna Fail.

Alan Dukes had struggled to persuade Austin Currie to stand for Fine Gael after failing over months to get a more heavyweight contender. Only a year earlier Currie had successfully switched out of Northern Ireland politics, where he had been a courageous civil-rights leader, to win a seat for Fine Gael in Dublin West.

Currie's presidential campaign struggled from the outset, with only token support from Fine Gael TDs and Senators. He came home third, winning just 17 per cent of the first-preference vote. The conclusion was worsened by director of elections Jim Mitchell advising his candidate not to attend the count.

At the moment Dukes received the call telling him about the no-confidence motion, he had been on his way to the count centre at the RDS in Dublin. He had turned back to hit the phones and assess his situation, unaware that his candidate, Austin Currie, would not be at the count either.

The absence meant that a bad Fine Gael election outcome looked vastly worse on the televised count declaration, with the party faithful largely absent. Dukes was gone within days. His colleagues had failed to appreciate the worth of his Tallaght Strategy, but most of them also felt his aloofness and apparently haughty demeanour had not helped him either.

Enda Kenny was among those in Fine Gael who shed no tears at the exit of Alan Dukes. He was very comfortable endorsing the unanimous choice of John Bruton as the new Fine Gael leader.

Kenny could look forward to a more rewarding career under Bruton as the party moved into a more harmonious phase. Well, that was the theory.

Reality would be somewhat different – on both counts.

PART 3

Getting Serious

CHAPTER 7

'Give The Dail A Ring'

It was the third time Enda Kenny had failed to win the confidence of a new Fine Gael leader.

On January 15, 1991, newly-elected leader John Bruton announced an expanded front-bench team of 21 out of the party's 55 TDs. But Kenny did not make the cut – he was named as junior spokesman responsible for job training and industrial relations.

First Garret FitzGerald, then Alan Dukes, and now John Bruton had shown that Enda Kenny did not readily spring to mind when picking their 'A Team'. FitzGerald only promoted Kenny at the very end of his 1982-87 government, Dukes did so in 1987 and then dropped him in 1988, now Bruton – whom he very definitely supported – did not pick him first off.

To assuage egos and keep idle minds away from plots, Bruton also set up four party policy-making committees. Kenny got to chair one of these, covering economic affairs; the other three chairmen were Ted Nealon of Sligo, Donal Carey of Clare and Jimmy Deenihan of Kerry.

It was also noticeable that Kenny's new Mayo rival in the promotion stakes, Jim Higgins of Mayo East, had made Bruton's front bench as Education spokesman. Higgins, who was increasingly getting noticed, had been a county councillor and Senator before winning a Dail seat from former Gaeltacht Minister Paddy O'Toole in February 1987.

Rated a very capable media performer, Higgins had been Fine Gael chief whip during the leadership heave against Alan Dukes in November 1990. At that time, many believed he did a good job as the 'honest broker' who eventually told Dukes he did not have the support to fight on.

Enda Kenny had no appetite for developing party policy in committee and had already discovered the benefits of delegation. A month later he announced that he had commissioned two reports for his new committee.

One of those would come from former party leader and economist, Alan Dukes, on the tricky political issue of the mandatory stopover by American flights at Shannon Airport. The second report, on the impact upon Irish farmers of EU Farm Commissioner Ray MacSharry's strategy in the global trade General Agreement on Tariffs and Trade (GATT) negotiations, would come from former MEP and now Senator Tom Raftery, who was also a university professor.

At the same time Kenny continued to up his constituency profile under pressure from rival Padraig Flynn, who was Environment Minister for the years 1987-1991 and later Justice Minister. Flynn had sanctioned funds for a remarkable campaign of road-building, a new Mayo County Council headquarters and a new county library, all in Castlebar.

Nationally, Flynn faced criticism as a minister – but locally he had the reputation of delivering. In June 1992, Kenny took on the issue of ground rents in Castlebar and the extraordinary case of Lord Lucan.

This was the story of the ultimate absentee English landlord, as it was by then 18 years since Richard Bingham, 7th Earl of Lucan, had disappeared without trace and was sought on suspicion of murdering his childrens' nanny.

Among the unfinished Lucan business were Castlebar ground rents worth an estimated IR£30,000 per year, which included Kenny's own constituency offices on Tucker Street, over which he also had a small flat.

For the more cynical observers, Lucan's rents in Castlebar were a summer story which filled space when the courts and the Dail shut down. But Kenny announced that he was visiting London to meet Lucan's son and later wrote to the-then British Prime Minister, John Major, on the issue.

Later that summer Kenny voiced strong views on the management of the Mayo county football side after another disappointing season and the departure of manager Brian McDonald. Kenny felt it would be a mistake to recruit outside the county as his analysis showed only one of the 10 previous All-Ireland winning teams had been managed by an outsider. That was Eugene McGee of Longford, who won with Offaly in 1982.

Furthermore, in comments which will still resonate with some GAA fans, he criticised what he called a "trend towards lucrative GAA contracts" for managers, which were harming small clubs. "The Central Council and Congress must insist on all such agreements being made public, including payments over and under the counter, benefits in kind etc," he said.

Back in Dublin, John Bruton was still struggling to keep order in the Fine Gael house as the party trailed in the opinion polls. But an even bigger drama was also unfolding inside the Fianna Fail-Progressive Democrats coalition – and it was making an early general election look unavoidable.

Things began to look up for Enda Kenny on September 30, 1992, when John Bruton named him as chief whip in a revamped Fine Gael front bench – almost two years after Bruton took over as leader. The new team saw the return of former leader Alan Dukes as environment spokesman and the retention of Jim Higgins as education spokesman.

Charlie Haughey had put together the coalition with his arch-enemy, Des O'Malley, after the June 1989 election. Against all predictions, Haughey had manoeuvred the change of approach within Fianna Fail politics with considerable skill and he was met with pragmatism by O'Malley on the other side.

But within Fianna Fail there was a deep-seated discontent at

155

having to give two cabinet seats to the Progressive Democrats. Finance Minister Albert Reynolds addressed a party rally in Kanturk, Co Cork, on Friday evening, February 16, 1990, and his comments drew wild applause.

"I hope that the temporary little arrangement which we have with our partners won't be there all that long and that we'll be back to where we were at the start," Reynolds said. His comments were picked up on tape by a local radio reporter, John O'Connor of Cork Sound, who duly relayed them countrywide.

It was the first of many public indications that Fianna Fail had not yet made the cultural transition to power-sharing and that Charlie Haughey's days as leader were numbered.

At the party's 1991 Ard Fheis, Maire Geoghegan-Quinn did things more subtly, with warm praise of Haughey – but framed in the past tense.

Kenny's Mayo rival Padraig Flynn – who had very publicly opposed sharing cabinet power in June 1989 – revealed the depth of his disillusionment and the extent of his instincts for power when he obliged Haughey to sack him from his government post alongside Reynolds in late 1991. By February 1992 Albert Reynolds was leader of Fianna Fail and Taoiseach.

The coalition with the Progressive Democrats would not last much longer. From the moment Reynolds took over, it became two parallel governments: there was the formal 15-member Cabinet and the Reynolds kitchen cabinet.

A bitter row over the State's Export Credit Insurance scheme, previously run by Reynolds as Industry Minister, was played out in 1992 at the notorious Beef Tribunal of Inquiry into allegations of serious corruption in that sector. At Tribunal hearings, O'Malley repeated on oath his view that Reynolds had been "grossly unwise, reckless and foolish"; Reynolds told the Tribunal O'Malley was "dishonest".

"I had no option but to get out," O'Malley recalled.

The government fell on November 5, 1992. Albert Reynolds, relying on advice from Padraig Flynn and others, was very bullish about winning an overall majority for his party. Polling was fixed for November 25.

On the campaign trail, Reynolds soon learned very brutally that he was utterly wrong to believe he could do what Charlie Haughey had failed to do in five attempts throughout the 1980s. The last time Fianna Fail won an overall majority was in June 1977 – Flynn and Reynolds had not learned how Irish politics had so fundamentally changed.

This was the second time Flynn had got it wrong in advising his party leader to risk all in an avoidable general election. In summer 1989 he was among those who urged Charlie Haughey to call an early election in a vain quest for an overall majority.

Now Enda Kenny, newly appointed Fine Gael chief whip, made another prediction. He said Fine Gael was the best-equipped and organised that it had been in years to fight an election and would be "in a commanding position" afterwards.

But this statement was made more in hope than in confidence and had little basis in reality.

****

As far as Enda Kenny was concerned, Fine Gael would "self-destruct" if it did not get into power.

"Fine Gael will have to get into government. If we stay in opposition the public will be asking who we are at the next general election," he rather too candidly told *The Irish Press* on November 30, 1992.

It was five days after the general election which had brought grief to John Bruton and the increasingly fractious Fine Gael party he had led for just two years. Power seemed to be the only remedy – but others, notably Labour and Dick Spring, who were in the driving seat, had very different ideas.

In Mayo, Enda Kenny had a very tough campaign. Padraig Flynn was at the height of his powers in a 25-year local political career. He had pulled in 9,629 first preferences, more than 2,000 votes above the quota, to top the poll and his surplus helped bring home a second Fianna Fail candidate, solicitor Seamus Hughes from Westport.

Flynn fought the election as Justice Minister, the post he got as reward from Albert Reynolds for helping to oust Charlie Haughey. A month after the election, Reynolds appointed Flynn as Ireland's EU Commissioner, a job worth IR£120,000 per year with perks and a generous tax regime.

Rumours of this European Union appointment were rife throughout the election. But with his characteristic third-person self-references, he managed to downplay it. "I am running a campaign to have Flynn elected to Dail Eireann. That's what Flynn is trying to do now," Flynn said dismissively.

To make matters worse for Kenny, he had a new Fine Gael running mate who was to prove a very different proposition from the gentlemanly fellow candidates of previous elections.

Michael Ring of Westport was just weeks short of his 39th birthday when he won the party nomination at the convention in the Travellers' Friend Hotel in Castlebar on Sunday night, November 8.

He defeated veteran Myles Staunton, also of Westport, who had come to Kenny's rescue as a late running mate in the previous election in June 1989. Kenny supporters voted for Staunton to be nominated – but the majority of delegates thought Ring a better prospect.

Ring was a natural political campaigner and he eventually polled 5,136, almost 50 per cent up on Staunton's 1989 vote but not enough for a seat. Patrick Durcan – who had clashed with Kenny after the 1987 general election – was one of Ring's key campaign organisers and was to take a similar role in every election from then until February 2011.

"Durcan's strategic and organisational skills, combined with Ring's energy and ability to connect with people, were a powerful combination," one local party activist remembered.

Ring's haul and Flynn's huge vote clearly depressed Kenny's vote.

He had to rely on almost 500 transfers from Flynn's surplus and the elimination of the dissident former Fianna Fail Independent, Paraic Cosgrove of Erris, to get him elected. Seamus Hughes took the final seat for Fianna Fail.

Nationally, Fianna Fail's campaign had been a directionless shambles as they took the brunt of the blame for the Beef Tribunal controversy and were damaged by other gaffes made by the Taoiseach. Reynolds' popularity rating, which had been 63 per cent in summer 1992, had slumped to 28 per cent by the eve of polling six months later. The party lost nine seats, bringing them to a low of 68 TDs – their worst election performance since 1927.

But John Bruton's Fine Gael fared worse: 10 fewer seats and just 45 TDs in the biggest reverse in half a century for a main opposition party. The Progressive Democrats, further emphasising that voters believed O'Malley over Reynolds, gained four seats for a grand total of 10.

Labour were the big winners, though, with Dick Spring's effective leadership of opposition performances really catching the public mood. They gained 18 seats for an all-time high of 33 TDs – and the driving role in fashioning a new government, with several options on coalition make-up.

Enda Kenny's Fine Gael colleagues knew he was right about his "self-destruct" warning – but many felt he was just too naive to be so public and forthright. The party's leader in the Seanad, Senator Maurice Manning, a good friend of Kenny's, described the comments as "nonsense", stressing they needed a good government programme as the basis of any coalition.

For Kenny and party colleagues, the shape of the government was obvious: it should be John Bruton leading a Fine Gael-Labour-Progressive Democrats coalition, which totted up to 88 Dail seats and created a comfortable overall majority capable of going a full term.

Labour could not overcome the legacy of the poor relationship between Bruton and Spring in the 1982-87 government and felt that Fine Gael presumed too much in expecting to lead in the current circumstance. Labour also had difficulty with the Progressive Democrats' free market rhetoric and were uncomfortable giving Democratic Left, with their four TDs, freedom in opposition to build a hard-left base.

Again speaking as Fine Gael chief whip, Kenny made it clear that Democratic Left – which had come out of the Official IRA and had until recently been called the Workers' Party – were not acceptable to his party. There could also be no question of Labour getting their way on a 'rotating Taoiseach', with Bruton and Spring taking turns.

"We made it crystal clear during the campaign that what we sought to do was to form an effective government with Labour and the Progressive Democrats," Enda Kenny stated on RTE radio, on December 3.

"Were we to form an alliance with Democratic Left, we would have to go back to the people whom we told quite clearly during the election on a number of occasions that we would not do so."

Bruton and Spring had a brief and tetchy meeting on Sunday morning, December 6, 1992, in the Constitution Room of the Shelbourne Hotel in Dublin. Spring did not even sit down, though this was because his back was extremely painful after a three-week campaign travelling the country, and it was clear both sides were more keen to score points off one another than talk coalition.

Just after that meeting Spring told his adviser Fergus Finlay that he had delivered some harsh truths to Bruton. "I told Bruton as straight as I could that he was impossible to work with before and I couldn't see any sign of change," Finlay later recalled Spring saying.

It all took weeks to play out and 1992 ended without a government. But Reynolds and Spring flung aside months of mutual political savaging – and the major basis for Labour's election campaign.

Spring's speech on November 5, the day Reynolds's first government collapsed, was rated one of the most anti-Fianna Fail Dail contributions of that era. He castigated Reynolds and then accused Fianna Fail of being blind to any kind of standards, and blind to the needs of the people they were supposed to represent.

"We will not support any government with the track record of this one," the Labour leader said. Then, just over two months later, Dick Spring became Tanaiste under Albert Reynolds as Taoiseach.

The first ever Fianna Fail-Labour government took office on January 12, 1993, optimistic that they could tap into an international economic upswing and spend an expected huge EU grant-aid windfall due to run for the next seven years. An EU leaders' summit on December 12 in Edinburgh agreed a total regional and social fund worth IR£65 billion, to be mainly shared among the 'poor four' countries, Spain, Greece, Portugal and Ireland, until the year 2000.

Reynolds had put the most optimistic and generous gloss on Ireland's expected share, claiming the country could take about one-eighth of the total. He announced an Irish take-up of IR£8 billion as fact – even though there was no agreement on how the aid cake would be divided and much tough negotiating lay ahead.

In the longer term, Reynolds was proved almost, but not quite, right about the EU grant-aid share for Ireland.

But the key point was that his handling of the summit outcome was crucial to his return as Taoiseach – and days after Edinburgh he was in talks with Spring and Labour. Spring later said he had also been keen to get involved in Reynolds's Northern Ireland initiatives.

The EU funds and the government deal brought a brief salvation for Reynolds and a whole heap of future problems for Spring and Labour. But, despite Albert Reynolds's profound dislike of giving two cabinet posts to the Progressive Democrats, he now had to give six senior ministries to Labour as the price of staying in power.

For Bruton, and the newly favoured Enda Kenny, it was a crushing blow. As predicted by Kenny, Fine Gael were now set to have a good go at self-destructing over the following two years.

****

Enda Kenny was John Bruton's chief whip through the trauma of the Fine Gael self-destruct years,1992-1994. But he was not Bruton's first choice for the job when the latter was elected leader in November 1990.

However, after taking on the pivotal role almost two years later, in October 1992, Kenny proved an invaluable and loyal ally to Bruton in his grim struggle for survival.

The year 1993 was all about mutterings and rumours of coups and heaves in Fine Gael, with the names Michael Noonan and Jim Mitchell featuring, plus that of former leader Alan Dukes.

In fact, Dukes was first out of the traps to attack his successor when Fine Gael TDs, Senators and MEPs met on January 21, 1993, to consider their position. The crucial meeting followed an election which had seen them lose 10 TDs, and government negotiations that left them marginalised in opposition.

Dukes opposed a motion of confidence in Bruton as leader, saying that if he had led the party to lose 10 Dail seats he would have resigned – and not sought a renewal of his mandate.

Kenny was clearly on Bruton's side: a photograph in the next day's papers showed him holding an umbrella while squiring his boss into the meeting. Six other TDs spoke up for Bruton, leaving Dukes in the minority and accused of sour grapes as a former leader drummed out of his job.

But Dukes was not that easily sidelined. He was a good media performer and an astute reader of policy issues on environment, for which he was party spokesman. The following Sunday he did a long RTE radio interview in which he made it clear that he was not going to recant any of his Bruton criticisms – and did not rule out the prospect of an eventual comeback as leader.

That intervention led another ambitious Fine Gael TD, finance spokesman Michael Noonan, to stir himself. He took some high-profile stances on various policy issues and then gave a long interview to his local newspaper, the *Limerick Leader,* on February 4, 1993, saying he was interested in the leadership.

Noonan said the confusion and speed with which Fine Gael changed leader in November 1992 meant he did not let his name go forward. He also felt the party needed to settle – and then got to the point.

"But if a vacancy occurred in the medium term – and it is unlikely to – then I would be putting my name forward," Noonan said.

Such things were duly noted by Bruton and his kitchen cabinet, who now included Dublin North TD and grand-niece of Michael Collins, Nora Owen, shortly to become deputy Fine Gael leader. On March 4 Bruton announced a long-awaited big front-bench shake-up which saw Enda Kenny continuing as chief whip.

Bruton shuffled his potential rebels, with Alan Dukes moved sideways from environment to agriculture, and Michael Noonan demoted from finance to transport, energy and communications. There was no place for Jim Mitchell, a former justice and later transport minister, but this was explained away by his planned appointment as chairman of the Dail Public Accounts Committee.

The Finance job went to young gun Ivan Yates of Wexford, who had briefly thrown his hat into the leadership race in November 1992 and was frequently cited as a future leader. But he was balanced by another ambitious Wexford TD, Avril Doyle, who got Dukes's old job as environment spokesperson.

The next anti-Bruton missile followed swiftly. On March 29, 1993, Jim Mitchell told his Dublin Central constituency party members that a new 20-member Commission of Renewal announced days earlier was probably Bruton's last chance to remain as leader and everything hinged on upcoming by-elections in Mayo West and Dublin South Central.

The Commission had some senior lawyers including Dermot Gleeson, a future Attorney General; economist Professor Patrick

Honohan, who became head of the Central Bank in 2009; former Irish ambassador to the USA Sean Donlon; Meath football coach Sean Boylan, and RTE's former London correspondent Mike Burns. It was to report on the calamitous events of the previous year and try to chart a new political approach for Fine Gael.

Mitchell sent his speech to all the newspapers. He was trying to give Bruton a deadline of the following autumn to shape up or quit.

"We cannot allow Fine Gael to die a slow death," he said in a later interview.

The rumblings dragged on well into the summer of 1993. But at a special Fine Gael parliamentary-party meeting on September 7, called to prepare for the new Dail year, Bruton challenged his colleagues to "put up or shut up". In response he got a series of declarations about the need for loyalty – so he said the issue of leadership was now "closed".

"The issue is now off the agenda," said party chairman and Tipperary North TD Michael Lowry, rather optimistically.

Waterford TD Austin Deasy commented that Fine Gael's problems were more about maintaining political relevance than about leadership.

The meeting also heard an interim report from the Commission on the Renewal of Fine Gael. Michael Lowry, who was also party director of finances, told them that the party's IR£1.2 million debt had been cut to IR£900,000 and the target of IR£500,000 could be achieved before the end of 1993.

The party was moving back from financial Armageddon, thanks to Lowry's fundraising flair – though this would also have a cost in the future. But the leadership issue was by no means "off the agenda".

****

It was 3.50pm on Thursday February 10, 1994, when the four Fine Gael TDs walked into the leader's office at Leinster House to have their requested meeting with John Bruton.

The four were more than surprised to see Bruton was not alone. Seated next to him were his chief whip, Enda Kenny, deputy leader Nora Owen, and National Executive chairman Donal Carey.

John Bruton had been hearing all the rumours of meetings in various Dail offices over the previous days. Confirmation that he was to be confronted came that morning when the four asked for the meeting. He had summoned his back-up team and was now ready to fight for his political life.

The four TDs – soon to be called the 'Gang of Four' – were from the party's solid middle ground and not the expected suspect rebels. They were Dublin South TD Alan Shatter, Jim O'Keeffe of Cork South West, Jim Higgins of Mayo East and Charlie Flanagan of Laois-Offaly.

Jim O'Keeffe was first to speak. He said they appreciated that Bruton was doing his best as leader but the party continued to slip in the opinion polls – even despite the unpopularity of the Fianna Fail-Labour coalition, which was floundering on unpopular issues such as a proposed property tax.

An opinion poll earlier that week had put Fine Gael's core support at just 13 per cent and there were fears that they could head into single figures. The four now believed John Bruton should "consider his position".

Kenny and his colleagues remained silent throughout the encounter. Bruton replied forcefully that he had no intention of resigning and would face down any and every challenge.

The four had been prepared to agree some breathing space to allow Bruton to mull things over. However once he came out fighting, they had no option but to tender their own resignations. They had gone there looking for him to quit – but they ended up by quitting themselves.

It was very much first blood to Bruton and Co. But the big question now was whether he could win a confidence vote from the 66 TDs, Senators and MEPs.

There followed four days of frenetic lobbying and canvassing, and Enda Kenny deployed all his skills with the parliamentary-party members, with whom he was still extremely popular. Kenny also formally proposed a motion of confidence in Bruton and made a strong defence to the party's 45 TDs, 17 Senators and four MEPs at their meeting on February 14.

In all, 41 people spoke and the meeting lasted over seven hours. Some of those present calculated that 20 people spoke for Bruton, 16 against and five speakers were noncommital. There were strong views put by both sides, with Jim Higgins, Kenny's most recent Mayo rival in the promotion stakes, asking members how many of them had used posters carrying John Bruton's photograph in the previous general election.

Senator Paddy Burke, a long-time ally of Kenny's in Castlebar and in the party at Leinster House, made a comparison between Fine Gael and the Mayo county footballers. He said they had sacked four managers in succession and then hired a Kerryman, Jack O'Shea, and still failed to win a match of any importance.

Michael Noonan, who had signalled his intention to stand for the leadership if the leader was ousted, said Bruton lacked the required media skills. There was some surprise when Frances Fitzgerald, promoted in her first Dail term by Bruton, announced that she thought a change of leader was needed.

The vote was by secret ballot and papers were counted by parliamentary-party chairman Michael Lowry and the grand old man of the party, Peter Barry of Cork, whose neutral credentials were enhanced by his intention to retire at the next election. They were both insistent that the detailed figures on the result would remain secret.

Bruton emerged from the meeting room at just after 6pm to announce that he had won the confidence vote and was pleased with the meeting and the verdict. "Things were said that needed to be said," he added, putting his best foot forward.

Those supporting Bruton put it about that it was a decisive 41-25 result in his favour. But the count took 22 minutes to complete and this allowed some anti-Bruton people to claim a much closer outcome of 35 votes to 31.

Whatever the specifics, the rebels accepted Bruton had won. "The party has spoken. I accept their decision," Charlie Flanagan said.

On the RTE Six One news Bruton said the leadership issue was "definitively put aside" and it was time to concentrate on policy.

"It is time for the party to stop looking in on itself and time for it to speak to the people," he stated.

Magnanimity was not on the agenda when John Bruton announced his new front bench a week later. Seven people were dropped – the gang of four plus would-be leadership contenders Michael Noonan and Alan Dukes and the surprise Bruton opponent, Frances Fitzgerald.

There were several new faces, but his key lieutenants got additional rewards. Nora Owen continued as deputy leader with responsibility for foreign and European affairs; Donal Carey continued as National Executive chairman and also became director of organisation; Enda Kenny remained as chief whip but with additional responsibility as regional development spokesman.

Bruton was proved right in his view that the leadership was sorted until after the next election. This was largely because things began to look up for the party, and their leader, in the following months.

The year 1994 would also prove a very good one for Enda Kenny. He had started very well by picking the right side in a heave – unlike his Mayo rival, Jim Higgins.

****

The man with the Fianna Fail badge had an urgent question for Padraig Flynn, the veteran Mayo politician who was now EU Commissioner for Social Affairs and Employment.

"Does this mean European funds for the West will dry up?" the man asked earnestly.

Flynn – who had just seen daughter Beverley lose in the by-election to choose his Dail replacement for Mayo West – had somehow maintained a smiling face at the count centre. But he was beginning to run out of patience.

"Don't be so stupid. This has nothing to do with that. I'm here in a private capacity to vote for my daughter. I voted a plumper for her, too," Commissioner Flynn replied.

It was June 10, 1994, and just 18 months earlier, at the same count centre, Padraig Flynn had been the poll-topping political king of Mayo West. Was it too much to expect that his clearly able and well-qualified daughter, Beverley, could take over the family seat?

The answer to that was a resounding 'Yes' – an abject lesson in how quickly political loyalties can switch, even in the traditional Mayo heartland.

There were several key reasons for this display of political in-gratitude. One was the 18-month delay in holding the by-election to replace Flynn, who had resigned from the Dail in January 1993. This was deemed an abuse of government power but, more importantly, it also saw a changed local political agenda.

An Independent candidate, Paddy McGuinness, caught the voters' attention with a strong campaign for the independent academic status of the new Regional Technical College (RTC) in Castlebar. Too many people felt it was being treated as an 'out-house' of its Galway counterpart and the blame for that rested with the Fianna Fail-Labour coalition government.

There was some dissent in the Castlebar Fianna Fail camp, with some critics feeling Padraig Flynn had swanned off to 'Euroland'. Then he parachuted in Beverley, who was working in banking in Dublin, to carry on his political fiefdom.

And last, but by no means least, the voters of Mayo West had met the political phenomenon called Michael Ring of Westport, who was standing for Fine Gael.

Beverley Cooper-Flynn had campaigned well, with a cheeky slogan, 'Up Bev,' a pun on the decades'-old mantra extolling the party's founder, Eamon de Valera. She was top of the poll but her almost-11,000 number one votes were not enough.

Ring, who had put in a huge rolling campaign lasting 14 months, was 600 votes behind 'Bev' on the first count. But McGuinness, whose slogan was 'McGuinness Is Good For You', polled a huge 6,275. It all hung on where these would transfer.

Also on the ballot was Dr Jerry Cowley of Mulranny, who stopped his canvass once the government approved IR£7.5 million in funding for a new development at Mayo County Hospital. Cowley, an Independent TD from 1997 to 2002, withdrew too late to take his name off ballot papers and on the day got 388 votes.

Cllr Johnny Mee, a well-known local historian and typesetter with *The Connaught Telegraph*, stood for Labour in one of the party's very rare outings in Mayo. Clearly damaged by Labour Education Minister Niamh Bhreathnach's stance on the RTC issue, he got 1,103 first-preference votes, similar to his last outing, in the 1981 general election.

With the quota at 14,562 votes, returning officer Patsy Murphy decided to eliminate the three lowest candidates – McGuinness, Mee and Cowley – all at once in the second count. It turned out to be nail-biting stuff.

At lunchtime, veteran Fianna Fail numbers man Seamus Brennan was on RTE radio logically arguing that first-preference votes for McGuinness and Mee, as Castlebar people, would heavily transfer to Beverley Cooper-Flynn and elect her. But Fine Gael tallymen had been noting all morning a heavy transfer rate – out of Castlebar town – to their man Michael Ring.

Phone calls were made to Fine Gael leader John Bruton, who was about to receive the best piece of news he got since taking over as party leader three-and-a-half years earlier. Bruton collected his wife, Finola, at their home in Dunboyne, Co Meath, and headed west – daring to hope that his luck might be on the turn.

There were 1,421 non-transferable votes. Of the remainder, Cooper-Flynn got 2,672 votes but Ring got 3,673. The Fine Gael man had it by just 424 votes, triggering huge celebrations in his native Westport, which had not returned a Fine Gael TD since 1973.

Ring had capitalised on his very respectable vote in the November 1992 general election. Fianna Fail predictions that this time he had peaked too early and canvassed too long were wrong.

His supporters believed that the atrocious rain of the previous general-election campaign had impeded him, along with not being well known enough in the Erris area, in the north-west of the constituency.

This time luck was with him and Bruton was very glad he had travelled to Castlebar for the victory declaration. It all had special relevance for his wife, Finola, better known as Finola Gill in her home town of Westport.

A rare good day for Bruton contrasted with a bad day for Padraig Flynn: the potential 'Flynnasty' appeared stuck at the starting gate. Both he and his daughter were a model of dignity and decorum – but the surprise and hurt also showed as the Fianna Fail post-mortems, better known as 'the blame game', began immediately.

Beverley wistfully noted that Castlebar had done well out of her father's term as Environment Minister. Padraig Flynn frankly said not enough Castlebar people voted for her.

"Nobody worked as hard as she did. But the vote in Castlebar, the home base, definitely let her down. We expected a much higher first-count figure than actually happened," he remarked.

Nationally, the outcomes of this by-election and another on the same day which saw Democratic Left candidate Eric Byrne elected in Dublin South Central were to change Dail arithmetic. These and other events would soon help to throw a lifeline to John Bruton and Fine Gael.

But for now, both Bruton and his colleagues were grateful for some good news to settle things down. Some within the party had been openly saying that a good performance – and probably a win – was necessary if Bruton wanted to continue as leader.

"John Bruton will be able to lead rather than cautiously look over his shoulder," veteran *Irish Independent* political correspondent Chris Glennon wrote.

Enda Kenny was among those credited with playing a wholehearted role in Ring's successful campaign – though he knew his new colleague's no-holds-barred attitude meant internal strife ahead. "Kenny knew things were going to be different from now on," one local party supporter recalled.

Ring's acceptance speech banished any naive thoughts that magnanimity might prevail in the wake of victory.

"I'm a fighter – and I proved it, too," he stated.

"I have told John Bruton I will not be happy with the back benches," he added.

This assessment of Michael Ring by Castlebar journalist Sean Rice and printed in *The Connacht Tribune* before Ring's first Dail election outing is extremely telling.

"Ever since he was first elected to Westport Urban District Council, Michael Ring has exuded a hunger for political fulfillment. And his steady climb up the ladder, to Mayo County Council last year with a huge poll, and now to the Fine Gael ticket for the Dail, has brought new spirit to the grass roots Fine Gael in the constituency," Sean Rice wrote.

The key phrases – which recur again and again – in descriptions of Ring are 'hunger' and 'a connection with the grass roots'. One of Michael Ring's campaign slogans had been 'Give The Dail A Ring'; another was 'Give Kenny A Ring In The Dail'.

Two busloads of people travelled from Mayo to Dublin for Ring's first Dail session and someone among them produced a handbell outside Leinster House. There was 'A Ring In The Dail' now – its peals continue to be heard to this day and often do not foretell happiness for Enda Kenny.

****

Mary Harney cast a sardonic look across the Dail chamber at the Fine Gael benches. The year 1994 was drawing to a close, with a turn of events that no thriller-writer would get away with advancing as any kind of believable plot line.

John Bruton was about to be elected Taoiseach, heading the most diverse band of people – many of them sworn political enemies until just weeks beforehand. Fine Gael were putting together a Rainbow Government with Dick Spring's Labour, who had been demonising Bruton up to 10 days before this, and with Democratic Left, whom Fine Gael had long insisted were political untouchables.

"If somebody told me a few months ago that a County Meath farmer would bring Democratic Left into his first government, I would have said, 'Bring the men in the white coats to see me.' I do not know if Pat Rabbitte will get the farm, but these are certainly extraordinary events," summed up Mary Harney, who had taken over as Progressive Democrats leader a year earlier.

The political picture changed very swiftly from the summer of 1994, when Bruton had got his first break with the June by-election win by Michael Ring. Most importantly, the Fianna Fail-Labour government broke up in a chaotic chain of bad-tempered events. These saw the fall of Albert Reynolds as Taoiseach and Spring balking at a renewed deal with Bertie Ahern, Reynolds's successor as Fianna Fail leader.

There was some improvement in Fine Gael's and Bruton's for-tunes: two more good by-elections significantly changed the Dail arithmetic. On November 10, Fine Gael gained a seat through Hugh Coveney in Cork South Central, while Democratic Left added another TD in neighbouring Cork North Central with Kathleen Lynch.

But the Fine Gael knives were still out for Bruton and were only stayed by the emerging chaos in the government. Even as late as the first week of December 1994, the media continued to specu-late that Bruton could not survive as party leader.

The events surrounding the collapse of Albert Reynolds's Fi-anna Fail-Labour coalition in November 1994 are complex and remain to this day a matter of dispute. But both Fianna Fail and

Labour people active in the period agree that the handling of the final report of the Beef Tribunal in July 1994 was a major factor in the government falling apart five months later.

Since joining forces in January 1993, the two parties had muddled through a series of problems. These included a currency crisis in the EU's Exchange Rate Mechanism which led to devaluation of the punt; a IR£600 million shortfall in Reynolds's claimed EU aid take; scandal surrounding the State sugar company, Greencore; a row over Irish passports granted to a Saudi Arabian family who invested in Reynolds's family business, C&D Foods Ltd, and a Fianna Fail-driven tax amnesty.

The Beef Tribunal had been set up on May 31, 1991, following an ITV television programme which made a series of allegations about Co Louth beef baron Larry Goodman and claimed links to senior politicians. Under the chairmanship of High Court President Mr Justice Liam Hamilton, it ran for three years and cost taxpayers IR£30 million.

On July 31, 1994, the report was published in two doorstop volumes. Labour were enraged, claiming Reynolds "hijacked" the report by promptly telling the press that he was "vindicated" in relation to alleged impropriety when he was Industry Minister. Others felt this was an exaggeration, as the equivocal findings were that Reynolds did act in the national interest – but there should have been more scrutiny before Goodman got export credit insurance.

Alleged financial links between political parties and Goodman companies were ruled as normal political donations by Mr Justice Hamilton. But the links between business and political parties – including those involving Fine Gael and John Bruton – would be the subject of subsequent tribunals of inquiry.

Enda Kenny was active as chief whip trying to ensure a full Dail debate on the Beef Tribunal, a debate which would include questions to the Taoiseach. All this controversy, however, was totally overshadowed by the announcement of an IRA ceasefire on August 31, 1994. This was a milestone on the road to a Northern

Ireland settlement and a great credit to all concerned, especially Albert Reynolds, who had courageously led efforts to break the deadlock.

But trust had irreparably broken down between Spring and Reynolds, and Labour and Fianna Fail. Their government fell after revelations of failures in the processing of extradition warrants for the notorious paedophile priest, Fr Brendan Smyth.

This fed into a row over Fianna Fail's insistence on appointing controversial Attorney General Harry Whelehan as the new High Court President. The six Labour ministers withdrew from government, leaving it unclear whether or not they had resigned.

On November 17, 1994, Reynolds abandoned his efforts to defend himself, resigning as Taoiseach. Harry Whelehan then resigned as High Court President and apologised for having overlooked a second paedophile extradition case involving a man named Duggan.

Whelehan stressed that he did not know of these cases until controversy erupted and he was resigning mainly to protect the office of High Court President from political controversy. Reynolds said he did not wish to see a general election as it would jeopardise the Northern Ireland peace process.

Bertie Ahern was elected Fianna Fail leader two days later, on November 19. The expectation was that he would do a new government deal with Spring and Labour, and talks on a joint programme soon began.

But on the eve of a Dail vote to elect a new Taoiseach, other revelations emerged which suggested Ahern knew more, and at an earlier stage, about the extradition controversies than he had led Labour to believe. Ahern's supporters argued that this was a Labour device to avoid renewing government with Fianna Fail as the information concerned matters of detail and was not especially new.

But Labour said they had broken with Reynolds because he had been less than candid about all he knew and when he knew it. Now Ahern was in the same boat. Labour would look elsewhere

174

for allies to make a government – and John Bruton had been thrown a lifeline, which he swiftly grabbed.

There followed a remarkable softening of relationships between the previously feuding parties, Fine Gael, Labour and Democratic Left. This was largely driven by politicians' hard-headed realpolitik views about an available deal to get them into power.

But Enda Kenny, still John Bruton's chief whip, was among those who acted as a political ice-breaker, using his people skills and relations with people in all parties at Leinster House to help get the talking started.

Kenny's range of social contacts extended to Democratic Left – he had long been friendly with Pat Rabbitte, one of their senior people and a fellow Mayoman.

"Kenny was always good pals with Pat Rabbitte. They are two Mayo fellows of similar age who like drinking pints and talking about football," one person close to the events revealed.

Things were helped by a much-improved personal relationship between Democratic Left leader Proinsias De Rossa and John Bruton. Bruton was from wealthy Meath farming stock and revered John Redmond and the old Irish Parliamentary Party. De Rossa was a Dublin potato-dealer who had been interned as an IRA member in the late 1950s.

But both now shared a similar view on the North's conflict, though they had arrived at their views in very different ways. "I particularly admire Deputy Bruton's thinking on Northern Ireland and his willingness to move beyond the shibboleths of the past," De Rossa told the Dail as he explained his reasons for allying with Fine Gael.

It was the first time in Ireland's history that a government changed without an election and the process took almost a month to complete.

In the Dail on December 15, 1994, at precisely 12.10pm, government 'teller' or vote counter Enda Kenny took possession of the result. It elected his boss, John Bruton, as Taoiseach by a score of 85 to 74.

John 'Phoenix' Bruton – as his deputy leader Nora Owen described him to much hilarity when proposing his candidature to the Dail – headed up to Aras an Uachtarain to get his seal of office. Two hours later he was back with his chosen cabinet, which included eight Fine Gael nominees, six Labour members, and one for Democratic Left – plus a 'super-junior' ministerial post for them which had a non-voting right of attendance at cabinet.

Labour's big prize was the appointment of Ruairi Quinn as Finance Minister, which spread the party's influence into every wing of government. Democratic Left leader Proinsias De Rossa was appointed Social Welfare Minister and his colleague Pat Rabbitte, as the aforementioned 'super-junior', ensured that the party would be represented at cabinet meetings if De Rossa were absent on business.

Enda Kenny was among Bruton's nominees – named as Minister for Trade and Tourism. It was a good appointment for someone representing a western constituency.

Nineteen years and almost one month after he first took his Dail seat, he was finally a member of cabinet.

CHAPTER 8

A Taste For Power

Enda Kenny's Department of Tourism and Trade soon became known across the civil service as 'happy valley'.

The designation was a mixed blessing. It certainly was a tribute to the new minister's sunny personality and courtesy.

It was also a recognition that Tourism and Trade were not blood-and-guts political operations but 'softer' departments with a lower profile and periodic opportunities for good-news media appearances. Enda Kenny's time at the Cabinet table – which spanned two-and-a-half years, from December 15, 1994 until June 26, 1997 – was also a very upbeat period in Ireland. The economy was on the mend, EU grant aid was boosting already growing national confidence and there was an emerging peace in the North.

But the term 'happy valley' also suggested a minister easily managed by his own officials who, in the fashion of the television political satire Yes, Minister, were the ones who called the shots. He did, however, follow Taoiseach John Bruton's advice and the example of government partners Labour and Democratic Left by appointing a non-civil servant, Fine Gael general secretary Ivan Doherty, as his key adviser or programme manager.

"The term 'nice' often gets a bad press in politics. When you hear someone say 'nice fellow' about a politician, nine times out of 10 it's followed by some criticism that he's not really at the races," a senior politician of that era commented.

A cabinet colleague of Kenny's from that time is more

trenchantly critical: "Was he all that interested? He certainly did not often give that impression," the former minister said.

It is clear that, at the very least, Enda Kenny's reputation persisted as an easy-going man who liked to party.

"He continued to suffer for his gaiety and socialising," another of his colleagues explained.

These critics' accusations of Kenny being a lightweight, set against supporters' arguments that he suffered unjustly for not being pompous, were still bouncing about 20 years after he had first arrived at Leinster House. It was the same dynamic which had followed his late father, Henry Kenny, throughout his 21-year Dail career.

But leaving those arguments aside, Enda Kenny's ministerial term was extremely busy, with a huge volume of foreign travel and a considerably higher national profile. He also used his time closer to the government levers of power to be seen as delivering for Mayo, and some supporters argue that the foundations for Fine Gael's ascendancy in that county were laid in this period.

****

The new minister got his retaliation in early. Just over one week in his new office, and two days before Christmas 1994, Enda Kenny was announcing details of IR£6 million worth of new tourism development projects which would attract IR£1.5 million in EU funding.

That happy task would be repeated again and again during his term, as there was IR£370 million in EU tourism development funding available to Ireland over the following five years.

Projects being grant-aided in that first announcement included new leisure facilities for a hotel in Cork, a new conference centre for a Killarney hotel and 15 new cruisers for the River Shannon.

It did not take him long to deliver closer to home. In Budget 1995, Westport and Achill were included in a list of 'traditional seaside resorts' designated for special development tax incentives.

The Irish Times snootily commented that Westport was a marvellous place – but "hardly bucket-and-spade territory", a comment which did Enda Kenny no harm at all.

In June 1995, Prince Charles, heir to the British throne, visited Ireland and John Bruton's government pulled out all the stops for the first official visit by a senior member of the British Royal family since the foundation of the Irish State.

Many deemed Bruton's speech at dinner in Dublin Castle – in which he said the visit did more to improve British-Irish relations "than any other event in my lifetime" – was too effusive and sycophantic.

Enda Kenny got by far the better end of the deal as the prince also visited scenic Delphi Lodge in southwest Mayo to do some quiet fishing. Prince Charles did not catch anything, but at least he was treated to some of the most beautiful scenery in the world.

"It is publicity for the western region which you just couldn't buy," the Tourism Minister insisted.

In January 1996 and obviously on the same principle, Enda Kenny was on hand to squire Prince Charles's younger brother Edward on a quick visit to Castlebar, which included a call into the new Mayo Regional Technical College. That visit was in connection with the Irish President's Gaisce Awards.

The minister also managed to brush off questions about opening a huge foreign holiday trade fair at the RDS encouraging people to go outside Ireland. Surely it was his job to promote holidays at home?

"True enough – but when you consider the quality and diversity of the total Irish holiday experience, that conflict of interest becomes largely irrelevant," he told reporters, and he got away with it.

Kenny also revamped Dublin's St Patrick's Day Parade, establishing a committee in autumn 1995 chaired by Gate Theatre boss Michael Colgan. Kenny joined Colgan and the parade grand marshal, soccer star Paul McGrath, to view the spectacle on March 17, 1996. The event was applauded in newspapers across the USA.

As time went on, a total of IR£20 million was pumped into tourism projects in Mayo, Roscommon and Galway. Scarcely a week went by without Kenny presiding at a launch or an opening of some kind. In June 1996 he opened the IR£250,000 Quiet Man Heritage Centre in Cong, Co Mayo, which celebrated the 1952 iconic movie that boosted Irish tourism across the world.

He had the pleasure of flying by helicopter into the north Galway village of Glenamaddy to open a IR£150,000 refurbished school, very close to his family's old home at Williamstown during the 1940s. He also gave a favourable hearing to grant applications by Williamstown handball club.

In autumn 1996 he supported the opening of talks which would lead to the famous Tour de France coming to Ireland in July 1998. He was later involved in preliminary talks on the Ryder Cup coming to Ireland.

The trade side of his portfolio brought involvement in world trade talks and collaboration with EU Trade Commissioner Leon Brittan. This work intensified in the six months from July to December 1996, when the Irish government acquitted itself well as holder of the EU Presidency.

On some of Kenny's frequent visits to Brussels, his reputation for doing Padraig Flynn impersonations enhanced his social standing with many in the EU capital who knew the Irish Commissioner.

He hosted several ministerial meetings in Ireland and on one occasion took his guests for late evening pints in Dessie Hynes's well-known pub at Baggot Street Bridge in Dublin. Even the usually stuffy and self-regarding Commissioner Brittan tagged along.

The demands of travel and his wife's work as the public relations executive for RTE took a very heavy toll on family life, especially as the couple now had three children. While rival politicians were muttering about his frequent absences from his Castlebar base, Kenny did not neglect Mayo politics or the grass roots.

He was in Brussels when controversy erupted about rat infestation in a school at Rathbane, in Bofeenaun, Co Mayo, in late November 1996. As luck would have it, Education Minister Niamh Bhreathnach was also in Brussels, and after talks between the two, Kenny announced that a new school would be provided as soon as possible, with interim accommodation immediately if necessary.

On the News At One on RTE radio, Kenny told presenter Sean O'Rourke he had first-hand experience of this problem as a teacher and had occasion to sneak back to school in the evening and shoot the rats. This surreal conversation then followed:

O'Rourke: "How many?"

Kenny: "I think I dispatched half a dozen."

O'Rourke: "How?"

Kenny: "By shotgun."

O'Rourke: "Politics must be quite boring by comparison?"

Kenny, laughing: "Well, it's a good thing to take out the odd rat."

O'Rourke, laughing even louder: "Well, I think we'll leave it there."

Also in Mayo, he tackled head-on the two major issues which threatened his own and Fine Gael's fortunes: the fractured relations with Knock Airport management and the status of the RTC in Castlebar.

From the moment he was appointed minister he worked at improving his relationship with the Airport board, to whom he had not been able to deliver funding when Garret FitzGerald was in power in the 1980s.

In the autumn of 1996, Kenny was at the heart of a potential airport-related development which could have meant hundreds of jobs for the area. Serious efforts were made to persuade the US freight group Alliance International to set up a major European hub at Knock. Kenny was among a group which travelled to Texas to meet one of the company principals, Ross Perot Junior, to discuss the idea.

Ross Perot Senior had made international headlines by standing twice in the US Presidential election, taking almost one-fifth of the popular vote on his first foray in 1992. Kenny and local rival Jim Higgins, by now a junior minister, successfully lobbied Finance Minister Ruairi Quinn to grant Knock Airport special tax reliefs in the Finance Bill approved on April 29, 1997.

That tax designation was hailed at the time as a deal-clincher. Kenny was heavily criticised by his Fianna Fail rivals for making "premature announcements" about the project and its potential.

But one Fianna Fail rival, Westport TD Seamus Hughes, came to his defence – a move viewed as being as much about annoying Michael Ring, who shared Hughes's Westport base, as anything else.

The timing of the tax designation and the Perot talks could not have been better for Kenny and Mayo Fine Gael, as a general election had been called for early June 1997. In fact the project would never happen for reasons beyond Kenny's control – but that did not become apparent until more than a year later.

As a general election loomed, the Mayo Regional Technical College action group remained extremely active and speculation continued that Castlebar businessman Paddy McGuinness would stand once again. In the June 1994 by-election, McGuinness had taken 6,500 votes and deprived Beverley Cooper-Flynn of a Dail seat by effectively helping to elect Michael Ring on transfers.

If McGuinness did stand, it was fair to assume that Fine Gael, as the government party, would take the brunt of the damage this time. Kenny announced that he had secured RTC funding totalling IR£1.8 million and the action group stood itself down, announcing that its work was done. Soon there would be more than 1,000 students on the new campus.

Paddy McGuinness is a native of Monaghan who lived most of his adult life in Castlebar, where he was active in both business and social initiatives such as the Castlebar International Song Contest. He now showed Kenny something which is often a scarce political commodity: gratitude.

McGuinness paid a warm tribute to Kenny's work, which he said was crucial.

"It had to be delivered at the cabinet table and Enda Kenny has done that," said McGuinness.

The McGuinness-Kenny relationship would continue to be a happy one for quite some time, with McGuinness successfully standing as a Fine Gael county council candidate in 2004 and later joining the party's Dail election-planning group.

In early 1997, Enda Kenny's wife Fionnuala decided not to return to work in RTE and the entire family relocated to Castlebar from their Dublin home. With his wife and three young children now in Mayo, there was an end to mutterings about him being an "absentee TD".

Kenny could look forward with some optimism to an election which had to happen by that year's end.

****

Being appointed to cabinet meant he could no longer be a county councillor. So Enda Kenny decided to keep things in the family as his older brother Henry became a co-opted member of Mayo County Council in February 1995.

"In politics, more than anything else, blood is thicker than water," Henry Kenny summed up some years later, reflecting on the Kenny family's political involvement in Mayo and Fine Gael. He frankly said that he had been happy to fulfill his promise made soon after their father's death in 1975 to defend his younger brother's political back.

Henry Kenny, named after his late father, a Mayo sporting and political legend, also frankly conceded that some local party people felt they had been passed over and resented the Kennys trying to build a dynasty. These local Fine Gael tensions had been fed by Henry's decision not to stand in the 1991 previous local elections, after he had failed to win a seat in the 1985 elections (he stood because of the defection of Cllr Frank Durcan).

Against all that, Henry Kenny handsomely beat four other contenders at a party selection convention to choose his brother's council replacement, held on Monday night, January, 30, 1995. Of the 232 Fine Gael delegates gathered at the Travellers' Friend, 104 voted for him in the first count, giving him more than twice his nearest rival's vote.

It is also clear that a strong acceptance – indeed, an expectation – of family succession in Irish politics was at play here. When Mayo County Council met in February 1995, another new Fine Gael councillor was co-opted with Henry Kenny. Nobody in any party raised an objection as Johnny Devaney of Lahardane took over the seat held by his recently deceased father Frank, for nearly 40 years.

Furthermore, Henry Kenny's experience was soon evident as he hosted a celebration at the Ballyvary Village Inn near his home outside Castlebar the week after his council co-option. It was billed as feting "Ballyvary's first councillor in nearly 50 years". He was re-elected to Mayo County Council at local elections in 1999, 2004 and 2009, and in June 2005 he was elected Cathaoirleach, an office neither his father nor brother ever held.

It soon became very clear why Enda Kenny appreciated having his big brother to watch his back in Mayo. Michael Ring unleashed a broadside on local radio in early August 1995, pointing to local grievances that tourism was in fact doing badly despite official statements from Bord Failte, which reported to Tourism Minister Enda Kenny.

Just weeks earlier, Minister Kenny had promised that Ireland was on target for its "best tourism year ever". He said visitor numbers for the first quarter of 1995 were up 16.7 per cent on the same period a year earlier.

Ring contradicted the national figures, and said Mayo was not reaping rewards, adding: "The figures are far short of what had been predicted earlier in the year."

The harsh criticism by Ring of party colleague Enda Kenny enraged the Castlebar wing of Fine Gael. It also delighted Ring's local Fianna Fail rival, Deputy Seamus Hughes, who was increasingly feeling the pressure of sharing his Westport base with the Fine Gael newcomer.

Hughes accused Ring of trying to "knife his fellow Fine Gael man". But Ring was unabashed and gave things another whirl, all the time insisting that his relations with Enda Kenny were "excellent as always".

"It was in no way disloyal to tell the truth as I see it. The people of West Mayo elected me to be truthful and honest. It suits Deputy Hughes to imagine 'knives' where there are none," Ring commented.

For Michael Ring, however, there could well be "knives out" inside Mayo Fianna Fail. He noted that Beverley Cooper-Flynn was determined to stand for the Dail next time out against Hughes and his two other party colleagues.

Clearly, not everybody was happy about Enda Kenny's 'happy valley' – and in Mayo it was already shaping up to be a very long and hard-fought general election campaign.

****

Amid all the political craziness of November and December 1994, few people other than full-time politicians noticed the announcement of a Dail Constituency Commission to update boundaries in line with population changes.

Chaired by Mr Justice Richard Johnson of the High Court, the independent Commission began work the following January and its report was published on time, on May 2, 1995. Overall changes were minimal – but Mayo was among the few exceptions.

Three-seat Mayo West, which had been basically unchanged since 1969, was amalgamated with neighbouring three-seat Mayo East to create a five-seat constituency covering the county in its entirety. Parts of Galway, which had been propping up Mayo to continue justifying these two three-seat constituencies, reverted to an enlarged Galway East, which gained one seat to make it a four-TD constituency.

Since the State's foundation, Mayo had been two constituencies. For all of Enda Kenny's career it had been divided between East and West – with him in Mayo West. For most of Henry Kenny Senior's time, Mayo was divided North and South, with Henry representing Mayo South for 15 of his 21 years in the Dail.

Now all Mayo politicians and their supporters were dealing with a very different political entity. Ireland's third-biggest county was a single political unit. For a director of elections, this was going to be very difficult to work, very difficult to canvass and, above all, very difficult to control.

It was soon clear that the six sitting TDs would be vying for the five seats. There were varying predictions about who among the West's sitting trio, Enda Kenny and Michael Ring of Fine Gael and Fianna Fail's Seamus Hughes, would lose out. Equally, analysts looked at the East's three, Tom Moffatt and PJ Morley of Fianna Fail and Jim Higgins of Fine Gael, to find a potential victim.

Some observers suggested that Castlebar, as the biggest town, could return two TDs, with Westport and Ballina having the potential to elect a deputy each and the final seat being a scramble involving someone from the southern or eastern parts of the county. Then Beverley Cooper-Flynn, battered by her by-election loss to Michael Ring in June 1994, upped the ante by signalling that she would definitely be in the race.

Everyone was conscious that Ms Cooper-Flynn had polled almost 11,000 first preferences in her unsuccessful by-election attempt to take her father's old seat. It was now very definitely seven candidates for the five seats making Mayo, often the most predictable and boring of contests, one of the more interesting battles in the country.

Beverley Cooper-Flynn reinforced her presence on the ground in Castlebar by being co-opted on to Mayo County Council in September 1996. She replaced the ever-colourful Cllr Dick Morrin, who had died earlier that summer after a short illness.

There were still tensions within the local Fianna Fail

organisation about Cooper-Flynn's Dail candidature, but for 'Flynnasty' supporters there was a certain symmetry in her taking Dick Morrin's council seat. The late Cllr Morrin had first got on Mayo County Council in April 1982 – co-opted to replace Padraig Flynn, who had been made a junior minister.

Cllr Cooper-Flynn announced that she would hold constituency clinics in Castlebar and that her employers in Dublin, National Irish Bank, were being very sympathetic and supportive.

But in January 1998, both Ms Cooper-Flynn and National Irish Bank hit the headlines as RTE journalists Charlie Bird and George Lee reported that she and others at the bank had helped customers evade tax through illegal overseas investments.

These reports were later upheld as true by both the High and Supreme Courts following legal action by Ms Cooper-Flynn. This decade-long controversy and legal battle fed into other problems faced by her father, Padraig Flynn, and ultimately left her liable for €1.2 million in legal costs.

But all of that was in the future. As the 1997 general election drew nearer, PJ Mara, Fianna Fail's director of elections and now speaking for Bertie Ahern's revamped party, recognised Mayo's importance, saying: "Without winning seats like the third one in Mayo we will have an uphill fight to form the next government."

****

John Bruton had spent his first four years as Fine Gael leader, 1990 to 1994, fighting for political survival. Once he was elected Taoiseach there was a complete transformation – he was sure-footed, competent and even stylish at times.

Approval ratings, previously on the floor, soared and were never below 53 per cent; in March 1997 they reached a high of 63 per cent. The economy was growing and Bruton surprised many by skilfully leading a three-party coalition, enjoying reasonable working relations with Labour leader Dick Spring and a surprisingly excellent relationship with the Democratic Left leader, Proinsias De Rossa, and his colleagues.

Bruton even made some headway on pushing forward Albert Reynolds's success on finding settlement in the North – though he suffered from a poor relationship with the Sinn Fein leadership and a perception that he was not sufficiently ardent in his nationalist views. Bruton also took more than his share of the blame for the message to republicans that their arms stocks were stymieing their involvement in settlement talks.

But Irish people were also heartily sickened by IRA treachery during Bruton's term of office. The IRA abruptly ended their 17-month ceasefire with a huge bomb at the Canary Wharf financial district of London on February 9, 1996, killing two people and doing IR£100 million in damage. On June 7, 1996, they brutally shot dead Detective Garda Jerry McCabe and seriously wounded Detective Garda Ben O'Sullivan in a post-office van robbery in Adare, Co Limerick.

Eight days later, the IRA bombed the centre of Manchester, injuring 212 people and doing IR£700 million worth of damage.

Bruton would have to look at things other than the North's peace process to show the results of progress.

But even though he did well in government, his cabinet was rather accident-prone. The first to fall at the ministerial jumps was Carlow-Kilkenny TD Phil Hogan.

Hogan had to resign as junior Finance Minister on February 8, 1995, when a budget fact sheet was inadvertently faxed to the *Evening Herald* newspaper before Finance Minister Ruairi Quinn even got on his feet to deliver his first budget. Hogan's calamity proved an opportunity for Kenny's Mayo rival Jim Higgins, rehabilitated after his role in the unsuccessful February 1994 leadership heave, to take Hogan's slot.

Cork TD Hugh Coveney was not far behind Phil Hogan. He was demoted from Defence Minister to a junior ministry in May 1995 over a phone call he made to the chairman of Bord Gais.

Coveney insisted that he did not intend anything improper when he inquired if there were plans to invite tenders for work at a new Bord Gais site in Cork. He had retained an interest in one of the country's biggest quantity surveying firms.

The capable Jim Higgins again benefited from Coveney's fall from grace as he moved on from his junior Finance Minister's job in May 1995 to become government chief whip and attend cabinet meetings. Some observers felt Higgins was one to watch as a potential future leader.

There were a number of near misses for the coalition.

Labour junior minister Eithne Fitzgerald, responsible for ethics legislation among other things, survived controversy surrounding her invitations to "a rare opportunity to gain access to the Finance Minister" at a IR£100 per head party fundraiser.

Arts Minister Michael D Higgins, also of Labour, was embroiled in a row when *Hot Press* magazine editor Niall Stokes, whom Higgins had appointed chairman of the Independent Radio and Television Commission, lent his name to fundraising for Higgins.

Proinsias De Rossa faced Dail questions about ministerial staff recruitment notices in his Democratic Left party newsletter.

Agriculture Minister Ivan Yates was in the wars over a Russian beef import ban arising from the BSE 'mad cow' crisis.

Health Minister Michael Noonan was the focus of heavy criticism over the handling of the cases of victims of the hepatitis C debacle.

Justice Minister Nora Owen was subjected to criticism over the botched handling of the delisting of a Special Criminal Court judge which resulted in prisoner releases.

Some of these controversies surrounding the other ministers could be put down to the rough and tumble of daily politics. However, they did also point to Kenny's trouble-free term as being competent and lucky.

But the biggest hit of all was taken by Michael Lowry, Minister for Transport, Energy and Communications and a staunch ally and defender of John Bruton. Lowry, along with Enda Kenny, Phil Hogan and Nora Owen, had formed an alternative 'Gang of

Four' to defend their leader when the four rebels – Jim Higgins, Charlie Flanagan, Jim O'Keeffe and Alan Shatter – set up a leadership heave in February 1994.

His fall was personal to Bruton and everyone close to him – including Enda Kenny.

"Lowry was very important in defending Bruton in the 1994 heave. He organised the canvass and identified weakness which could be used to 'encourage' some people to vote the right way," one senior Fine Gael figure recalled.

On Friday November 29, 1996, journalist Sam Smyth revealed in the *Irish Independent* that Dunnes Stores had paid IR£200,000 for a major extension to Lowry's home outside Thurles in Co Tipperary. For all of that day Lowry tried to cling on to his job and at one stage Bruton defended him by saying the disputed payment happened before he was appointed minister.

On the Saturday afternoon of November 30, 1996, Lowry and Bruton met at Government Buildings and later both emerged to say Lowry had resigned as minister.

As photographers asked Bruton and Lowry to pose for photographs, Lowry said: "Yes, indeed, I'll pose with my friend. Best friend. Friend for life."

Bruton's initial defence of Lowry was mild by comparison with what Enda Kenny had to say.

On December 3, 1996, during the Dail debate on the nomination of Lowry's successor Alan Dukes, Kenny lamented the departure of Michael Lowry from government and strongly defended the Tipperary TD, saying: "I very much regret the departure of Deputy Michael Lowry from cabinet. I have known him for many years, both as a member of Fine Gael and as a government colleague, and he is a man of the highest integrity and honour."

These comments would come back to haunt Kenny in March 2011 when, just three weeks after he was elected Taoiseach, the Moriarty Tribunal report made some very damning findings against Michael Lowry.

At that point, Fianna Fail leader Micheal Martin would enjoy repeating Kenny's words about Lowry's integrity and honour.

More immediately, fuller facts on Lowry emerged in August 1997, after a six-month tribunal presided over by Mr Justice Brian McCracken which also examined Ben Dunne's payments to Charlie Haughey, the leader of Fianna Fail for more than 11 years and taoiseach three times. In all, Dunne gave Haughey a total of IR£1.3 million in various amounts over several years.

Much of the material came to light as a result of a bitter family row which ultimately led to Ben Dunne quitting the firm. That had its origins in Dunne being arrested for possession of cocaine in the company of a prostitute at a Florida hotel in 1992.

The McCracken Tribunal found that the Lowry affair centred on the extremely close relationship between Dunnes Stores and Lowry's refrigeration firm, Streamline Enterprises, which did all the fridge installation and maintenance for Dunnes Stores in Ireland. In essence, Mr Justice McCracken found that Dunne and Lowry worked it so Lowry could dodge tax.

According to the McCracken Tribunal report, Lowry "operated his business on two levels, on one level through the company, which made a small profit and duly paid its taxes, and on a second level whereby large sums of money were paid to him personally in a clandestine manner". The bill for works done at Lowry's home turned out to be IR£395,107 in total – it was paid by Ben Dunne but booked in as 'refrigeration work' at his stores.

Fine Gael had been in deep financial trouble, still suffering the tailback expense of three general elections in the 18 months between June 1981 and November 1982. It also had a poor organisation, so money generally was scarce and difficult to raise. Fine Gael party chairman Michael Lowry was the gifted organiser and fundraiser who, as Tipperary GAA chairman, had cleared a huge building debt at Semple Stadium in Thurles.

Like other businessmen, Ben Dunne had given generously to various political parties and his initial contact with Fine Gael was through Dublin TD Jim Mitchell. From 1991 onwards he began channelling money to Fine Gael via Michael Lowry, and at one meeting Dunne gave John Bruton IR£50,000. He gave smaller election donations of IR£3,000 and IR£5,000 to Lowry, to Michael Noonan, to Noonan's Limerick East organisation and to Ivan Yates.

In May 1993, Dunne, Lowry and Bruton met again and this time Dunne gave Fine Gael IR£100,000. This was handled by Fine Gael secretary general Ivan Doherty, who was soon to be Enda Kenny's ministerial programme manager. Doherty respected Dunne's wish that it be treated confidentially in the Fine Gael accounts.

Mr Justice McCracken stated in his report that the donations were made without the knowledge of the other Dunne family members. He also made it clear that neither Ben Dunne nor his family ever sought any political favours in return for the money. But he also stressed the vulnerable position that Lowry, a government minister, had placed himself in by his behaviour.

Lowry resigned from Fine Gael altogether when he was told he could not stand for the party in the 1997 Dail election. He has continued to prosper politically in Tipperary North, where he and a number of supporting county councillors have built a mini-independent political organisation of their own. In autumn 2000 John Bruton raised eyebrows within Fine Gael and outside when he suggested that, in the fullness of time, Lowry could be accepted back into Fine Gael once he had paid all his taxes, back taxes and penalties and made amends for any wrongdoing which might be established by the tribunals.

"I don't think in any society we should stigmatise people forever. That would be totally unchristian," Bruton told *The Irish Times*.

Lowry's relationship with another Irish business mogul, Denis O'Brien, was the subject of the 14-year Tribunal of Inquiry chaired by Mr Justice Michael Moriarty.

In July 2010, in advance of that tribunal's report, Enda Kenny caused some consternation when, in a speech at Phil Hogan's 50th birthday party in Bennettsbridge, Co Kilkenny, he remarked to Lowry: "Is that an application form I see in your top pocket?"

It was among three references to Lowry by the Fine Gael leader during the event.

Fine Gael insisted that Kenny's comment was a joke made at a social function. But at the time there was plenty of speculation as to whether Kenny's comments had any further significance.

There were 150 guests at Phil Hogan's function, with some very senior people including future ministers James Reilly, Frances Fitzgerald and Paul Kehoe. Hogan has remained friendly with Lowry over the years and several ministers subsequently defended meeting the latter about constituency business on the grounds that he was still an elected representative.

Fine Gael figures also argue that Lowry benefited from supporting the 2007-2011 Fianna Fail-Green Party coalition government, during which time he held regular meetings with ministers and officials. Others point to the extent of the trenchant findings of the Moriarty Tribunal and that these caused Taoiseach Enda Kenny to call on Lowry to resign as a TD.

In March 2011 the Moriarty Tribunal concluded that Michael Lowry, as Communications Minister back in 1995, influenced a public tendering process to help Denis O'Brien's consortium get a new mobile phone licence being awarded by public tender.

Mr Justice Moriarty found that Lowry's influence upon the licence allocation had been "insidious and pervasive" as the-then minister responsible. He also concluded that O'Brien afterwards either made or facilitated payments to Lowry. Between May 1996 and December 1999 IR£147,000 and STG£300,000 was paid to Lowry, and O'Brien also supported a STG£420,000 loan for Lowry, according to the Moriarty Tribunal Report.

The Tribunal also found that in 1996 Lowry had corruptly sought to double the rent being paid by the-then State agency Telecom Eireann for a building in Dublin owned by one of Ben Dunne's companies. Ben Dunne rejected this finding as "opinion – not evidence", and challenged Mr Justice Moriarty to ensure he was prosecuted to properly test the issue.

Both Lowry and O'Brien also vehemently rejected and continue to reject the Moriarty Tribunal findings. Denis O'Brien has insisted he never gave "one red cent" to Michael Lowry.

But O'Brien's links to Lowry and Lowry's past close links to the top of Fine Gael continue to cause embarrassment – despite the party's assertion that Lowry was swiftly forced out of their ranks 16 years ago.

On St Patrick's Day 2012, Taoiseach Enda Kenny formally opened the New York Stock Exchange to mark Ireland's national saint's day. Denis O'Brien was in attendance and was photographed among a business group with Mr Kenny. Simply the appearance of O'Brien in the same photograph offered an opportunity for the opposition to embarrass the Taoiseach.

Sixteen years on, the issues surrounding Michael Lowry continue to bedevil Enda Kenny.

****

In Mayo, the June 1997 general election count was all about Michael Ring. He topped the poll with 10,066 votes, 300 over the quota, and was elected on the first count.

It was a phenomenal performance and down to Ring's sheer slog in covering every inch of the county over the previous two years, coupled with his extraordinary personality.

"Michael was out there hoovering up votes. He was a bit like a demented Nilfisk," his party colleague Jim Higgins told reporters at the count centre.

The tallies showed that Ring had taken votes all over the county. In June 1992 Ring had had a very weak showing in Erris and Belmullet in the northwest. Now it was the total opposite. Castlebar tallies showed he took 1,137 number one votes in the Kenny and Cooper-Flynn home base.

A flavour of Ring's attention to constituency detail was caught by journalist Sean Rice in *The Connacht Tribune*: "Nothing went unnoticed. A cow calving was almost deemed worthy of a letter of congratulations. If a funeral was missed, he called later to the house of the bereaved."

Ring also made it known to local reporters that he had turned down interesting trips abroad because of his commitment to the constituency. At the same time Tourism and Trade Minister Enda Kenny was rarely in Ireland for a full week due to travel engagements.

Like Jim Higgins, Kenny decided to allow Ring to bask in victory at the count centre, and told *The Connaught Telegraph*: "Somebody had to head the poll and Michael Ring is entitled to his hour of glory."

Kenny had come second to Ring on the first count, with a creditable 8,568 votes.

Michael Ring was his usual boisterous self and he used the RTE airwaves to send a promotion application to Fine Gael leader John Bruton, announcing: "I have been a curate long enough with two parish priests – now I want to be a canon."

Kenny, Higgins and Beverley Cooper-Flynn – the other big Mayo election story – were all elected at the same time, on the seventh count. Cooper-Flynn was accompanied by a beaming Padraig Flynn and his wife Dorothy, as they regained the 'family seat' lost in June 1994.

Beverley Cooper-Flynn had put in a huge campaign and celebrated her 31st birthday by being elected Mayo's first woman TD. *The Connaught Telegraph* suggested that she must be cabinet material sooner rather than later. Many agreed, but events were to dictate otherwise.

The Mayo Dail quintet was completed by Fianna Fail's Dr Tom Moffatt of Ballina. There were two notable casualties: PJ Morley of Claremorris, who had held the seat for Fianna Fail since 1977, and his party colleague, Seamus Hughes of Westport, who had served just one term.

The Mayo campaign had been fraught for the two big parties because of television deflectors. Kenny was himself heckled and jeered at a meeting on the issue in Westport on Friday evening,

March 21, 1997.

That meeting heard that 30,000 Mayo homes had been unable to receive British television channels because of the forced closure of illegal deflectors and the move towards a new cable system. Kenny told the meeting that his office had taken 247 calls on the issue.

"Fifty of these were from women who said that for the first time in a long time there was more talk in the household than there had been for years," he said. A stunned silence was followed by uproar from the 700 people at the meeting.

All six sitting TDs for Mayo attended that meeting and pledged to work towards a compromise which would swiftly restore the channels. Many party people feared that Mayo could have a candidate representing this group – especially as it could have been combined with another difficult issue: reduced support for water schemes.

In Donegal South West, farmer and school caretaker Tom Gildea was elected to the Dail in the 1997 election as a television deflector candidate on an independent ticket. But, in the end, nobody representing these groups stood in Mayo.

The Mayo Fine Gael campaign's unsung hero was director of elections Jim Nally, who quietly said the party had a plan and a territorial divide framed 18 months previously. The strategy was largely kept – up to a point.

There were reports that Ring was upset by rumours about him in Erris and Achill allegedly circulated by Kenny supporters. Kenny joined the high-tech age by posting a video cassette about his achievements to supporters deemed to be wavering.

Ring supporters were enraged that some of these videos were sent into his Westport territory. It was Kenny supporters' turn to lose their tempers when Ring was seen canvassing the main street in Castlebar.

It was all part of the showbiz in which prospective voters' glory and the keen internal rivalry helped Fine Gael. In the previous six elections since 1977, Fianna Fail had taken four of the six seats in the two Mayo constituencies. On this occasion Fine Gael had 49 per cent of the vote and three out of five seats.

Kenny's Mayo supporters said the three-out-of-five outcome fully justified the arguments he had been making for years: that once he was given promotion by the Fine Gael party leader nationally, he would deliver the extra seats locally.

Clearly, Ring and Higgins were very strong candidates in their own right – but Kenny had used his cabinet presence to deal with two huge problems, Knock Airport and the Regional Technical College.

Enda Kenny was entitled to kudos for leading Mayo Fine Gael. But the only problem was that the local result was not matched in national terms.

Bertie Ahern's Fianna Fail party pulled off a considerable coup in June 1997. They won, even though they were fighting against the backdrop of shocking revelations in early 1997 that Charlie Haughey had received IR£9 million in cash gifts. This came to light as part of the interlinked investigations into Dunne, Lowry and Haughey, which would be further probed later.

Many Fine Gael politicians feel they were hampered in 1997 by the Lowry allegations, which prevented them mounting a no-holds-barred attack on Fianna Fail and the Haughey legacy. Fianna Fail strategists have long argued that the extent of their achievement in that election risks being airbrushed by hindsight.

Bertie Ahern moved about the country like greased lightning in a brilliant personalised 'blokish' campaign. But in the end he owed his win to meticulous vote management.

In November 1992, Albert Reynolds's Fianna Fail had just 68 TDs and 39.11 per cent of the vote. In June 1997, Ahern's Fianna Fail added nine seats – yet still only had 39.33 per cent of the vote. A new era of organisation had arrived for Fianna Fail which would take them through two more general election wins, and add considerably to Fine Gael's woes.

The Rainbow Government bloc of Fine Gael, Labour and Democratic Left had a combined total of 75 seats, too few to put together a new government. Dick Spring's Labour took a ferocious kicking and dropped from 33 TDs to 17 – effectively this level of Labour losses meant the end of the Rainbow. Democratic Left lost two seats but Bruton's Fine Gael gained nine, making a total of 54 TDs for them.

Mary Harney's Progressive Democrats had a disastrous, gaffe-strewn campaign and dropped from 10 to four TDs. But they were vital to Ahern if he was to get to Government Buildings. With a combined Fianna Fail-Progressive Democrats total of 81, Bertie Ahern quickly assembled from among the 10 independent TDs the three more votes he needed to be elected Taoiseach.

The irony of it all for Kenny in Mayo was summed up in a rather cynical but accurate comment from one Mayo Fianna Fail stalwart at the Travellers' Friend count centre in Castlebar as proceedings ended in the early hours of Saturday, June 7, 1997.

"Sure all they have done is elect three members of the opposition," the Fianna Fail supporter said.

It was true. Enda Kenny was back on the opposition benches.

****

On an afternoon in August 1997, Enda Kenny was contributing by telephone to a long-forgotten RTE Radio 1 afternoon programme called Daily Record. The news topic he was discussing is also long forgotten, though the programme presenter, Joe Duffy, has since become a household name in Ireland.

What many people recalled for quite some time afterwards was that in the background the Kenny children could be heard engaging in what increasingly began to sound like a mini World War III. The eldest child, Aoibheann, was approaching her fifth birthday; her brother Ferdia had recently celebrated his third, and the youngest, Naoise, was two months shy of his first birthday.

"If Brian Cowen ever quits as Minister for Children – I'll nominate you," Joe Duffy quipped, as they abandoned the interview and allowed Enda Kenny to investigate how adaptable his political skills might be on the home front.

With three children all under the age of five, a return to the backbenches in the summer of 1997 had personal advantages for Enda Kenny and, more especially, his wife, Fionnuala. He also could increase the visibility on local political projects – and surely this ramshackle 'three-legged stool' – Bertie Ahern's Fianna Fail-Progressive Democrats-independents coalition – would only last months, perhaps even weeks?

With the summer holidays over, Fine Gael leader John Bruton announced his new front bench in September 1997. Enda Kenny was included as spokesman on arts, heritage, Gaeltacht and the islands – clearly expected to deploy his Irish-speaking skills. His Mayo party colleague and rival Jim Higgins was given the more senior position of justice spokesman.

But Michael Ring – poll-topping record and radio-promotion application to Bruton notwithstanding – did not make the first team and was appointed junior agriculture spokesman responsible for livestock and horticulture. It seemed a reasonable call. Kenny had 22 years' Dail experience and Higgins first came to Leinster House as a Senator in 1981, while Michael Ring had been a TD for just three years.

In the end, Bertie Ahern had mustered 85 Dail votes to get himself elected Taoiseach, defeating John Bruton on 78 votes. The Ahern voters comprised the 77 Fianna Fail TDs, four Progressive Democrats, and three Fianna Fail-friendly independents: Jackie Healy-Rae from Kerry South, Mildred Fox from Wicklow and Harry Blaney from Donegal North East. The final Ahern vote on the day was that of Sinn Fein's sole TD, Caoimhghin O Caolain of Cavan-Monaghan, who made no formal arrangement but often voted with the government.

This solid voting bloc of TDs was later joined by Donegal South West TD Tom Gildea, an independent campaigner for multi-channel television. The four independents were assigned a civil servant to liaise with government, additional secretarial back-up, promises that they could deliver constituency results such as roads, schools and bridges, and guaranteed access to ministers in case of problems.

The relationship was managed with consummate skill by government chief whip Seamus Brennan and the Taoiseach's programme manager, Gerry Hickey. It caused periodic dissent among Fianna Fail backbenchers – but it endured a full five years, confounding most observers and critics.

However, as the Dail returned in September 1997, Bertie Ahern's government looked anything but secure. On August 7, Foreign Affairs Minister Ray Burke, Ahern's trusted lieutenant and number three in the government ranking, issued a statement saying he had received IR£30,000 in an election donation from Joseph Murphy Structural Engineers in 1989.

Burke clung to the political mantra of the time, insisting that "no favours were asked or given". But a series of other money revelations continued and on October 7, 1997, he quit politics for good, resigning his cabinet post and Dail seat.

It was a body blow for Ahern and the opposition parties felt this development, which compounded his slight and less-than-reliable majority, meant he could be taken out. But they were wrong – Ahern and company quickly steadied the ship.

Ahern's first big win was the October 1997 presidential election, in which he showed a ruthless streak by shafting former taoiseach Albert Reynolds for the Fianna Fail nomination. His preferred choice, Mary McAleese, a journalist and academic lawyer from Belfast, kept her nerve and won through in a very acrimonious campaign.

But on this occasion Fine Gael's candidate, Dublin MEP Mary Banotti, took a creditable 30 per cent of the vote and second place. The real casualty of this presidential election was Dick Spring and Labour, whose candidate, Adi Roche, came home on seven per cent – half the vote of independent Catholic conservative and one-time singer Dana Rosemary Scallon.

Ahern and his cabinet settled down to government in what would prove the most golden decade to be in power. The economy was thriving and tax revenues continued to outstrip all optimistic predictions. The IRA's ceasefire was restored in July 1997 and gradually all-party talks began, culminating in a marathon session at Hillsborough Castle and a deal on Good Friday 1998.

Bertie Ahern's reputation began to grow as the "architect of the peace". The Northern feel-good factor fed into the economic buoyancy, which in turn allowed the government to cut taxes and increase spending; among other things, this made generous public service pay deals possible.

It was a hard time to be in opposition and Fine Gael's internal convulsions proved to have been merely suspended for the duration of their period in government. Bruton tried to concentrate on quality-of-life issues like health and education standards, environmental problems, traffic congestion and house prices, which were spiralling by the week.

Enda Kenny, doubtless conscious of the need to keep up his profile in Mayo, remained quite busy locally and was also hitting national newspaper pages from time to time. Criticisms began to mount that Fine Gael and Bruton were ineffective in opposition, and there were also charges that Kenny was not pinning down the lacklustre Arts, Heritage and Gaeltacht Minister, Sile de Valera.

Part of Kenny's problem here was that the issues involved are rarely central enough on the political stage to allow for the showing of results. Also, de Valera, who had almost no Irish, left all the heavy lifting on Gaeltacht and western-development issues to her first cousin and junior minister, Eamon O Cuiv of Galway West. O Cuiv has superb Irish and operated very skilfully through those years.

Kenny twice took on the government over the issue of the Irish language in this period.

In October 1998 he accused the government of abusing Bord na Gaeilge funding for an advertisement in the All-Ireland football final programme which depicted Charlie McCreevy in the Kildare colours and Eamon O Cuiv in the Galway colours.

In September 2000 he made similar criticisms when the All-Ireland programme carried a Foras na Gaeilge advertisement including only Fianna Fail personalities.

"It is ironic at a time when our government has a Taoiseach, a Tanaiste and a Minster for the Gaeltacht who are unable to answer a single question in the Dail in Irish," Kenny said.

In June 2000 Kenny became Fine Gael education spokesman but managed to show few results. In August, along with the party's policy director Richard Bruton, he launched a scheme which would pay pupils at risk of dropping out of second-level school IR£36 per week and he made a trenchant attack on the government's record in tackling educational disadvantage.

Kenny managed to show more sparkle on broader political issues. He accused Taoiseach Bertie Ahern of "hypocrisy" after he visited Eddie Jordan's Formula One racing team, which had links with tobacco giant Benson & Hedges. For Kenny this made no sense at a time when the government was trying to restrict availability of cigarettes to young people.

On the local front, as is frequently the case, he also showed a bit more heart, backing campaigns for Castlebar Hospital and a safer location of the local main post office. In January 2000 he castigated the government for wasting taxpayers' money by holding a series of cabinet meetings outside of Dublin, and one specifically in Ballaghaderreen.

"It's a waste of money: 17 State cars rolling into town for this stunt," he told reporters – doubtless happy that Ballaghaderreen, in Co Roscommon was safely outside his constituency and he no longer had a State car.

He was on firmer ground when he criticised the National Lottery in May 1998 for revelations about a mystery winner who scooped IR£1.8 million in Geesala, Co Mayo.

"There were only 100 Lotto tickets sold in Geesala last night and yet the National Lottery announce that the winner is 'male and single'. You don't have to be Sherlock Holmes, and while it is good National Lottery propaganda – it could have very serious consequences for the security of the person involved," Kenny said.

There were other local political staples. He championed the

need for an open drain to be filled in at Rathbawn housing estate in Castlebar to resolve a recurring problem with rat infestation and supported a campaign to keep open the 130-year-old St Mary's Church in Castlebar.

Kenny also had the pleasure in May 2000 of delivering good news, via an answer to a Dail question, to a Castlebar campaigner whose worthy cause he and other politicians had backed for 20 years. Ernie Sweeney, who had battled with illiteracy, finally got the authorities to allow candidates' photographs on ballot papers to help those with reading problems.

But while Kenny was keeping the Fine Gael door open and the lights on in Mayo, on the national stage they were going nowhere. Fine Gael was about to major in internal conflict once more.

****

The end for John Bruton was centred on a snail – or, to be more precise, the Fine Gael party's IR£160,000 outdoor-advertising campaign headlined 'It's Time To Eradicate The Celtic Snail.'

It was an attempt to cadge some of the British Conservative party's success in 1979 when their 'Labour Isn't Working' slogan, illustrated by a snaking dole queue, caught the public imagination. Fine Gael was trying to tap into discontent at quality-of-life issues like traffic congestion, and general delays in delivering on government promises.

It was the brainchild of Dublin advertising agency DDFH&B and a clear play on the Celtic Tiger, which had become shorthand for the economic boom. The kinder assessments suggested it was a reasonable idea, poorly executed; harsher judgements were that it was nonsense from start to finish.

The reality was the message failed to reach Irish people, who suddenly had vastly more money to spend and far better cars in which to sit out those pesky traffic jams. It rebounded on John Bruton who, his critics later said, had just presented it as a done deal to an increasingly fractious front bench keen to blame their leader's 'charisma deficit' for their woes.

Bruton's leadership had delivered nine extra seats in the previous June 1997 election. The party won in a Cork South Central by-election in October 1998 when Simon Coveney replaced his father, Hugh, who had died in a tragic accident.

In the June 1999 local elections there was a small gain of seven seats and an increase in vote share, to 28 per cent. In June 2000 Fine Gael surprised everyone when its candidate Tom Hayes strongly challenged for a seat in a Tipperary South by-election, with an encouraging 27 per cent of the vote.

But these were deemed small gains by many within the party. By mid-November 2000 Fine Gael was trailing in opinion polls and John Bruton was least popular of the main party leaders.

That was when Enda Kenny's old drinking buddy, former Agriculture Minister Austin Deasy of Waterford, shocked everyone by putting down a motion of no confidence in the leader. Yet again, Enda Kenny, who had fallen out with Deasy over Bruton and the leadership issue, was among those manning the defences.

Earlier that month, on Friday, November 10, Bruton was in Castlebar presiding at a function to celebrate Enda Kenny's 25 years in Dail Eireann and Senator Paddy Burke's 21 years as a member of Mayo County Council. Bruton was given a royal welcome and the local media coverage was very positive.

On November 23, 2000, Deasy's challenge was soundly defeated by Fine Gael TDs, Senators and MEPs at a meeting at Leinster House. Only six deputies spoke against Bruton as, for the fourth time, he faced down a leadership challenge.

Thus, Bruton appeared secure as Fine Gael leader before an election expected by many to take place in the first half of 2001. Both assessments were quickly proved wrong.

Fine Gael was about to turn in on itself, with some of the bitterest infighting imaginable. And Enda Kenny was about to vault into the forefront of all those struggles.

CHAPTER 9

'I'll Electrify Fine Gael'

"Enda, where did this come from? I mean, if he had only given us some inkling over the years. I love the idea. But this comes right out of the blue. There's so little to back it up."

Those were the words of one Fine Gael parliamentary party member spoken to this writer at Leinster House on the afternoon of February 1, 2001. In the early hours of that day Enda Kenny had put out a statement saying he would contest the party leadership and the above speaker's reaction summed up the views of almost all of his colleagues.

The majority liked him as excellent company, many rated him as a long-time parliamentary colleague, but few, if any, saw him as their potential party leader. He had been a TD for 25 years and had acquitted himself well for a year as a junior minister and over two-and-a-half years at the helm of Tourism and Trade – but that was some distance from being Taoiseach.

Even his wife, Fionnuala, was surprised by his decision to stand for the Fine Gael leadership. He rang her at 1.30 that morning, February 1, waking her up at their home in Castlebar to tell her of his decision and get her opinion.

Before phoning home Kenny had been talking for quite some time with John Bruton and others. "They were in Bruton's office. It had been a long and bruising day and there was a share of whiskey drank after it all," one contemporary recalled.

The day had resulted in Bruton losing a confidence vote after a decisive seven-hour meeting of Fine Gael TDs, Senators and MEPs at Leinster House. "You could describe the atmosphere as vengeful. There was a lot of talk about betrayal. There was also a determination that there would be no 'coronation' for Michael Noonan – that somebody from the Bruton camp would oppose him," another person close to those events explained.

After the experience of long absences when he was a minister just three years earlier, his wife wondered again about the dreadful impact on their family life with three young children.

"Do we need this grief?" she is quoted by writer Kevin Rafter as asking her husband on the phone. Fionnuala also pledged to back him to the hilt – a pledge she faithfully kept through the demanding years that were to follow.

The huge surprise element aside, Enda Kenny had publicly declared that he wanted to lead Fine Gael – and, by extension, be Taoiseach. It would take him precisely 10 more years to fulfill his goal.

****

He had remained loyal to party leader John Bruton right until the very bitter end.

The final heave had begun bubbling only days after Bruton defeated a poor and surprise challenge by Waterford dissident Austin Deasy in late November 2000. This time it was local Fine Gael activists voicing serious discontent to their TDs that proved the tipping point for this final and very swift, very clinical leadership heave.

Even in Mayo – where Bruton had been feted barely two months earlier – the mood was rather anti-Bruton. Two hundred Mayo Fine Gael members gathered in Castlebar on Monday, January 29, 2001, two days before Fine Gael TDs, Senators and MEPs took their decisive vote of confidence in Bruton.

Mayo, with three TDs and two senators – all with leadership votes – was very significant in this battle to be decided by the

72 parliamentary party members. It was also the only constituency in the country where Fine Gael held three out of five seats. The Mayo membership did not instruct their five representatives on how they should vote, but they did make their view clearly known.

Tom Kelly, writing in *The Connaught Telegraph* that week, noted that 30 people spoke at that Castlebar meeting and the ratio was six to one against John Bruton. But Kenny and stalwart backer Senator Paddy Burke were still strongly supporting Bruton.

"He is the best man for the job. That's why I'll be supporting him," Enda Kenny said after the meeting. He strongly defended Bruton on local radio and later told reporters that his stance was not just about personal loyalty.

"In politics you stand for what you believe in and you are respected for that. That is what John Bruton has done," Kenny later told reporters.

Kenny's Mayo rival Jim Higgins was keeping his powder dry. Equally, Michael Ring was weighing up his options, though perhaps leaning towards voting against Bruton.

"The silent majority has to be taken into account and I will be considering all aspects before I make up my mind. The whole business is difficult and unpleasant," Michael Ring said.

The fifth Mayo Oireachtas member, Senator Ernie Caffrey from Ballina, favoured a change of Fine Gael leader.

Dublin Central TD Jim Mitchell and Limerick East deputy Michael Noonan were jointly behind the final move against Bruton. There were contacts between dissident TDs and senators plus other senior party figures over the Christmas holidays and the plotting began in earnest in January, with intensive canvassing of undecided backbenchers and Senators.

Matters came to a head on the evening of January 25, 2001, when *The Irish Times* published their usual opinion poll before the return of the Dail. It showed that six out of 10 people were happy with Bertie Ahern's Fianna Fail-Progressive Democrats minority government – giving it every chance of being re-elected.

It was terrible news for Fine Gael and John Bruton. The party was down four points to just 20 per cent. In Dublin it was on 11 per cent, two points behind Labour. John Bruton had an approval rating of 37 per cent – his lowest since before being elected Taoiseach in late 1994.

Fine Gael heavy hitter Alan Shatter was on RTE television when the survey figures came in and he told programme presenter Olivia O'Leary it was time for John Bruton to "consider his position". History was to repeat itself and Enda Kenny would have the same experience in June 2010, when an opinion-poll result would be the catalyst for a leadership heave against him.

But, for now, things quickly gained momentum and that momentum was with the anti-Bruton camp. On Sunday afternoon, January 28, Michael Noonan and Jim Mitchell held a press conference in Buswells Hotel in Dublin, just across the street from Leinster House. They announced that they would be tabling a motion of no confidence in Bruton, to be taken the following Wednesday.

Thereafter, both Noonan and Mitchell would stand as party leader. But their platform would be united in that each pledged that if they won, they would appoint the other as deputy.

It was a formidable challenge, with both Noonan and Mitchell representing the provincial and Dublin wings of the party and each with decades of political experience, including senior government office. They gathered around them a team which met several times a day to discuss each potential voter and how he or she could be influenced.

But Bruton, with the help of people like Enda Kenny, mounted a brilliant rearguard action. They clung to the hope that Bertie Ahern, whose party was afflicted by serious allegations of sleaze, could be beaten in the next election and that John Bruton would be Taoiseach again, with his key lieutenants senior members of government.

The 72 Fine Gael TDs, senators and MEPs met at 2.45pm on

Wednesday, January 31, 2001, in an airless dungeon of a room in the parliament's new wing called Leinster House 2000. It took seven-and-a-half hours to reach an outcome because 48 of those present spoke, some of them at length.

Enda Kenny was first on his feet and spoke for 15 minutes in defence of John Bruton. But his speech is remembered by some as having irritated younger TDs, as he questioned the need for such a challenge.

Bruton gave a very strong emotive message which resonated for all who attended; opponents acknowledged the power of his contribution.

The extent of Bruton's ability to 'box off the ropes' can be gauged by Noonan's frustration at one point in the preceding days when he described Bruton as "a good defender" but stressed Fine Gael's need for people "to get scores". However, many of those present felt that minds had been made up the previous day and oratory was surplus to requirements.

The final 39 votes to 33 against John Bruton was a very close-run thing. Just three people changing their minds could have allowed him to hang on for another while at least. The surprise was not that he lost – but that he was so hard to beat.

The die was cast, however, and Bruton's stormy decade at the Fine Gael helm was over. Fine Gael's parliamentary party would meet again on Friday, February 9, 2001, to pick a new leader.

****

For years afterwards, his sometime media tormentor Vincent Browne liked to mockingly recall that Enda Kenny had threatened to "electrocute" Fine Gael.

In fact he said he would "electrify" the party. Enda Kenny was formally launching his bid for the leadership on RTE Radio 1's News At One on Friday, February 2, 2001, where he was put through the hoops by presenter Sean O'Rourke. He claimed that he had been approached by people who had both supported John

Bruton and voted against him.

"They wanted me to stand on the basis that I provided a fresh face with long political experience, somebody who has the energy and the stamina to re-energise and revitalise the Fine Gael electorate.

"This row, if you like, was about lack of image, lack of style, a different form of leader, a new face. I have electoral contact with people in a way that, I believe, Jim Mitchell or Michael Noonan do not have.

"I'm going to electrify the Fine Gael party," he said.

News anchor O'Rourke asked Kenny about claims that he was a political lightweight who had not been rated by two previous Fine Gael leaders, Garret FitzGerald and Alan Dukes. Kenny said he had been expected to get a government post in 1982 in FitzGerald's second coalition with Labour – but had remained loyal to the party even though he had been disappointed.

Kenny also argued that the only reason he was not retained on Alan Dukes's front bench was because he had loyally opposed the removal of family friend Deputy John Donnellan from the Fine Gael parliamentary party. "Alan Dukes, with whom I have a strong relationship, deposed me from the front bench when I openly supported John Donnellan not being fired from the Fine Gael party. I did so because I am a person of conviction," Kenny insisted.

It was a strong performance, although Enda Kenny appeared to have caught a little of the penchant of long-time Mayo adversary Padraig Flynn for speaking about himself in the third person.

"I know from the calls around the country that Kenny is in this to win. He is not just an outsider putting his name on the ticket. He is out to win and he will win it," Enda Kenny said.

"I don't know where this notion of Enda Kenny not having dealt with the substantial issues over the years has come from. When I became Minister for Tourism, Bord Failte was in chaos after Charlie McCreevy. The industry was in a very fragile state. I dealt with that sure-footedly, very competently, brought people with me, restored confidence.

"As Minister for Trade, I chaired the Council of Ministers for Trade for Europe very competently, very successfully, brought people with me," he argued.

And then he came right out with the argument used by his supporters back then and up to the present day: he suffered unduly for his failure to appear pompous and his sense of humour and light-touch approach to politics were used against him.

"So, just because one has a sense of humour and is not weighed down by the troubles of the world does not mean that one doesn't have a conviction, a commitment or a competence to do the job in a proper manner," he said, emphatically.

Enda Kenny went on to say that as Fine Gael chief whip he could claim "central credit" for starting the dialogue which brought Democratic Left into the Rainbow Government in December 1994. He said he shared the same nationalist views on Northern Ireland as Michael Noonan and agreed that John Bruton did not make himself clear enough on this issue, especially by not showing that Fine Gael was always a nationalist party.

"Fine Gael's nationalism was not spelled out clearly enough by John Bruton and, when it was spelled out by him, it was not always understood," he summed up. It was a strong campaign kick-off.

That same morning Kenny had received a morale boost when a former Fianna Fail Mayo rival, Denis Gallagher of Achill, who had been Gaeltacht Minister, went out of his way to issue a warm tribute and wish him good luck. The Gallagher statement also again underlined how Kenny had benefited over the years from a benign attitude in the 'non-Padraig Flynn' Fianna Fail element in his home county.

But, while he began strongly on RTE radio, the range of media commentary elsewhere was rather derisory. Vincent Browne, writing in *The Irish Times* on February 7, acknowledged that Kenny was "a nice fella" and might even be nicer than Bertie Ahern – but he insisted Kenny was an unknown and unlikely candidate.

"His name would not have been the first, or the second, or even 23rd that would have occurred to me as a future leader of Fine Gael," Browne wrote, also stressing that the major problem was a lack of direction in the party.

A more satirical take on Kenny's candidature, just days earlier, had come from the pen of Miriam Lord, writing in the *Irish Independent*. Lord conjured up a scenario of dejected John Bruton supporters casting about for a new champion, when a shaft of moonlight falls upon their hero.

"'Indakinny!' they shout. 'Young and blonde and will keep his mouth shut. He's the boy for us.' And so it came to pass that a mere stripling of 50 years of age, with 25 years of Dail experience, emerged as the fresh youthful face of Fine Gael, the young fella who will scupper the leadership plans of Michael Noonan and Jim Mitchell," she wrote.

The piece quickly and pithily covered a lot of ground: Kenny was a sort of 'elderly youth' and an unlikely person to be on such an errand of internal party vengeance on behalf of the John Bruton rump. It also caught something of the bitterness of this intense election.

Such writings are discounted to one degree or another by politicians. But the term 'Indakinny' – a sort of cheery bumpkin image – persisted and became a bugbear.

As days wore on it became clear that there would be four names on the ballot paper, the interlinked 'dream team' of Michael Noonan and Jim Mitchell, Enda Kenny, and Cork North Central's Bernard Allen, a former junior sports minister. Wexford TD Ivan Yates, often been cited as a future prospect, caused major surprise by announcing that he was quitting politics at the next election to concentrate on his bookmaker business.

A private opinion poll, controversially carried out for Jim Mitchell by marketing company MRBI, found Mitchell to be the most popular candidate among ordinary voters, with a strong showing for Noonan just behind him. These positions were reversed, with Noonan ahead, when the poll was confined to Fine

The newly appointed Taoiseach after receiving his Seal of Office at Aras an Uachtarain with President Mary McAleese and *(below)* Taoiseach Enda Kenny with Labour leader and Tanaiste Eamon Gilmore and the new Government top table at their first Cabinet meeting on March 9, 2011

US President Barack Obama with Enda Kenny in Farmleigh; *(inset left)* Mr Obama after receiving a hurley from Mr Kenny; *(inset right)* Mr Kenny with

...itain's Prime Minister David Cameron at Government Buildings prior to a State ...nner for Queen Elizabeth II

Taoiseach Enda Kenny meets Queen Elizabeth II at Government Buildings during the second day of her State visit to Ireland in May 2011

Taoiseach Enda Kenny greets Queen Elizabeth II and the Duke of Edinburgh, with President Mary McAleese and Dr Martin McAleese, at Aras An Uachtarain on the first day of the royal visit and *(below)* Taoiseach Enda Kenny listens carefully to the historic speech by Queen Elizabeth II at Dublin Castle during her State visit

Enda Kenny at the Dail with Gay Mitchell (left), Phil Hogan (right) and Richard Bruton (far right) after his election to Fine Gael leader on June 5, 2002, and *(below)* Taoiseach Enda Kenny in Government Buildings on December 4, 2011, delivering a live televised address to the nation on the economic crisis facing Ireland

Enda Kenny with GAA President Christy Cooney at the All-Ireland Senior Football Championship semi-final in Croke Park on August 21, 2011 when Kerry beat Mayo. A few rows behind, former Taoiseach Bertie Ahern checks his phone

Enda Kenny with party members after introducing the new team for the Senate at Dail Eireann on August 7, 2002

Gael voters only.

But the survey fieldwork had been done before the race hotted up. The third candidate included in the survey was Ivan Yates and Enda Kenny did not rate a mention.

This once more showed that Mitchell's and Noonan's supporters had been plotting for some time – and that they had not expected Kenny to contest the leadership.

A *Sunday Independent*/IMS poll on February 4 gave Kenny grounds for optimism. While he trailed both Noonan and Mitchell among general voters, he was rated at 25 per cent among Fine Gael supporters and within striking distance of his two rivals.

Chief whip Charlie Flanagan was mentioned as a strong potential candidate as were other names in the melting pot, including that of Kenny's Mayo rival Jim Higgins. Part of Kenny's calculation in standing for the leadership was a fear that, if he did not, Higgins might well go forward and steal a march on him in terms of national profile and party pecking order.

Those close to Kenny at that time concede that he felt that Noonan, especially if Mitchell stood aside at the 11th hour and backed him as expected, could not be beaten. "The reality is that Noonan had by then been engaged in the longest ever campaign to become the leader of Fine Gael. He had been at it on and off from the early 1990s – it looked like his time had eventually come," one party veteran recalled.

Noonan had set out to meet every member of the parliamentary party, in their home base where possible. In the case of Cork South West TD PJ Sheehan, it was at one of his clinics – where Noonan waited in an ante-room along with some of the supplicant constituents.

This scenario fed the more imaginative Dail bar wags, who scripted how they imagined Noonan being engaged in idle conversation by one of PJ Sheehan's constituents. "I'm here about the medical card – what are you after yourself?"

Kenny's campaign was being organised by local political ally Senator Paddy Burke, who also tried to ensure that Kenny got to speak personally to all 72 potential voters. Burke argued that Kenny had for too long been underestimated, adding a little-commented-upon fact – that Kenny had been Fine Gael national director of elections in the previous June's general election, when the party gained nine seats.

In fact, Kenny had chaired the 1997 election-strategy committee. But Burke's point had been that the national election role had given Kenny an added burden as he tried to get to grips with a new all-Mayo constituency. Burke insisted that Kenny had to attend meetings all over the country.

"As well as fighting his own corner, he had to fight everybody else's. As it happens he filled both roles rather well," Paddy Burke said, arguing that this should debunk claims that Kenny was "lightweight".

"I know there are those who question his laid-back style. In my view there are few harder workers in politics than Enda Kenny," Burke argued.

Senator Burke also caused some laughter in Mayo by telling *The Connaught Telegraph* how well Ring and Kenny got on together. "I accept there is a perception that himself and Michael Ring don't always tango. But that's only a perception. They are very friendly and get on very well," Burke said.

Along with Paddy Burke, Mayo deputies Jim Higgins and Michael Ring and Senator Ernie Caffery all came out strongly in favour of Kenny. They had no choice but to park whatever rivalries or misgivings they might have and be seen to support the home team. On the day, Enda Kenny was proposed by Michael Ring and seconded by Jim Higgins.

But Higgins was either damning Kenny with faint praise or else being too honest in his comments to local Mayo journalists. "Enda is in with a right good shout. It's a fantastic achievement to come from nowhere and build up a bloc of over 30 votes," he said.

There was sharp criticism by Kenny supporters of Sligo-Leitrim TD Gerry Reynolds, who had openly backed Jim Mitchell's candidature. "Public representatives from the West can hardly complain about the region being neglected by government if they won't vote for one of their own as party leader," Michael Ring said.

Kenny had the backing of many of the Bruton grouping and he now began to canvass more widely. In the final days his supporters produced a telephone poll, apparently done as a gift by a firm called Stone Consulting, which showed that out of 100 respondents, 29 chose Kenny, 28 opted for Noonan and 22 went for Mitchell. In the last days before polling, over 30 TDs, MEPs and Senators had yet to publicly declare a preference, so canvassing focused in on those.

But Kenny did himself huge damage on the eve of the vote by putting in a disastrous performance on RTE's Prime Time programme, during which he failed to state clearly why he should lead the party. Later, recordings of this show would be used by his media coaches in 'how not to do it' lessons.

Bernard Allen, whose candidature was never taken seriously, announced on the eve of the election that he was withdrawing. On the day itself, Jim Mitchell announced he was pulling out in favour of Michael Noonan, making the outcome a foregone conclusion.

Nobody could face the gruelling seven-hour meeting of 10 days previously, so party chairman Phil Hogan got agreement that only proposers, seconders and candidates would speak.

It was done quickly, with a verdict inside two hours. Noonan got 44 votes of the available 72 – Kenny got a creditable 28, five fewer than had backed John Bruton a week earlier, but still about 40 per cent of the vote.

Twelve people had publicly declared they were voting for Kenny: the five Mayo representatives; western neighbours Joe McCartin MEP of Leitrim and John Perry TD from Sligo; Cork deputies Bernard Allen and Liam Burke; Wexford TD Avril Doyle, and long-time friends of Kenny's, John Farrelly of Meath and Dun Laoghaire TD Sean Barrett.

After the vote, Senator Maurice Manning, another close friend, also said he had voted for Enda Kenny.

Once the verdict was known, Kenny kept the tone of his response as good-humoured as possible. He cited one of Fine Gael's all-time irrepressible characters, Pat Lindsay, who had shrugged off his rejection by the voters of North Mayo in June 1938 with the words: "They will never know what they missed."

Outside on the Leinster House plinth party chairman Phil Hogan appeared, flanked by the two contenders, and quickly announced the result. Noonan had a smile as wide as the Shannon Estuary on whose banks he was raised. He was easily prevailed upon by photographers to raise his arm in acclamation.

The third act of this three-act drama – which had already seen Bruton ousted and Noonan take the crown – was to be the selection of Noonan's new front-bench team. That was billed for the following Thursday, February 15.

Everyone agreed that Enda Kenny, with 40 per cent of the vote, had to be given a prominent role by Noonan. And, one more time, everyone was wrong.

****

Enda Kenny picked up a voicemail on his mobile phone at 1.45pm on February 15, asking him to go and see Michael Noonan. The pair had what Kenny later described as a "direct conversation", lasting 10 minutes.

"Sorry, I have no place for you on my front bench," Kenny later quoted Noonan as telling him. Kenny's home-town newspaper, *The Connaught Telegraph*, which adopted the most outraged tone in defence of their local man, added that Noonan had used "his barky Limerick accent" to convey his message.

There was genuine outrage on behalf of Enda Kenny among some of his parliamentary colleagues. "It was one thing that Noonan shafted John Bruton – but now he was shafting somebody just for the sake of it," one colleague recalled many years later.

216

Kenny told Noonan that he was making a mistake – sending out the wrong signal at a time when he should be about healing and unity. "I had contested an open leadership contest. It was not a heave," Kenny told reporters.

For his part, Noonan insisted that he acted without malice and would have liked to include Kenny on his first team. But he wanted a reduced front bench of 16 people working on a focused opposition agenda and he had to achieve a balance which took account of geography and gender.

"I had to make a decision in Mayo who I would put on my front bench and I opted for Jim Higgins," explained Michael Noonan.

Kenny supporters were further enraged that Higgins had tourism, Kenny's former minstry, added to his responsibility for public enterprise.

Not even Noonan's close supporters could believe his line about "gender and geography" obliging him not to pick Kenny. That said, he had chosen a reasonably balanced team overall, though he leaned towards the 'Munster mafia' of politicians from Limerick, Cork and Clare, who were seen as his main support base.

Kenny could not disguise his dismay at being excluded by Noonan. But he maintained a dignified presence and answered all journalists' questions directly in the yard of Leinster House.

While Kenny was speaking to reporters his mobile phone, now ubiquitous in daily politics, kept ringing. As the impromptu journalists' interview drew to a close, Kenny answered the phone and spoke to someone called Denis. It was clearly Roscommon Fine Gael TD Denis Naughton, then aged 27, who had also been passed over by Noonan.

"You're a young man in politics, Denis. If you want to talk to someone about how to take a knock in politics, Kenny's your man," the defeated candidate was clearly heard to say.

It was apparent that feelings against Noonan were running very high in Kenny's Mayo camp and the new leader was due there two weeks later for the Fine Gael meeting to pick their next general-election candidates. But it was also abundantly clear that Noonan had simply 'played the Jim Higgins card' in a county which was very precious to the organisation.

The brutal reality was that Higgins, an able performer locally and in the Dail, could attract more support in Mayo by being identified as a future government minister if Noonan's Fine Gael could win. Kenny already had the tireless Michael Ring on his back on home turf. Now things could get very tricky indeed.

For all his talk about a slimmed-down front bench, Noonan was actually providing as much occupational therapy as he could for his troops.

He proposed that each of the 16 spokespeople should recruit two others as assistants, in what he called a "cabinet system".

In the ensuing days, there was a marked reluctance among Noonan's new team to recruit Enda Kenny as a junior. This changed when the education and youth affairs spokesman, Michael Creed from Cork North West, asked Kenny to come on board. However Kenny graciously declined, preferring the backbenches.

The big question everyone was asking Kenny all that week was: "What now?"

Would he return to the backbenches? Would he quit politics and leave Noonan with an immediate by-election headache? Would he investigate the prospect of trying the European Parliament?

"I'm going to drive back to Castlebar and think about it," was Enda Kenny's only reply.

****

Michael Noonan knew he faced the prospect of loud protests and a walk-out by Kenny loyalists angered at his treatment of their man just 10 days before. So he wisely decided to be otherwise engaged on the evening of Sunday, February 25, 2001, when Fine Gael members gathered in Castlebar to pick their candidates for the next election.

The previous night Noonan had been in Cahir, where Tipperary South activists chose Senator Tom Hayes to contest a by-election caused by the tragic death of Fine Gael TD Theresa Ahearn. It was going to be a serious test of Noonan's leadership and he was justified in tarrying a while in Tipperary South to boost the canvass preparations.

For Kenny, it was a good opportunity to make it clear that he was hanging in there. Friends say that he steeled himself and prepared a brave public face.

"But it was just a face. He was really bruised, and colleagues found him awkward, cranky and difficult for months afterwards," one contemporary remembered.

"While I accept that people are angered by what has happened to me, I am a championship player and I'm taking it on the chin," Kenny told the meeting in the Travellers' Friend Hotel.

"Don't be disillusioned and don't wallow in self-sympathy. It's vital to focus on the real agenda. Let nobody doubt my loyalty and my ability to serve under Michael Noonan.

"I will work harder than ever. I love Fine Gael for what it stands for and I'll be ready to serve in the next government," Kenny insisted.

There was a good deal of venting against Michael Noonan on Kenny's behalf. But just weeks earlier the assembled Mayo membership had unanimously favoured a change of leader – so now they had to live with the outcome of that process.

Unsurprisingly, the Mayo beneficiary of the new leader, Jim Higgins, fronted a strong pro-Michael Noonan message. He said that towards the end of John Bruton's term as Fine Gael leader he had been a figure of derision.

"The sniggering is over now. So is the derision. Michael Noonan is outfoxing and outboxing Bertie Ahern. The media like his style – and that's half the battle," Higgins told delegates.

For Jim Higgins, Noonan's move to refuse all corporate donations to Fine Gael was a central symbol of change. "In banning corporate donations, he got to the core of the difference between

Fianna Fail and Fine Gael. When Fianna Fail accept a corporate donation, there is always a price to be paid," he said.

"Deals were done and land was rezoned on the back of how much you could pay. Power meant millions of pounds to them. That was the basis of their ferocious hunger for power. But that greed led to corruption which sullied the name of politics. That culture put off young people.

"Now Fine Gael has taken the moral high ground from the Labour Party and the Progressive Democrats. The Fine Gael wagon is going in the right direction," Jim Higgins said.

The third Fine Gael candidate nominated, the redoubtable Michael Ring, was least enamoured of all with Michael Noonan and gave a very simple message to the meeting. "He should have put me on the front bench. I am tired of being on the hind tit. I am as capable as anybody. I am as able as Jim Higgins or Enda Kenny," Ring insisted.

But the Westport politician evened things up with a good strike at the performance of local Fianna Fail junior minister Tom Moffatt. He also had a two-for-the-price-of-one attack on the coalition government, calling Finance Minister Charlie McCreevy an uncaring Progressive Democrat at heart.

The meeting took place in the aftermath of a local Mayo Fine Gael dispute about who should be the fourth candidate on the ticket. The local party's officer board had resigned en masse the previous October after the Dublin HQ had very belatedly cancelled their selection convention because they disliked the expected outcome.

Dublin Fine Gael organisers felt that 29-year-old Ballina solicitor Michelle Mulherin was a better fourth candidate than Senator Ernie Caffrey, who had already been beaten three times. Kenny and the others had to intervene, encourage the local officers to return to the fold and re-fix the selection convention.

His brother Henry Kenny had given a long and revealing interview to *The Connaught Telegraph* when the row first blew up in October 2001. Henry had lavished praise on the local Fine Gael officers and especially acknowledged their fundraising efforts.

At the reconvened convention, the local view won out and Senator Caffrey was nominated to try one last time. Even back in spring 2001, Mayo Fine Gael fancied the notion of bagging four out of the five Dail seats.

But no such thing was going to happen in the next election, played out in May 2002. In fact, Fine Gael's vote was about to go through the floor, curiously bringing about both danger and opportunity for Enda Kenny.

****

As spring moved into summer in 2001, it became clear that Enda Kenny was very lucky not to be Fine Gael leader, as misfortune followed woe for Michael Noonan and his team.

On the very day he named his front bench, Noonan brushed off questions about who was behind the private survey which his deputy leader, Jim Mitchell, had published during the party leadership campaign.

Mitchell later said about 20 friends put up IR£450 each to cover the cost. It was a small enough issue but Fianna Fail kept bringing it up in efforts to knock the gloss off Noonan's pledge to foreswear all company political donations.

A large *Sunday Independent* cartoon depicting Noonan being crushed by a container full of Fianna Fail company donations summed up some Fine Gael members' fears. "No point in you doing the 'right thing' if the other crowd still have all that cash," a veteran Fine Gael member commented.

Noonan's efforts to maintain momentum were also immediately impeded by the foot-and-mouth crisis scuppering travel in case the virulent animal infection spread throughout the country. The restrictions meant his first Fine Gael Ard Fheis, on March 3, 2001, had to be scaled back to a Dublin regional conference. Noonan did avail of a 50-minute televised address to the nation, though, and his speech was well received.

However, the first of several political body blows came his way just days later, on Tuesday, March 6, 2001, and a mere 25 days after his election as leader. Michael Noonan had to admit that Fine Gael had received US$50,000 from Norwegian telecoms firm Telenor, partners with Denis O'Brien in their successful quest for Ireland's second mobile-phone franchise.

The full extent of the value of the franchise had emerged a year earlier, when it was sold on to British Telecom for IR£1.9 billion.

The bizarre saga surrounding the payment was as damaging as the money itself. It had been routed through offshore banks in Jersey, and then back to the party via two wealthy supporters. Noonan said they had believed the money was from the party supporters and they had been trying to give it back for several years once its origin became clear.

At 5pm on Friday, May 11, 2001, Noonan arrived at the political correspondents' offices at Leinster House to make another confession in a vain attempt to blunt an expected Sunday newspaper revelation. The Fine Gael party had, years previously, paid staff 'under the counter', cutting their PAYE and PRSI costs. It was something else which long predated his leadership and a IR£110,000 settlement had been paid over to the Revenue Commissioners in 1999.

Then the Telenor cheque and the under-the-table staff payments were added to by a third issue about the party receiving IR£90,000 in so-called 'pick-me-up' or delayed donations through the paying of specific bills for printing, travel or other expenses.

Suddenly Michael Noonan's Fine Gael felt exposed and cold on the moral high ground they had sought to take from Labour and the Progressive Democrats. They looked like Fianna Fail – but without the competence and winning ways.

Noonan's only real boost came in June 2001, when Tom Hayes handsomely won the late Theresa Ahearn's seat for the party in Tipperary South with the help of director of elections Charlie Flanagan, who was working on his second back-to-back campaign there within a year. However it was only a brief intermission in a continuing grim tale for the party and its leader.

Noonan and Fine Gael also faced a legacy issue from his period as Health Minister during the 1994-1997 Rainbow Government. Early in 2002 RTE screened a fictional drama series called No Tears based on the life and suffering of Brigid McCole, a mother of 11 children who eventually died from Hepatitis C contracted from infected blood products.

Brigid McCole's and other victims' redress claims had come to a head under Noonan's term in Health and he and his officials handled the matter very badly. But the unnamed minister in the RTE drama series was depicted doing things which never occurred and it was a very dubious call by the national broadcaster to allow it to be screened so close to an election, especially as the timing of that election was not in any doubt.

"I'll put it this way to you – RTE would not have done that if they thought Michael Noonan and Fine Gael were going to win the next election," a senior Fianna Fail figure told this writer in late 2002. That view is, unsurprisingly, shared by many politicians in Fine Gael.

But it was clear for a long time that Michael Noonan's Fine Gael could not win the May 2002 general election, which turned out to be the most predictable in the State's history.

Their problems were compounded by Labour leader Ruairi Quinn keeping his options open on coalition – strongly signalling that he was available to Ahern and Fianna Fail. The Labour stance meant that whatever government line-up emerged it would not include Fine Gael.

And Enda Kenny sounded more than a little smug in one of his few national newspaper interviews, in mid-April 2002, a month before the general election. He was very critical of party proposals to compensate those who lost on shares they bought in the Eircom privatisation and taxi drivers who took a hit on deregulation.

Kenny recognised that Fine Gael deputy leader Jim Mitchell had been "through the mill" with ill-health but nonetheless felt

Mitchell should be more careful in his public utterances. He also had some advice for his beleaguered Fine Gael colleagues, as a plethora of local opinion polls predicted they would lose their seats.

"If a politician opens a newspaper and sees himself eliminated in the fifth count, that becomes fact. It has got to the point where they would be better off not even reading those polls," Kenny told *The Sunday Business Post*.

As the person who chaired the party's election-strategy committee at the previous general election in 1997 when Fine Gael gained nine seats, Kenny also criticised overall strategy. Clearly seeing the advantages of backbench banishment, he said it was wrong of Jim Mitchell to openly seek an alliance with Labour or even a 'Tallaght Strategy Against Terrorists' – supporting a Fianna Fail minority administration to keep Sinn Fein out of government.

For Kenny there were many ways, short of a formal Labour pact, to signal that a rainbow government was a credible alternative. "The last time Fine Gael supported the Haughey Government with the Tallaght Strategy, we were well thanked!" Kenny also stated.

It was by now very clear that Michael Noonan did not connect with voters and that many Fine Gael proposals smacked of desperation. But it is also worth summarising the economic and political backdrop against which Noonan faced Bertie Ahern's Fianna Fail.

The Irish economy had shown more sustained growth than any other OECD nation, unemployment was down to four per cent or effective full employment, emigration had been reversed, national debt was under 35 per cent of GDP, the top tax rate had been cut from 48 to 42 per cent and the lower rate from 26 to 20 per cent.

There was peace in Northern Ireland and industrial peace in the Republic. Welfare rates had shot up. Irish people were prosperous and bullish facing into polling day on May 17, 2002.

The only thing that stopped Bertie Ahern from winning an overall majority, a first since 1977, was the intervention of Michael McDowell of the Progressive Democrats with his apocalyptic warnings.

The final result was Fianna Fail, 81 seats; Fine Gael, 31; Labour, 21; Progressive Democrats, eight; Green Party, six; Sinn Fein, five, and others, 14.

Bertie Ahern was back as Taoiseach and Mary Harney as Tanaiste – the *Irish Independent's* headline read 'Same Again Thanks'. But Fine Gael's meltdown was the news story of Election 2002: the party lost 23 seats, bringing it to a level not seen since the 1940s, and with only three seats in Dublin.

The heavy losses also pointed up a sort of 'hidden penalty clause' in the proportional-representation system. The party had lost 20 per cent of its vote share – but over 40 per cent of its seats. Clearly, as vote losses increased the seat-loss rate escalated even more.

The party's entire leadership structure was also wiped out.

Michael Noonan held his Dail seat but quit as leader the night of the count. Other senior figures – deputy leader Jim Mitchell, former leader Alan Dukes, and former deputy leader Nora Owen – all lost their seats, along with key figures like Charlie Flanagan and Brian Hayes.

"For the first time in electoral history, the electorate voted out the opposition, not the government," wrote Geraldine Kennedy as editor of *The Irish Times*.

Enda Kenny was very lucky indeed not to have been anywhere near the leadership of Fine Gael for this political carnage. But he was also lucky in another way in May 2002 – in fact, he barely held on to his Dail seat.

****

By early afternoon on the day of the 2002 count, many of Kenny's most loyal supporters had abandoned hope. Kenny himself alternated between faint hope and increasing fatalism.

"Listening to the pundits, I found it too close to call. It was the longest day of my political life. I had resigned myself to a fate that looked inevitable," he said later. It was May 18, 2002. Forty-eight years ago to the very day, his father, Henry Kenny, had been elected to Dail Eireann, thereby establishing the 'Kenny family firm'.

The Castlebar count venue was the familiar, though now re-vamped, Royal Theatre at the Travellers' Friend Hotel. It took the counting staff 15 hours to separate 14 candidates over 10 counts and allocate the five Dail seats.

On the first count, Enda Kenny came in seventh on a disap-pointing 5,834 votes – barely over half a quota. Jim Higgins was 24 votes ahead, in sixth place.

By the seventh count, Kenny was 400 votes behind Higgins. But his luck changed with the sequence of eliminations as re-turning officer Fintan Murphy announced that the eighth count would distribute the vote of Fianna Fail's Senator Frank Cham-bers from Newport, which is about 10 miles from Kenny's family home at Derrycoosh, Islandeady.

Kenny got 600 of Chambers's transfer votes while Higgins got just 120. So now Kenny was 87 votes ahead of his long-time rival. It meant Higgins was eliminated and Kenny elected on the next count, thanks to a massive 4,615 transfers from Jim Higgins.

The story was made all the more remarkable by the fact that Frank Chambers had been in hospital in Galway for the final week of the campaign following a car accident – and only 108 votes behind Kenny on the first count. Chambers was also behind his Fianna Fail colleague John Carty of Knock, whose elimina-tion at that point would certainly have elected Jim Higgins – who also hails from that eastern side of the county.

Right up to the outcome of the eighth count in Castlebar, Hig-gins was recorded as one of the Fine Gael party's few good per-formers and someone who could figure as a leadership candidate. His narrow Dail defeat would gradually render him a peripheral figure in Fine Gael and national politics over the ensuing years. He was initially elected to the Seanad in 2002 and in 2004 successfully contested the European Parliament election. By autumn 2012 he was still a sitting MEP.

The other big stories of the Castlebar count centre were a renewed poll-topping performance by Fine Gael's Michael Ring and the emergence of Dr Jerry Cowley of Mulranny as an Independent TD. He had impressed with years of social and community work, including the imaginative Safe Home sheltered-housing scheme for distressed Irish emigrants.

Mayo Fine Gael were hit by the showing of Cowley on almost 9,000 votes, and another Independent, Michael Holmes, whose campaign for better roads netted almost 2,000 votes. They were also badly affected by the national slump: their fourth candidate, Ernie Caffrey, got half his previous election vote.

Beverley Cooper-Flynn, in the middle of a marathon court battle with RTE, was also re-elected and Bertie Ahern promised a reconciliation for her with Fianna Fail. The contest also saw newcomer John Carty of Fianna Fail take a seat but party colleague Dr Tom Moffatt lose.

The Kenny-Higgins tale became a subset of Fine Gael's national disaster. Each candidate was publicly a model of gracious behaviour at the Castlebar count centre.

Kenny said it was disappointing to see a party colleague lose and that took the gloss off his narrow victory. "I had resigned myself to losing the seat," Kenny told journalists.

Higgins was gracious, saying he was pleased to see Enda Kenny elected to continue his family's record of service in public life. He was also pleased that his party vote had transferred so remarkably solidly.

"I'm very disappointed. I didn't think the national trend would be repeated in Mayo. But it was and I'm the casualty here," Higgins added.

Higgins also acknowledged the speculation about himself and the Fine Gael leadership. "I had been mooted as a possible leader.

I'm not sure I would have gone for it – but it doesn't arise now," he stated.

Fine Gael's Mayo story – with a seat lost and an 11 per cent drop in the vote – was bad, but vastly better than the situation nationally. Inevitably, Kenny faced reporters' questions about ambitions to try again to lead what was now a very battered party. But he said now was not the time to discuss such things.

Kenny said it had been depressing for him to watch the television reports from around the country. He noted that Michael Noonan had taken full blame for the outcome – but said it could not all be laid at the Limerick man's door.

"It has been a failure of the party over the last 18 months to demonstrate that this was and is a credible alternative to Fianna Fail. With politics you never know what lies around the next corner and what fate lies in store for Fine Gael," he said.

****

Bertie Ahern was busy putting together his second coalition and Fine Gael were busy trying to find their political 'black box' among the election crash debris.

But the Irish people had only one thing keeping them busy – the unholy civil war between soccer manager Mick McCarthy and player Roy Keane and its impact on Ireland's World Cup hopes in Japan and Korea. That was the backdrop against which Enda Kenny tried once more to become leader of Fine Gael in late May and early June 2002.

Journalists filing political stories about the coalition negotiations and/or the Fine Gael post-mortems were met with a certain impatience from the news desks. "See if you can get political reaction to Keane's latest outburst. Any move on Bertie mediating between the sides?" was a common enough response from their editors.

Such was Bertie Ahern's walk-on-water status that there was a national hope that the incoming Taoiseach could help persuade

Roy Keane to return to the Republic of Ireland camp he had so angrily abandoned. All that would remain to be done then would be to have Mick McCarthy accept Keane and restore a good general working relationship inside the squad.

There was total silence in bars when news reports of the soccer saga came on. Everyone, irrespective of age, class or sporting interests, had a strong personal opinion.

This slightly muted political-news spotlight helped the remaining Fine Gael TDs take stock of the ruins. The 31 TDs, 14 senators and four MEPs gathered for their first parliamentary party meeting on Friday May, 24, 2002, precisely one week after the general election. It was also the day news came back that Ahern's delicate Keane-McCarthy overtures, via FAI officials, were a total non-starter.

As Fine Gael tried to pick up the pieces, two stumbling blocks emerged in relation to the immediate election of a new leader. The first was a decision in principle by the Fine Gael members at their Ard Fheis in February 2002 to change party-leader elections and involve local councillors and the 25,000 grass-roots members.

Fine Gael headquarters and many senior party figures had huge practical and principled problems with this extension of party democracy. These problems were compounded by an additional obligation to hold a leadership election every two years, irrespective of whether the party was in power.

The party brass could point to the general election run-up as a good reason for not changing the rules to make the Ard Fheis decision a reality. It was in legal limbo and had been referred back. A second practical consideration was whether or not a Fine Gael leadership election should wait until new Seanad elections were held in the coming weeks.

If the leadership contest went ahead sooner, it would fall to the outgoing senators to choose a leader, whom their successors – potentially a much-changed batch – would then have to deal with. Equally, some recently defeated TDs, now without a vote, could expect to win Seanad seats which would give them a say in the leadership choice.

This procedural confusion was compounded by a suggestion that parliamentary-party chairman Padraic McCormack's term had expired due to the general election. McCormack countered that he could only be replaced at an annual general meeting – and that AGM could only be held after the new senators were elected. He refused to vacate the chair.

These issues tapped into a more general feeling among some Fine Gael politicians and activists that there was no need to rush choosing Michael Noonan's replacement. If needs be, a senior party figure could take over on a caretaker basis until a more considered debate and decision was possible.

But the parliamentary-party members emerged from their meeting on Friday, May 24, with three clear decisions. Firstly, they would go ahead and pick a leader soon. Secondly, they would try to do this by agreement rather than having a divisive election. Thirdly, they would hold a two-day meeting at Citywest Hotel on the outskirts of Dublin the following week to have further discussions.

Enda Kenny looked to be in pole position as the new leader. But he avoided such speculation. "We have an Everest to climb," he said, as he left the meeting at Leinster House.

Former leader John Bruton – who made it clear that he did not want to return to office – suggested they should try at all costs to agree a leader. Others pointed out that the history of the party suggested that unanimously chosen leaders were more likely to succeed.

There was also a suggestion at the meeting that it might be time to "skip a generation" and choose a younger person – a move which would have blown Enda Kenny out of the reckoning. The younger names being floated were Simon Coveney of Cork South Central, aged almost 30, and, more notably, Denis Naughten of Longford-Roscommon, who was close to his 29th birthday.

Others of the older guard being mooted, along with Kenny, were Phil Hogan of Carlow-Kilkenny, John Bruton's brother

Richard, from Dublin North Central and Gay Mitchell, of Dublin South Central, a brother of Jim Mitchell. Since the party had been left with only three Dublin TDs out of a potential 47 seats in the capital, there were good grounds for choosing a Dublin deputy.

Attempts began over that weekend to ensure the idea of 'skipping a generation' was seen off amid fears that an untested and inexperienced politician could not cope with the huge task ahead. Phil Hogan phoned Denis Naughten in efforts to ensure the required outcome on that issue.

The Fine Gael parliamentary party regrouped at Citywest Hotel the following Tuesday, May 2, for several marathon sessions. Some impromptu straw polls were taken to show each prospective candidate where they stood. There were long discussions about the future direction of the party and its reason for existing.

Well in advance of the close of nominations on Tuesday, June 4, 2002, it was clear it would be a contest between Kenny, Hogan, Bruton and Mitchell. Everyone believed it would be Kenny – though Hogan or Bruton both retained the capacity to surprise.

But Young Fine Gael activists strongly campaigned for a delay in electing a new leader. Two key members of Young Fine Gael and future cabinet colleagues of Enda Kenny – Leo Varadkar of Dublin West and Lucinda Creighton of Mayo – wrote to the parliamentary-party chairman, Padraic McCormack, asking for a stay on the matter. "This is not the time to rush into a leadership election," Lucinda Creighton told reporters.

At the monument in Beal na Blath in West Cork to commemorate the Fine Gael party's claimed founding father, Michael Collins, one activist kept a vigil of protest. Richard Deasy from Nenagh was largely ignored as he warned that party democracy was more important than a quick leadership decision. There was a steady stream of phone calls and messages to Fine Gael's Dublin HQ urging a stock-taking delay.

The election went ahead. Michael Noonan had handed in his formal resignation the previous Wednesday. Fine Gael TDs, senators and MEPs said they could not face into the new Dail term without a leader.

They waited until the Republic of Ireland had played out a dramatic 1-1 draw with Germany in the World Cup and then convened to pick their new leader at 2.30pm.

The process took two hours and there were no slip-ups – Enda Kenny emerged as leader.

Kenny was once again proposed by constituency sparring partner Michael Ring, and seconded by newly elected TD Olwyn Enright. At the end of three counts he was declared the winner, with nine votes to spare over his nearest rival, Richard Bruton.

In the first count both candidates had shown strongly – 17 votes for Bruton and 16 for Kenny. Phil Hogan had nine votes and Gay Mitchell, seven. When Mitchell was eliminated and his votes distributed, Kenny led by 19 votes to Bruton's 18, with Hogan on 12.

In the final count only two of Hogan's votes went to Bruton while 10 went to Kenny – the clear winner on 29 votes.

The party then presented a strong and positive image to the public and tried to cadge some of the Ireland soccer squad's feel-good factor as they met journalists. And Enda Kenny spoke strongly.

"Fine Gael's political mourning is over. This party is getting up off the floor and we are determined to demonstrate all over Ireland that we are a force to be reckoned with in the future," he said, to loud cheers from colleagues.

So, on June 5, 2002, 26 years and six months after he was first elected a TD, Enda Kenny took on the leadership of Fine Gael.

He was their third leader in 16 months. The party had been in power for an accidental two-and-a-half years out of the previous 15 years. They had last won a general election almost 20 years earlier, in November 1982, under Dr Garret FitzGerald.

Their Dail strength had been reduced to a level not seen since 1944. Among the consequences of the recent general-election meltdown was a one-third cut in taxpayer funding to the organisation. An ageing and disengaged party membership felt demoralised and disregarded.

Arguments that Fine Gael had fallen as far as it could and the only way was up rang hollow. History showed that political parties can and do vanish into the mists of time.

As the new Dail assembled on June 6, 2002, being the leader of Fine Gael seemed anything but a glittering prize.

CHAPTER 10

Two 'Nice Guys' Square Up

He began his first political term as party leader with an apology.

It started in the basement bar of Buswells Hotel, opposite Leinster House, on Wednesday evening, September 4, 2002, at a farewell drinks party for Fine Gael's outgoing press director, Niall O Muilleoir.

Earlier that afternoon, Enda Kenny had received the dreadful news that his former colleague and close friend David Molony had died suddenly in Thurles at the age of 51. Molony, a former senator and TD, was among Kenny's first friends at Leinster House in the mid-1970s, but had quit politics in 1987 to return to his solicitor's practice, leaving the way open for Michael Lowry to win a Dail seat.

The Buswells gathering was very laid-back as O Muilleoir, who had previously worked for the Irish Farmers' Association, was popular with journalists. When it came to saying a few words of farewell, Kenny was both relaxed and in a mood to reminisce about his deceased friend.

He told a story about David Molony on a short 'lads' holiday' in Portugal in the late 1970s. It went like this: Molony, Kenny and Senator Maurice Manning were in a bar one evening when they noticed the drinks menu included a 'Lumumba Cocktail'.

The name of Patrice Lumumba, the first democratically elected premier of newly liberated Congo but murdered in 1961, had huge resonance for Irish people of that generation. The Congo was the Irish Army's first major overseas peacekeeping mission in 1960, and 26 Irish soldiers were killed there down through the years.

Maurice Manning asked the barman whether the cocktail was named for the tragic Congolese leader. The barman, whom Kenny described as "a Moroccan with shiny teeth", laconically told Manning the drink was named after "some nigger who died dans la guerre [in the war]".

While he was telling the anecdote, Kenny eyeballed several journalists in the crowd, and three times said he did not expect to see this yarn reported in print.

Those working for daily newspapers, radio and television accepted his injunction – but the following weekend three Sunday newspapers carried it, complete with condemnations by various civil-rights groups of this use of 'the N-word'. The *Sunday Independent* used it as its lead story.

At first Kenny's press spokeswoman had fought with the Sunday newspaper journalists who had phoned seeking reaction. She argued that Kenny had been off the record on a social occasion and now his comments were at risk of being taken totally out of context.

Then Enda Kenny issued the following statement:

"I used a word I should never have used and apologise unreservedly for it. Some of the people in whose company I used this term have gone to great lengths to explain that the word was used in recounting a true incident in the past. The fact is that I used the word and no context can excuse it. I failed to exemplify my own standards and that of a party absolutely committed to diversity. I'm sorry."

There were no further attempts at justification. Kenny had never previously been reported as uttering a racist statement and was not known to harbour such views.

It was clear that the joke turned, not on Kenny's use of the N-word, but on the indifference of a fellow African to Lumumba and his apparent licence to use a taboo word which the three 'white guys' would not dare to utter. Apart from overtones of racism, the anecdote had aged and travelled badly and was no longer funny in this setting over 20 years later.

But veteran Mayo and national journalist Tom Shiel had an interesting take on matters in the following week's *Connaught Telegraph*, which was normally quite positive towards Kenny. The writer noted that Kenny loved telling yarns and mimicking accents in pubs.

"Ask any patron of various Castlebar pubs that he has frequented over the years," Shiel wrote. The writer felt that Kenny's 'laddishness' meant an incident such as this was no surprise.

"Truth is that he has sailed close to the wind in matters of political correctness before," Shiel noted. He went on to recall an incident at Kenny's triumphant homecoming function in the Travellers' Friend Hotel the previous June.

On that occasion, the new Fine Gael leader had regaled the crowd in Castlebar with a tale of a woman capable of eating hay who was chosen to be the Rose of Bangor Erris.

"'To make matters worse,' he continued, 'she was pregnant.' The crowd hooted and cheered but many women present felt, quite rightly, that the tale was demeaning to women. After the events of last weekend, I'm sure the Fine Gael leader has learned his lesson," Tom Shiel concluded.

The minor furore soon passed and it was filed alongside other political foot-in-mouth occasions. What was left was a lesson in how things had changed now that Kenny was leader of the opposition – and a forceful reminder that Irish media conventions were changing rapidly.

It would be no longer possible to say things in front of journalists and expect them not to be reported. Foibles and gaffes, tolerated even among relatively senior politicians, could not be as easily shrugged off when you put yourself forward as a potential Taoiseach.

Henceforth there would be few, if any, 'private occasions' for Fine Gael leader Enda Kenny.

****

But, apart from publicly telling the odd joke in questionable taste, Enda Kenny had in fact begun to work very hard as Fine Gael leader. His first task was about healing and unity among the depleted group of TDs, senators and MEPs.

In the Dail he was trying to square up to Bertie Ahern in what would turn out to be a slow and lacklustre contest. Both were the perennial 'nice guys' of politics, whose style was to avoid direct conflict unless really necessary.

But in this squaring up of two 'nice guys', Ahern got the better of things over the longer term. In his autobiography, written by historian Richard Aldous and published in 2009, Ahern is typically gracious about Kenny – but adds a definitive assessment.

"I don't think Enda ever managed to lay a glove on me. He certainly never got a knockout punch," Ahern said. Few day-to-day observers in Dail Eireann would disagree.

One week after his election, Kenny appointed his front bench and avoided the disastrous mistake of his predecessor, Michael Noonan, by giving prestigious posts to the three who competed against him for the leadership. He also appointed Mayo constituency sparring partner Michael Ring as spokesman for social welfare and family issues, a post to which Ring could bring his passion for championing the underdog.

He appointed Richard Bruton, runner-up in the leadership election, as deputy leader, while Gay Mitchell was appointed foreign affairs spokesman and Phil Hogan was appointed to enterprise, trade and employment. Michael Noonan was invited to join the team but declined for the time being.

Two newcomers were also promoted: Olwyn Enright from Laois-Offaly took on education, and John Deasy from Waterford was appointed justice spokesman. Denis Naughten and Simon Coveney, two other young TDs, were also named on Kenny's first team.

Former leader John Bruton joined the front bench, without

a specific portfolio but named as director of elections for the upcoming rerun of the EU Nice Treaty referendum. Kenny also promptly ended Fine Gael's boycott of the Forum On Europe, a consultative body set up after voters had rejected the Treaty in June 2001.

Ending that boycott was a politically astute move by Kenny in the medium to longer term as the party had been heavily involved in all EU activities for a long time. He had also pledged that Fine Gael would take a positive role in the Nice referendum, which was to run again on the basis of extra guarantees given at an EU leaders' summit in Seville in June 2002.

While leading the Fine Gael group into the Forum On Europe, Kenny also managed a few deft cuts at Fianna Fail and the Progressive Democrats. He argued that past governments had fuelled public doubt about the EU by blaming Brussels for bad news and claiming credit themselves for positive developments.

"But I suppose that might not be entirely unexpected given that the government feels more at home in Boston than it does in Berlin," Kenny said. This was a reference to various ill-judged speeches by members of the previous government and it helped Fine Gael further strategically stake out their pro-EU ground.

But, far more importantly than all that, Kenny began to meet Fine Gael members old and new as part of a long and tough rebuilding initiative. By the end of June 2002 he had addressed large gatherings in many corners of the country, drawing notable crowds in Kilkenny, Galway and Cork during eight regional members' meetings which brought him into direct contact with 4,000 members.

At these gatherings he also met city and county councillors to push his strategy that Fine Gael Seanad candidates must be Dail material for the following general election. "It was vital to ensure that the Seanad was ruthlessly used as a forum to return defeated party TDs or 'blood' newcomers with a real chance of making the Dail the next time," a party insider of those times explained.

"It is impossible to tell councillors what to do – so Enda gave no instruction. He just explained the party aim of rejuvenation and left them strongly with that thought. The key word was 'survival' for the party," the Fine Gael source added.

The Seanad result was spectacularly good from Kenny's point of view: Longford-Roscommon contenders James Bannon and Frank Feighan were elected; so, too, were Joe McHugh of Donegal North East, Kenny's defeated Mayo constituency rival Jim Higgins, Brian Hayes of Dublin South West, Ulick Burke of Galway East and Noel Coonan of Tipperary North.

Others elected as senators and rated good Dail prospects at the time included Maurice Cummins of Waterford, Fergal Browne of Carlow-Kilkenny, Sheila Terry of Dublin West, Paul Bradford of Cork East and Michael Finucane of Limerick West.

The Seanad success showed that Kenny was lucky in that he now had widespread party unity, based on the simple need to survive. Unlike his predecessors, all members accepted that Kenny was the only leader available and they needed to support him if Fine Gael had any hope of a future.

There were two notable 'Seanad lifer' exceptions to the 'Dail material' rule among Kenny's 15 Fine Gael Senators elected in July 2002. One was Senator Paddy Burke of Castlebar, who had long been Enda Kenny's back-up man in Mayo, and would become increasingly important in the coming years. The other was Senator Paul Coghlan of Killarney, a seasoned and wily campaigner who defied the odds by defeating former Fine Gael TD Deirdre Clune of Cork South Central.

"Coghlan was the one fish who got away – he's just brilliant," an associate of Kenny's said at the time. Coghlan would repeat that feat in the 2007 and 2011 Seanad elections.

For the members' meetings, Kenny equipped himself with what politicians call the "Single Transferrable Speech", which he belted out with fervour again and again. The speech he made at the Menlo Park Hotel in Galway on Monday evening, June 24, 2002, captures the essence of his 'shrive and revive' message, which borrowed heavily from a revivalist preacher's lexicon.

Kenny acknowledged the "pain and frustration" of good party people who had seen Fine Gael bomb in the previous month's election. He frankly confessed that as opposition TDs and senators they had, to borrow Bertie Ahern's phrase, failed "to lay a glove on the government over the past five years".

"I hear you. And I promise you change," Kenny told the 500 people crammed into the hall.

"For five years the people of this country watched breathless as Burke and Foley and Lawlor were paraded before them, living examples of all that was wrong at the heart of government then – the same government that we have now," he continued.

"We made the fatal mistake of behaving, not as an effective opposition – but as a government-in-waiting," he summed up. It is interesting that this point had also been forcefully made by Kenny's party rival Michael Ring on the evening of the election count in Castlebar five weeks before.

Kenny pledged as Fine Gael leader to take every opportunity to expose "the crassness and contempt that lies at the heart of the Fianna Fail-Progressive Democrats coalition".

In future the 'Teflon Taoiseach' – as Bertie Ahern had long been known – would not have things his own way.

Kenny was voicing a view that, with economic storm clouds gathering in the post-election aftermath of 2002, Bertie Ahern's new government could finally be seriously challenged through targeted and effective opposition. He acknowledged that Ahern's Fianna Fail was "one of the slickest operations in Europe" – but therein lay the challenge.

"There will be no talking down to members of Fine Gael. This is your party," he vowed.

The audience loved it – they gave him a prolonged standing ovation. Then his real evening's work began as he mingled and talked to all comers.

"He's at his happiest meeting people. He was born to do that. No Fine Gael leader had ever really done that to this really popular extent before – certainly not the Cosgraves, not Garret, not

Bruton, not Michael Noonan," a senior party figure argued.

"The years that followed were all about that. Kenny went from town to town, from meeting to meeting, spending endless hours talking and listening. He was brilliant at it. From the moment he was elected leader he became a model of application – a workaholic," the Fine Gael person added.

Kenny's great ally on these occasions was Liam Coady, who took on the role of official driver soon after his election as Fine Gael leader. Coady was a lifelong trusted friend and Fine Gael activist who served for a time on Castlebar Urban District Council. His family ran a bar and undertakers on Linenhall Street, close to Kenny's constituency office on Tucker Street in the town.

Liam Coady was also a popular figure at Leinster House, where he was well known to politicians and journalists for his courtesy and gentle good humour. Enda Kenny was devastated by his sudden death, at the age of 64, while on holiday in London in August 2010.

Another Fine Gael politician from that early period of Kenny's leadership recalled his boundless energy and tolerance of late nights. "The problem half the time was to try to get him to go home. He'd linger on and on, talking with people and keep on saying, 'Come on, have another pint.' He had Liam Coady, who was ever-patient, to drive him," the politician revealed.

****

But Kenny and people like Phil Hogan knew that Fine Gael needed more than revivalist rhetoric and blokey chats in hotel ballrooms around the country. The party badly needed a total overhaul of structures and a long hard look at how it was financed.

When TDs, senators and MEPs gathered for a private meeting at the Knockranny Hotel in Westport on Friday afternoon, October 4, 2002, Enda Kenny presented them with their new survival manual.

The punchily written 70-page report called 21st Century Fine Gael had been produced over the previous 14 weeks under the guidance of Frank Flannery and party general secretary Tom Curran, who had overseen a group of 12 people with various levels of expertise and experience.

Frank Flannery was a central figure in the revival and maintenance of Fine Gael's fortunes. He worked closely with Kenny, who often took his advice – but the pair also had a fractious relationship at times, with some major divergences of opinion.

A native of Kiltullagh, near Athenry in east Galway, Flannery was involved in Fine Gael during his time at University College, Galway, and also served as national president of the Union of Students in Ireland in the academic year 1970-71.

In 1973 he joined Rehab, a leading non-governmental group which provides services to people with disabilities, and was its chief executive for 25 years. By the time he stood down, in December 2006, Rehab had 3,000 staff serving 60,000 people in Ireland and Britain, and an annual turnover of €160 million.

Flannery had worked closely with Garret FitzGerald's Fine Gael in the early 1980s and was part of a core advisory group dubbed the "national handlers". He faded from the party but in 2002 was brought back by Phil Hogan, a man who would also gain hugely in influence under Kenny's leadership.

The Flannery Report delivered many harsh home truths set against practical remedies and signposted a long road of hard work ahead. The report was largely kept under wraps for another month when it was leaked to the *Sunday Tribune* on November 17, 2002. Enda Kenny did a radio interview on RTE's This Week programme that same day.

On the airwaves Kenny conceded that he had not yet "electrified" the party as promised, but argued it was now "plugged in" at least. "If the party is not prepared to move and to change radically, then it is going nowhere."

In fact the Flannery Report in essence said 'change or die'. It pointed to the experience of the Canadian Conservatives and the British Tories, still floundering after their May 1997 election catastrophe.

Every day, in Ireland and across the globe, well-established brands disappeared. "Whatever happened to the Irish Press Group with its three strong titles and its thousands of readers? Why should a political party be any different?" the report asked.

The document included an analysis of past election figures and some projections for future elections. In a worst-case scenario, Fine Gael could be reduced to attracting just one in eight voters by 2020.

"The current image of Fine Gael is wholesome, healthy, traditional and boring. It seems to belong to another age," the document stated.

Inevitably, the report looked at what perennial rivals Fianna Fail stood for – and concluded it was everything and nothing at one and the same time. That, in a nutshell, was the key to Fianna Fail's success with voters.

"Fianna Fail is now no longer a political party but, in fact, a coalition of different political parties. It has become a populist party where Wolfe Tone, John Maynard Keynes, Charlie Mc-Creevy and Westlife enjoy equal status. Quite simply, Fianna Fail is everything and anything when required," according to the Flannery Report.

The document strongly hinted at the entry of research focus groups, which would soon become central to Fine Gael's future workings. "The starting point is no longer where the politician stands but from where the voter is looking at him/her. We are not telling them what they like or should like – they are telling us."

This was something John Bruton, when Fine Gael leader, had derided as "followership – not leadership". Privately, some Fine Gael activists often liked to characterise this as the "Fianna Fail approach", articulated in a stage rural accent: "Show me the biggesht crowd and I'll folly it."

Flannery proposed borrowing some things from Fianna Fail's approach of travelling light politically – but not totally taking it all on board by adopting their 'stand for everything and nothing' attitude.

In fact, the report stressed the need to retain Fine Gael's core values and combine "the best facets of Fianna Fail populism with a rejuvenated expression of the great ideals which Fine Gael stands for". The core values were upholding the institutions of State, responsibly managing taxpayers' money, reforming public services and especially the health services, sustaining and developing the education system, fighting crime and caring for the environment.

As well as taking on Fianna Fail, Fine Gael had to compete with niche parties such as the Progressive Democrats, with their business appeal, and the Green Party, who attracted voters concerned by environmental issues.

Fine Gael's target market was the 'progressive centre' or slightly left-leaning middle-class voters, the ones Garret FitzGerald appealed to in the early 1980s.

The Flannery Report also pointed up just how much of Fine Gael's fortunes were riding on the shoulders of their new leader, Enda Kenny. "A lousy party can succeed with a brilliant leader – the opposite does not work."

In the future Enda Kenny would embody Fine Gael. "In two years' time, what must be achieved is that when people on the street are asked what image do the words 'Fine Gael' summon up, they will mostly answer that Enda Kenny is doing a really good job; he has lots of good ideas; he sounds like he knows what the country needs," Flannery concluded.

The gap between this plan and its implementation was illustrated by an incident on Wednesday, December 18, 2002, when Fine Gael held their media Christmas party in the Shelbourne Hotel, Dublin. Entertainment was by the Sons of Erin, fronted by Derek Warfield, who previously led the traditional republican ballad group The Wolfe Tones.

They treated the astonished audience to songs which included Celtic Symphony, with its repeated chorus line 'Ooh, ah, up the

'RA'. Enda Kenny was played into the room to strains of A Nation Once Again.

Surely this was more Sinn Fein than Fine Gael – and a woeful media gaffe? The event organiser was Kenny confidant Deputy John Perry of Sligo-Leitrim, who took full responsibility for booking the band. Perry insisted Kenny would not have known who was playing – much less what songs they would feature.

Enda Kenny's own words after the May 2002 election debacle were: "We have an Everest to climb." By that measure, such gaffes meant that base camp was still a very distant image, much less the peak itself.

****

When Jim O'Brien answered his mobile phone early on Monday, May 31, 2004, he immediately recognised the voice of Phil Hogan, who had a very simple message which brooked no discussion. "Get those fucking posters down. And get them down before fucking lunchtime," Hogan blasted.

O'Brien was director of elections for Mairead McGuinness's European Parliament campaign, which ran from March to June 2004. Both the director of elections and the candidate were journalists and fully appreciated that there was no avoiding the 'cat fight' story of McGuinness versus Doyle.

For the five-year term 1999-2004, Avril Doyle had been the Fine Gael MEP for the four-seat constituency of Leinster, which comprised all that province's counties except Dublin. It was bad enough that the newly named East constituency had been reduced to just three seats for the 2004 elections – now, thanks to Enda Kenny and advisers Hogan and Frank Flannery, Doyle had to live with a big-name running mate.

Mairead McGuinness had a very high profile as farming editor of the *Irish Independent* and presenter of the RTE rural-affairs television show, Ear to the Ground. Kenny found that her addition to the European ticket had hugely boosted party morale

246

– she had offers from the Progressive Democrats, who had successfully recruited Irish Farmers' Association leader Tom Parlon to take a Dail seat in May 2002.

Kenny was even more enthused by the 'Avril versus Mairead' stories, which dominated news reports in an otherwise slow campaign. It was a colour writer's dream. Lines such as 'Designer handbags at 100 paces', 'political catfight' and 'horseboxes drawn' overwhelmed more worthy commentaries about trivialising women politicians and avoiding the real European issues.

For Kenny and his back-room team it was simple: friction meant publicity and publicity meant votes. But keeping a lid on a furiously boiling pot was easier said than done. The geography was perfect. McGuinness was based in the north of the constituency on the Meath-Louth border; Doyle was in the far south, in Wexford.

The only thing each side could agree on was that Meath was off limits to Doyle and Wexford was off limits to McGuinness. Well, that was the theory, but there was controversy in April 2004 when Doyle's portable electronic advertisement was placed outside Fairyhouse Racecourse in Co Meath.

McGuinness's supporters covered the electronic hoarding with their candidate's posters. But some were keen to take the matter further.

In late May 2004, two weeks from polling day, the McGuinness camp got new posters and her more robust and renegade supporters were keen to display them everywhere – including Wexford. The Doyle camp, many of whom had warned Kenny they would abandon Fine Gael if his strategy lost their woman her seat, were absolutely enraged.

Phil Hogan, national director of elections, had to take swift action. His blunt message to McGuinness's director of elections, Jim O'Brien, was accompanied by a warning that the party's HQ personnel would take down the offending posters in Wexford if necessary.

But both O'Brien and Hogan were undoubtedly also pleased

with the showing the invading posters got in the newspapers the next day.

Over the following days, opinion polls suggested that the unthinkable was possible and that both Doyle and McGuinness just might win, giving Fine Gael two out of three seats in that East Euro constituency. Throughout the other three constituencies, the poll findings were also good for Kenny's Fine Gael. It was the very first inkling of a Kenny revival.

In Dublin Gay Mitchell, a strong vote-getter in elections over the previous two decades, was going very well. The same was true of Jim Higgins in Connacht-Ulster, now renamed North West and with Clare taken from the former Munster constituency, and Simon Coveney in Munster, now newly named South.

Kenny was very closely associated with all these candidate choices. He had approached Jim Higgins as early as October 2002 to sound him out. The other Mayo Fine Gael rival, Michael Ring, was annoyed to see Higgins issue a statement saying he would give "serious consideration" to the idea of standing in place of veteran MEP Joe McCartin of Leitrim, who was retiring.

Ring made it clear he wanted to be considered for the Strasbourg assembly post – and was not fazed by the party leader approaching Jim Higgins. "It is the members at grass-roots level who will select Joe McCartin's replacement, not the party leader or officialdom," Ring said in October 2002.

But by the time the 1,300 Fine Gael delegates gathered at the Sligo Park Hotel on February 1, 2004, to choose their Euro candidates, Senator Jim Higgins was the one. He was joined on the ticket by Cllr Madeleine Taylor-Quinn of Clare, a former TD, senator and junior minister.

Simon Coveney had been identified as the best bet in the South, though veteran Bernard Allen was also in the frame for a while. After much deliberation, it was also decided to let Coveney stand without a running mate.

Former leader John Bruton was identified as a likely candidate in Dublin but it became increasingly clear that he would soon be appointed to the prestigious post of EU Ambassador to Washington, taking him out of electoral politics. So Kenny then spent a lot of time and effort successfully persuading Gay Mitchell to run.

At the same time, the new back-room team put in some very painstaking work in choosing candidates for the local council elections, to be held on the same day as the European Parliament vote. Over two years, Kenny's criss-cross tours of the country included meeting after meeting with councillors, local constituency officers and prospective candidates, all focused on the June 2004 local council elections.

Fine Gael general secretary Tom Curran was deployed along with party strategist Frank Flannery to interview every single candidate who would stand in those elections. The party's five full-time regional organisers also played a critical role here. "It was very time-consuming work. But they did it – and it was to pay off handsomely," one party stalwart recalled.

The party team was beefed up by the appointment of Ciaran Conlon as head of media and Gerry Naughten as political director. Both were experienced professionals without a previous link to Fine Gael and thus capable of telling home truths.

The pair worked well together and their efforts were augmented by some outside professionals, including public-relations expert Mark Mortell, who had previously worked for Fine Gael and had been appointed chairman of Bord Failte when Kenny was Tourism Minister.

Conlon began to seriously work with the tabloid newspapers – something Bertie Ahern's Fianna Fail had been doing effectively since his election as leader in November 1994.

Also at Fine Gael headquarters, organiser Terry Murphy headed up a special project to rebuild the party in Dublin. The three remaining Dublin TDs – Gay Mitchell, Richard Bruton and Olivia Mitchell – were also involved.

Enda Kenny showed an ability to delegate and empower people to get on with the job. His predecessor, John Bruton, was remembered as someone who tended to micromanage and sometimes meddle.

"Kenny would say to you: 'Get on with it. That's your job. But for God's sake don't have it landing back on my desk.' He had an ability to indicate from time to time that he was keeping tabs by asking a key question," one member of his Dail front bench revealed.

But the biggest change within Kenny's Fine Gael was that it had a secure income. He promptly reversed Michael Noonan's ban on corporate donations, a move endorsed by the other three candidates who had challenged for the party leadership against him in June 2002.

Even more significantly, Kenny implemented a Flannery Report recommendation that the party hire a full-time fundraiser. Anne Strain, one of the organisation's most formidable characters, joined the party from the Alzheimer Society of Ireland in January 2003. Since then she has organised the annual Fine Gael members' draw – one of the most successful in Ireland, and which pulls in an average of over €1 million per year.

The draw is confined to party members, who can buy tickets at €80 each. First prize is €20,000, with 19 other prizes ranging from €10,000 to €1,000, and a selection of smaller ones. By December 2011 total proceeds since the draw began were put at €11.4 million.

Fine Gael also charge an annual membership fee of €15 from their 35,000 members. Under Kenny's leadership, the number of members has almost doubled, from a low of 18,000 in 2002.

In addition, Anne Strain organises the party's annual €120 per head dinner each November and is in regular contact with Fine Gael TDs, senators, MEPs and councillors, who take the bulk of the tables. In November 2011 this event attracted 1,200 guests and grossed over €140,000. Corporate tables were also available and groups represented included the Irish Farmers' Association, the Vintners' Federation of Ireland and prominent accountants Grant Thornton.

Party organisers argue that these events have brought in cash and also created space between politicians and donors.

But critics point to a lack of transparency in all political-party accounts and argue that there is considerable scope for business groups and individuals to contribute to dinners, the draw and other fundraising efforts. Once amounts were kept below the €630 individual limit and €5,000 per company, a declaration was not required.

Given the history of controversies about political sleaze and two major tribunals of inquiry, this would remain a hot issue for Enda Kenny as Taoiseach and critics within his own party on the funding issue included Lucinda Creighton. But as he moved to rebuild Fine Gael, regular funding meant money to spend on broader-ranging research – for the first time taking in lifestyle and views on many issues well beyond voting intentions.

A regular relationship was opened up with Washington-based consultants Greenberg Quinlan Rosner, which continues to the present day. This followed on the example of Fianna Fail who, in 1996, retained renowned US political consultants Shrum, Devine and Donilon to guide their research plans.

"Without research, you were just taking a series of shots in the dark. With research, you could form coherent plans and stay with them," a Fine Gael strategist explained.

The *Irish Independent* headline on Monday, June 14, 2004, read 'Bertie's Blackest Day'. The Fianna Fail-Progressive Democrats coalition had suffered a serious reverse, with the combined loss of 20 per cent of their council seats, both city and county. Sinn Fein gained 33 seats, bringing them to 55 councillors in total.

But the big winner of those council elections in 2004 was Enda Kenny and Fine Gael. The party gained 16 council seats and stood at just 11 seats behind Fianna Fail, with a total of 293 councillors across the country.

And the really good headline-grabbing news came for Kenny and his party in the European Parliament contest. They beat Fianna Fail in a nationwide election for the very first time in almost

80 years. Five of the six candidates they fielded were elected; they were finally ahead of Fianna Fail, who had four MEPs.

Avril Doyle was elected to the last of the Republic of Ireland's 13 European Parliament seats just after 1am on Tuesday, June 15, 2004. She would join her constituency rival, Mairead McGuinness, along with Gay Mitchell, Simon Coveney and Jim Higgins. There was even the bonus that, with Jim Higgins safely 'exported' to mainland Europe, Kenny had only Michael Ring to rival him on Mayo home turf.

It was a huge contrast with Kenny's position one year earlier, in May 2003, when a poll in *The Irish Times* put Fine Gael support on 20 per cent and Labour on 22 per cent. In the Dail, Labour leader Pat Rabbitte was the star while Kenny appeared hesitant and ineffectual.

In just two years, Enda Kenny had led the party from the brink of disaster back to properly compete with Fianna Fail. Labour had also done well, with a gain of 18 council seats.

Suddenly, the idea of an alternative to a Fianna Fail-led government under Bertie Ahern did not seem such a fiction. But very many people, including those inside Fine Gael, still doubted whether Enda Kenny would head such an alternative.

****

Glorious sunshine greeted Bertie Ahern and his Fianna Fail parliamentary party on Monday, September 6, 2004, when they decamped to Inchydoney in west Cork to regroup after their summer election kicking.

Ahern had invited economic justice campaigner Fr Sean Healy to discuss poverty and the-then Taoiseach told *The Irish Times* he was "one of the few socialists left in Irish politics".

But Ahern was not the only one bent on delivering media surprises that sunny autumn day. By mid-afternoon heavy hitters from Labour and Fine Gael began ringing the political journalists who had followed Ahern to west Cork.

Both Enda Kenny and Labour leader Pat Rabbitte were in Mullingar "talking about talks for a potential political alliance", the hacks were told. It was a turn-up for the books.

The pair had gone there to give a boost to a local Fine Gael-Labour co-operation arrangement on Westmeath County Council, where their combined parties held the majority.

Now Kenny and Rabbitte surprised everyone by talking openly about making that local deal a national line-up. They were opening up an old game called '83-Plus'. The two Mayo guys were now discussing more than football and pints, and they were eager to steal Ahern's limelight.

"For good political strategists it's always about getting the 'magic 83', or more TDs required as a minimum to form a government in a Dail of 166 TDs. The calculation was that Fine Gael could gain 20-plus seats, bringing them into the early to mid-50s, Labour could go up five more seats to 25, the Green Party could have five or more. Bingo – a government." That is how one Fine Gael veteran summed up the thinking of all the key people in the opposition parties in autumn 2004.

The road ahead was long, however, because this time, unlike in summer 1997, everybody believed Bertie Ahern when he said he'd take his second government through the full five-year term. There were over two more years of solid politics to be slogged through before the political machines went into general-election mode for a contest in late May 2007. Certainly Bertie Ahern was not to be underestimated, even though he was bidding for a third consecutive election win.

Kenny's problem would be to maintain impetus as leader of the opposition – a task which most observers agree is very difficult. But he had two small bonuses in October 2004, when he announced a reshuffled front bench.

In a popular move, he recalled former leader Michael Noonan and made him chairman of the Public Accounts Committee, the biggest plum in his gift at that time as opposition leader. He appointed a new recruit to Fine Gael, the former Independent

Wexford TD Dr Liam Twomey, as health spokesman – and then he dropped a bombshell.

There would be no place for Michael Ring on his front bench because Ring had been offered and refused the job of marine spokesman. Ring claimed it was "a demotion" from his previous job as welfare and family affairs spokesman, in which observers agreed that he had shone.

"I'm hurt and disappointed – I'm gutted today," Ring told reporters, stressing that Dr Twomey had only just joined the party, whereas he had been elected a town councillor in Westport back in 1979. It was notable that Kenny had taken out insurance with Wexford Fine Gael grass roots by promoting Enniscorthy TD Paul Kehoe as his chief whip.

Kenny was apparently upfront about Ring's situation. Marine was an important post, responsible for thousands of jobs in a €500 million industry and with particular importance for the western seaboard. He said he could not understand why Ring would refuse it and let it be known that he had spent 90 minutes trying to reason with him on the issue.

For those close to Kenny around Dublin and in Mayo, this was a triumph as it showed steel. It compared with Kenny's prompt front-bench sacking of Waterford dissident John Deasy in April 2004 for flouting the new smoking ban by repeatedly refusing to put out his cigarette in the Dail bar.

But it was also just the latest in the Kenny-versus-Ring series, now 12 years old and dating from the 1992 general election. There had been three recent flashpoints in that saga.

The first was Ring's strident stance in unsuccessfully seeking the European Parliament nomination over Jim Higgins.

The second was Ring's insistence on taking an unsuccessful High Court challenge in late 2003 to the new ban on TDs and senators holding council seats, even though Fine Gael had supported that ban.

The third was Ring's call for party councillors to be allowed to support Dana Rosemary Scallon's efforts to win a nomination for a presidential election "in the interests of democracy".

Ring was still a force in Mayo, where many voters swore by him. But Kenny could hope to be contesting the next election in Mayo as a potential Taoiseach and was in a good place to stand up to his local rival.

Kenny had also already sidestepped the idea of a presidential election by supporting the return of President Mary McAleese, elected as a Fianna Fail candidate in 1997 for another seven-year term. He saw no benefit in engaging in an expensive campaign which Fine Gael were most unlikely to win and recalled the acrimony and internal party fallout from previous presidential elections.

Kenny drew some media criticism for failing to contest the presidency. But in the main, as McAleese got her renewed term, the criticisms fell on Labour and the Green Party, who had each mooted the idea of running a candidate and then backed out for various reasons.

In October 2004, Kenny was somewhat reassured by an opinion poll which put Fine Gael on 24 per cent. The party was already planning for two upcoming by-elections: in Meath, where John Bruton had resigned to become EU Ambassador to the USA, and in Kildare North, where Fianna Fail Finance Minister Charlie McCreevy had quit to become Ireland's EU Commissioner.

The two by-elections were held in March 2005 and they resulted in a handsome win in Meath for Fine Gael's Shane McEntee and a good vote in Kildare North for Naas town councillor Darren Scully. Kenny felt emboldened enough to publicly warn the Fianna Fail-Progressive Democrats coalition that "their days were numbered".

Fianna Fail's heavy hitter in Meath, Noel Dempsey, confidently said they would win the next election. "We still have two years – we can turn this one around," he told reporters.

Despite the by-elections there was evidence that the government's 'caring-sharing image' was bearing some fruit. McCreevy's successor as Finance Minister, Brian Cowen, put tax cuts for the low-paid into his first Budget.

Ahern was also slowly but surely gaining ground on completing the Northern Ireland peace process, which led to IRA arms decommissioning in 2005 and Ian Paisley of the Democratic Unionist Party finally sharing power in Belfast with Sinn Fein in the build-up to a deal that formally emerged in 2007.

The next election was slowly but surely shaping up to be a real battle. Kenny was going to give Ahern a run for his money.

****

The political year 2006-2007 opened with what at first looked like a major unexpected bonus for Enda Kenny. On Thursday, September 21, 2006, *The Irish Times* reported that the Mahon Tribunal, which was examining planning corruption, was investigating payments of between €50,000 and €100,000 made to Taoiseach Bertie Ahern.

The payments dated from 1993 and 1994, when Ahern was Finance Minister. It was a political sensation: Bertie Ahern was no longer the 'Teflon Taoiseach' and the stability of the coalition was in doubt, especially as Ahern's Progressive Democrats colleagues were now led by the combative Michael McDowell, who had taken over from Mary Harney just weeks earlier.

Ahern confirmed the reports in principle but challenged the reported amounts as the issue dragged over several days. Taoiseach Ahern went on the attack, appealing directly to the people in a pre-recorded interview at his own constituency offices, St Luke's, for RTE's Six One news with anchorman Bryan Dobson, on Tuesday, September 26.

It was an effective and emotive performance, playing on popular respect and affection. Ahern styled the money, equivalent to about €50,000, as a gift or "dig-out" from a number of friends at a time of great stress and expense as he negotiated a judicial separation from his wife, Miriam.

There were holes in his story, especially in relation to a revelation that he also received Stg£8,000 for speaking at a dinner in Manchester in 1994 which involved a man named Micheal Wall, who later sold him a house.

The Progressive Democrats were very uneasy, especially about the Manchester revelation, and considered quitting government. Ahern's relations with his partners were irreparably damaged and controversy would again surface in the general election the following summer.

But the public appeal succeeded for Ahern and Fianna Fail, as several opinion polls in October 2006 astonishingly showed the party's fortunes had improved by between four and eight per cent. Those polls showed the public did not believe Ahern, but that the people were prepared to give him a sort of fool's pardon.

Fianna Fail personnel were very agreeably surprised. "It turns out that the way out of a popularity downturn is to get yourself embroiled in a cash gifts row. Then you go up and the other crowd go down," one Fianna Fail TD summed up.

One opinion poll for the *Sunday Tribune* newspaper put Fianna Fail on 42 per cent, perhaps even enough for single-party government. The combined would-be Rainbow were on 36 per cent: Fine Gael, 20, Labour, 10 and Green Party, six. Kenny and Fine Gael were rocked and held back on further strong attacks on Ahern, sensing they were entirely counter-productive.

As news of this poll circulated at the Fine Gael presidential dinner at the Burlington Hotel in Dublin on Saturday evening, October 14, 2006, the party faithful's mood was despondent, despite the abundance of Ahern dinner, dig-out and donation jokes. Phil Hogan told the attendance they were adding a new prize of dinner for 25 in Manchester to the Fine Gael members' draw.

"But you must be good pals with the people in the room, deal only in cash and have no bank account," Hogan joked.

That evening Enda Kenny did his best to rally the troops. He referred to a very poor All-Ireland football-final display by Mayo weeks earlier. "But the next Mayo team that will take the field, Pat Rabbitte and myself, will not lie down," he pledged.

And, for home consumption, he ventured one last attack on Ahern. "The message coming from the centre of government is not the message with which I was raised. It isn't the message for the country I want to live in. I intend to change that," he said.

Kenny got a standing ovation from the party faithful. But few beyond the vast hotel dining room were listening.

****

Enda Kenny was in bed in Castlebar early on Sunday morning, April 29, 2007, when Taoiseach Bertie Ahern surprised everyone by going to Aras an Uachtarain and asking President McAleese to dissolve the 29th Dail. The President signed the order just before 8am and resumed her preparations to fly to the USA later that day for an official visit.

Kenny was on a flight at 9am out of Knock Airport and was smiling from ear to ear at noon in Dublin as he addressed the assembled press outside Fine Gael's swish election headquarters at Fitzwilliam Hall, near Leeson Street Bridge in Dublin 4.

"Today marks the end of 10 years of Fianna Fail-Progressive Democrats broken promises. Their time is up," he all but chanted, before offering his contract for a better Ireland.

Kenny predicted that Fine Gael would get anything up to 29 per cent of the vote and oust Ahern's coalition. He said the party were ready, with an army of 25,000 canvassers preparing to hit the 43 constituencies nationwide, and he challenged Ahern to debate "any place, anywhere, any time – in English or in Irish".

Purely to demonstrate his point, a number of jeeps liveried in Fine Gael colours arrived. Kenny and prominent Dublin candidates including Lucinda Creighton and Paschal Donohoe headed for the gates of Government Buildings in nearby Merrion Street to unveil a giant P45 form to officially sack Ahern's coalition.

By comparison, Bertie Ahern's start did not look too impressive. He had said nothing to the select band of journalists tipped off and present for his early-morning visit to the Aras. Later that morning he formally launched proceedings by reading a prepared script and refusing to take questions.

This was astonishing behaviour from a politician who often did an impromptu 'doorstep' with journalists on his way in and out of press conferences. In marked contrast to his 1997 and 2002 campaigns, when he toured the country, Ahern began to ration his public appearances.

The-then Taoiseach became the focus of a stepped-up media frenzy – for all the wrong reasons. The Mahon Tribunal was due to meet the next day and make an opening statement on his finances. There were weekend newspaper reports predicting detailed evidence around how he had bought his house from Micheal Wall and about "suitcases of cash" being stored by Mr Ahern in a safe at his constituency office.

Next day the Tribunal met and adjourned proceedings until after the election. But for the following fortnight all Fianna Fail's press occasions were dominated by questions about Ahern's finances.

On the first full weekend of the campaign the Progressive Democrats considered formally pulling out of the government, which was continuing in a caretaker capacity until the new administration after polling day. After a series of meetings, party leader Michael McDowell demanded a full statement from Ahern during the campaign and the Taoiseach agreed to do this.

By contrast, Enda Kenny was zipping around the country in a clear imitation of Ahern's previous campaigns. It was all photo opportunities and glad-handling – the kind of thing his advisers rightly believed he was born to do. He was frequently pictured holding his fist aloft; he skipped and ran whenever he could, to show he was fit and vigorous despite his 58 years.

But Bertie Ahern had three trump cards left to play. His backers called them the "statesman cards" which harked back to his years of slog in Northern Ireland. On Tuesday, May 8, he took a break from electioneering to travel to Belfast and witness Ian Paisley of the DUP and Martin McGuinness of Sinn Fein take office in the restored power-sharing government.

Three days later he welcomed Paisley to the historic Battle of the Boyne site in Co Meath in a visit full of ceremonial resonance. Then, on Tuesday, May 15, he addressed the joint Houses of Commons in London at the invitation of British Prime Minister Tony Blair, with whom he was friendly.

Enda Kenny made a virtue of necessity and accepted an invitation to attend Ahern's speech. Kenny managed to claw back what ground he could by showing that he could be statesmanlike also: he praised Ahern's work. Fianna Fail pressed home their advantage by running a party-political broadcast which featured tributes to Ahern the peacemaker from former US President Bill Clinton, former peace-talks chairman Senator George Mitchell and Tony Blair.

Ahern's statement on his finances begged even more questions and he then had to explain that Micheal Wall gave him money to refurbish the house which Wall later sold to Ahern.

But by then Finance Minister Brian Cowen, backed by Dermot Ahern and Noel Dempsey, had begun to score some points against Fine Gael's election promises and how they would be funded.

"In the final week Fianna Fail managed to switch the debate back to the economy. The lack of strength in the Fine Gael team began to show. Richard Bruton had been carrying the economic debate and he was tiring. We did not have people of Cowen's and Dempsey's calibre to robustly step into the breach," a senior Fine Gael figure conceded afterwards. He did not add that the party strategists generally kept Kenny away from economic issues and indeed most hard policy matters during the campaign.

Then came the televised leaders' debate on Thursday night, May 17. It was a turning point. Enda Kenny looked good and performed quite well – but he lost to Ahern, who showed a better and deeper grasp of the issues. Some journalists called it for Kenny and some fell back on the old reliable, "too close to call".

Subsequent opinion polling by TNS-MRBI suggested that

Ahern won by a margin of three to one among voters, who were taking a more detached view. "On the night, Ahern came across as the more competent, the more informed, the more controlled. Kenny scored points with his composure and his enthusiasm, but did not succeed in convincing voters that he had all the answers," MRBI pollster Damian Loscher wrote afterwards.

Opinion polls in the final days showed a surge towards Fianna Fail and away from Fine Gael and Labour. At 7am on the day of the count – even before boxes were opened – exit poll results on RTE radio correctly predicted that Bertie Ahern had achieved an historic three-in-a-row victory.

Three hours later, at the count centre in Castlebar, the tally-men correctly predicted that Enda Kenny was head of the poll and Fine Gael would take three out of five seats. Mayo voters had flocked to Kenny as someone who could be Taoiseach. Much of the local canvass was done by his team of backers, who were increasingly becoming known as Kenny's 'Castlebar cabal'.

The 'former potential Taoiseach' had almost 15,000 votes, Michael Ring was behind him on 11,412, and the county's football manager, John O'Mahony, was to take the third seat with almost 7,000 votes. The fourth Fine Gael candidate, Michelle Mulherin, got an impressive 5,428 votes for good measure.

The vote in Mayo also showed the diminished political impact of the Rossport Shell gas terminal dispute as the two candidates most closely associated with the opposition fared badly. Outgoing Independent TD, Dr Jerry Cowley, lost his seat while Sinn Fein's Jerry Murray also got a poor vote. Kenny had led local Fine Gael well on this issue backing the release of five jailed protestors and thereafter urging mediation.

Mayo Fine Gael, with 54 per cent of the vote, were beneficiaries of a phenomenal internal Fianna Fail dispute centred on Beverley Flynn, who had dropped the 'Cooper' after separating from her husband. Her prolonged legal battle with RTE had led to her expulsion from Fianna Fail and she won her seat in this election as an Independent. The fifth seat was taken by the talented Dara

Calleary of Fianna Fail, who is based in Ballina.

When all the national counting was done, Fianna Fail took almost 42 per cent of the vote and 78 Dail seats – just three seats fewer than in 2002. Given the storm of scandal allegations surrounding Ahern and general claims of government fatigue after a decade in power, it was a remarkable outcome.

The result for Enda Kenny's Fine Gael was equally remarkable, however, with an extra five per cent and 20 more seats than 2002. It was the biggest-ever seat gain by any party – larger increases achieved in the past had involved an increase in the overall number of TDs. Labour came back with 20 deputies, the same number as in 2002.

The Green Party had battled through a tough election and returned six seats. But the combined Fine Gael-Labour-Green Party total was 77 seats – far off that 'magic 83', the minimum for government formation.

Enda Kenny continued to maintain that a Fine Gael-led government was possible. Bertie Ahern simply went ahead and opened up contacts on a number of fronts.

Ahern's third government took in three other elements to supplement his Fianna Fail TDs. The two remaining Progressive Democrats TDs, Mary Harney and Noel Grealish, were taken on board, with Harney returning to cabinet. Party leader Michael McDowell had lost his seat and dramatically quit politics at the election count centre.

The Green Party joined government after a week of negotiations and an overwhelming vote in favour from the party membership. Deputies John Gormley and Eamon Ryan got the key senior ministries of Environment and Energy and Communications, respectively.

Four Independents – Jackie Healy-Rae of Kerry South, Finian McGrath of Dublin North Central, Michael Lowry of Tipperary North and Beverley Flynn of Mayo – all announced that they had deals with Ahern. They supported him when the Dail returned on June 14, 2007, and so Bertie Ahern was elected Taoiseach by

89 votes to 75.

After the vote, Enda Kenny rose to his feet for the customary words of congratulation. He commended his adversary's "persistence and permanence" and wistfully acknowledged Ahern's "infernal ability to construct a government of incompatibles".

"We should be thankful for small mercies that you have started your long glide to retirement," he said in reference to Ahern's recent comments about his future.

Later he spoke to *Irish Independent* writer Lise Hand. "There's 100 weeks to the local elections, and we're already working on that. We're going after specific issues and we'll be ready.

"Anyway, anything could happen with this government," Kenny added – signalling he was definitely still hanging in for the long haul.

CHAPTER 11

The Great Escape... to Government Buildings

RTE news cut into the afternoon television schedule to carry live coverage of Enda Kenny standing on the plinth at Leinster House. It was after 5pm on Thursday, June 17, 2010.

Appropriately enough, the interrupted programme was an episode in the series called The Great Escape – and Enda Kenny had just beaten a heave against his party leadership driven by a huge majority of his key lieutenants and fronted by his deputy leader, Richard Bruton.

It was less than eight months before the general election which would take him to Government Buildings as Taoiseach at a time of the biggest economic crisis in Ireland's history. Yet 11 of the 19-strong front bench, whom he had chosen himself, had publicly told him he would not get to be Taoiseach.

Kenny fought an admirable rearguard action routing the conspirators in a counter move 'from the outside in'. As his own top brass turned on him, he successfully appealed to backbench Fine Gael TDs, to his Euro MEPs, and even to the senators whose jobs he had, without any prior consultation, pledged the previous year to abolish.

On the Leinster House plinth Kenny spoke strongly to the nation saying he would go on from here to become Taoiseach and address the real issues facing the Irish people. Supporters pointed to two precedents in the party history – in 1972 Liam Cosgrave had seen off a potential heave and become Taoiseach within 12 months, while in 1994, John Bruton had done something similar in even more unlikely circumstances.

Enda Kenny took great strength and kudos from the events of the days June 14 to 17 in 2010. He showed a cool head, courage and considerable strategic judgment, qualities few people realised he had, and left his rivals in the halfpenny place. And, like Cosgrave and Bruton, he went on to become Taoiseach within the following 12 months.

But this heave against Enda Kenny by his own people also pointed to those doubts about ability and commitment which had followed him, through successes and reverses, over the previous 34 years in politics. It also destroyed the carefully cultivated image of Kenny as 'manager of a talented team' since those team members had turned on him.

****

Brian Hayes was director of elections for the June 2009 by-election in Dublin South. As most of the ballot boxes were opened at the RDS count centre, the Dublin South West TD was ecstatic.

Hayes phoned the Fine Gael candidate, George Lee, otherwise known as the 'nation's economist' for his superb work over years explaining economic complexities on RTE radio and television. "You're on 51 per cent," Hayes sang into the phone.

"Is that good?" Lee asked, rather overwhelmed by the events of the previous weeks.

Fine Gael general secretary Tom Curran and strategist Frank Flannery had persuaded George Lee to come on board to fight the by-election caused by the death of the popular veteran Fianna Fail TD, Seamus Brennan. Lee said he was motivated by the need for everyone to play their part in tackling the extraordinary economic crisis facing the nation.

His vote of 27,768 first preferences was spectacular, even allowing for by-election vagaries and the notoriously volatile nature of Ireland's poshest constituency, Dublin South. Lee had almost doubled the percentage vote that three Fine Gael candidates achieved in the previous general election in May 2007.

As the day wore on, Brian Hayes did a radio interview which was quite upbeat until a question about continuing doubts over Enda Kenny's leadership of the party.

"What does this man have to do before people get off his back?" Hayes responded with an exasperated question of his own. Just a year later Brian Hayes would be among a group telling Kenny he had to go.

The throng of journalists at the RDS count centre had another question for Enda Kenny, who was whiling away the time until a formal result was declared. Would George Lee be on his front bench and be in line for a Government job in due course?

"You would love me to answer that question here and now. Let the man be declared. I will use all of the talent and expertise available to me in the best interests of the party," Kenny replied – just ever so slightly edgily.

George Lee was the story of the day. But the local council and European Parliament elections on June 5, 2009, on to which two by-elections were added, were in fact a bumper victory for Enda Kenny.

Fine Gael emerged as the biggest party in the local elections, with 32 per cent of the vote and a total of 340 city and county council seats. This compared with 25 per cent and 218 Fianna Fail seats, whose loss of 84 seats came on top of their loss of 80 seats in 2004. It was the first time ever Fine Gael had beaten Fianna Fail in nationwide council elections.

In the European Parliament elections, Fine Gael also emerged on top with 29 per cent of the vote and four seats to Fianna Fail's 24 per cent and three seats. The headline news here was Fianna Fail's loss of their Dublin Euro seat held by Eoin Ryan.

The second by-election of the day, in Dublin Central, was won by Maureen O'Sullivan, a long-time collaborator of independent socialist Tony Gregory, whose death caused that vacancy. Fine

Gael's Senator Paschal Donohoe got a good vote, boding well for the next time. Maurice Ahern, the brother of former Taoiseach Bertie Ahern, who was still a sitting TD for this constituency, fared very poorly for Fianna Fail.

The transformation in the Irish political party landscape which would come in the 2011 general election was already being flagged. The *Irish Independent* headline of the following Monday, June 13 – "Why Taoiseach Enda doesn't sound so funny" – summed things up.

The headline and underlying article explained that Enda Kenny had a tough time battling doubt inside and outside his own party since his return to the Dail in autumn 2007 with a rejuvenated and strengthened Fine Gael party.

The upside of having 20 extra TDs was that he had more personnel options and new talent. The downside was that some of the newcomers – notably 'Young Fine Gael graduates' Leo Varadkar of Dublin West and Lucinda Creighton, originally from Mayo and now TD for Dublin South East – were wayward and took a deal of managing.

Strategist Frank Flannery was working on plans to take the party up to 70 TDs in the next election. Again, this was excellent news in theory. But in practice constituency sharing is always tricky.

Established TDs know that the push to take an extra Dail seat could well conclude with the loss of their own seat. In Galway East the sitting deputy, Ulick Burke, was enraged by the recruitment of his recent local opponent, the former Progressive Democrat Senator Ciaran Cannon in March 2009, months after that party was disbanded.

By spring 2009, Cannon was described by some Government TDs as 'a walking pub quiz question' as only true 'political anoraks' would in future recall him as the last ever leader of the Progressive Democrats. That party's members had voted in November 2008 to disband and Cannon's recruitment symbolised the end of 23 years of national torment on Fine Gael's right flank.

In the Dail, Enda Kenny was making better inroads in his attacks on the new Taoiseach, Brian Cowen, who had taken over in a blaze of popular acclaim from Bertie Ahern on May 7, 2008. . Kenny could claim some credit at the end for continually attacking Ahern amid ongoing money revelations and Ahern's failures to give credible explanations.

But it was really Cowen's more aggressive responses which gave Kenny some real opposition traction at last. Defeat in a referendum on the EU Lisbon Treaty on June 10, 2008, just weeks after his election as Taoiseach, put an abrupt end to the Government honeymoon.

But the Fianna Fail-Green Party coalition's slide in the opinion polls was all about the major banking crisis which led to a Government blanket bank guarantee in September 2008 and later bank bailouts. There was also rising unemployment, vanishing tax revenues, and the beginnings of cuts in social services. In sum, the Irish economy was suddenly falling apart.

A rushed budget brought forward from December to October 2008 led to political calamity when changes to pensioners' medical benefits brought thousands of older people on to the streets in a display of 'grey power'. From then onwards there was an unavoidable and growing sense that things were spinning out of the Government's control.

The first cracks in the Government showed in the wake of the budget as Fianna Fail lost one backbencher, Joe Behan of Wicklow, and also the support of Dublin North Central independent TD, Finian McGrath.

By February 2009, one opinion poll showed nine out of 10 voters were deeply dissatisfied with the Government – and many of the very few not registering dissatisfaction put themselves down as 'don't know'. Kenny and Fine Gael were showing well in opinion surveys with a long series of polls putting the party in an unprecedented first place. But alarmingly, the trend of Labour leader Eamon Gilmore being named as the country's most popular leader began to emerge.

Fianna Fail's woes were not entirely Fine Gael's joys and there was growing evidence that Enda Kenny was not capitalising on Taoiseach Brian Cowen's misfortunes. Cowen was getting continual media drubbings but these were not matched by positive media for Kenny.

Interviews like the one he gave Jason O'Toole in the *Irish Daily Mail on Sunday* on September 27, 2009, made it hard at times to take Kenny seriously. Again he harked back to his 1996 tales of rodent-killing heroics, when he had been a teacher in a rat-infested school in Mayo before entering politics.

Kenny explained that he had been secretary of the local gun club and the staff and pupils in his school were very disturbed by rats under the floor.

"I waited in the evening there one time and I took half the pellets out of the cartridge and I just waited for 'my friends' to arrive and I blew them into oblivion. I got three or four. They got their own back because you could smell the things in the floor for months afterwards," Kenny recalled.

For Fianna Fail TDs all this smacked of Kenny's well-known love of a good yarn. They also recalled that in June 2006 he had excoriated the Government about crime rates, pointing to 500 burglaries per week in Ireland, and drawing on his own horrific experience of being mugged by two knife-wielding attackers "high on drugs".

Kenny said he could never forget the rasping sound of a knife being drawn from a scabbard. Closer inquiry revealed the incident had not taken place in Ireland – but while he was on holiday in Kenya.

"He is stoking up people's fears about crime with this half-true tale of being attacked," Fianna Fail TD Billy Kelleher said.

But Kenny supporters argued that much of this was just continuing anti-Kenny media prejudice and they pointed to journalist John Drennan's continual depiction of him as 'Kenny Lite'. Drennan began this persistent reference in the *Sunday*

Independent soon after Kenny's election as party leader in summer 2002.

The term arose from Fine Gael people privately putting their leader forward 'as a kind of Bertie Lite'. The nickname had stuck and followed Kenny like an albatross – it dovetailed with political columnist Miriam Lord, who had moved to *The Irish Times* in 2006, making periodic references to 'Indakinny'.

It is very true that Kenny went through long periods of never being able to do the right thing in the eyes of most of the political journalists. It is also true that politicians of all parties have found being leader of the Opposition a role in which it is hard to show results. The plain fact also was that he was under a lot of pressure at this point as he had done another set of regional party conferences and countrywide meetings in late 2008. The late nights and early mornings took a toll.

"My own view is that he was tired and even more disinclined than usual to give the necessary attention to policy matters. You can't do everything. He was coming to parliamentary meetings and 'winging it'. Something had to give," a senior member of the Fine Gael parliamentary party recalled.

That assessment was shared by politicians in the Government.

"One of our very few saving graces right now is that Kenny is still not really credible," a senior Fianna Fail Cabinet minister confided to reporters in the wake of that February 2009 opinion poll.

But surely, after Fine Gael's huge gains in these by-elections and local and European elections in June 2009, everything would settle down and Fine Gael would rally round their future Taoiseach? The arrival of George Lee was a national coup as much as a local seat gain.

Politics, however, is rarely that neat. And ironically, George Lee was linked to Enda Kenny's next set of problems.

****

The year 2010 started very badly with a particularly hopeless performance by Enda Kenny on the Late Late Show on RTE on Friday, January 14. He again ruled out any coalition with Sinn Fein, but appeared very unfocused when presenter Ryan Tubridy sought his specific reasons for this, given the vastly-changed political situation in the North.

"There were some matters that were not cleared up... matters that related to republicanism," was all Kenny could manage vaguely. He refused to give any more details – and even made comparisons with the need for secrecy around the budget for not being more specific.

Kenny had often struggled with this Sinn Fein issue. While he always tended towards old Fine Gael values of 'having no truck', others in the party felt that inflexibility might not be realistic when it came to putting together a Dail majority for government.

He had demoted and reprimanded strategist Frank Flannery in June 2009 for publicly suggesting they could "do business with Sinn Fein". Those close to Kenny at the time insisted that he was "livid with Flannery" and others believe that relations between the two have never entirely recovered from this incident.

Kenny made an even bigger mess of things on Newstalk radio's Breakfast Show almost two weeks later, on Thursday, January 28, when talking to presenter and former Fine Gael Cabinet colleague Ivan Yates, with whom he had once shared a Dail office. Just days earlier, Environment Minister John Gormley had put forward plans for domestic water meters and water charges.

Yates insisted that voters were entitled to know if Fine Gael favoured these water charges. Kenny dodged, floundered and tripped over his words. Newstalk widely circulated the transcript which read as badly as it sounded on air.

The incident was not forgotten by Kenny and his advisers. He did one more Newstalk interview with Ivan Yates, on February 1, 2011, the day the general election was called. After that he was "unavailable" when subsequent interview requests from Yates were put to him.

But the real horror story came on February 8, 2010, when the party's national star and most recent recruit, George Lee, announced he was returning to RTE, quitting Fine Gael, the Dail and politics generally. It was just eight months since Lee had been the toast of Fine Gael as he swept into the Dail.

The row raged for a few days. Lee said he was disillusioned with having no real input into Fine Gael policy and had been "frozen out" by the party's finance spokesman Richard Bruton, who was unduly protective of his turf and saw Lee as competition. Fine Gael countered that Lee had not done enough to assert himself as a TD and had gone into politics without fully realising what the job really entailed. The party also insisted that he wanted to return to RTE before a 12-month grace period elapsed and his job would be no longer open to him.

The Government was delighted to see the media spotlight focus on another party's problems. But nobody in any party at Leinster House had much sympathy for George Lee as he left politics.

There is no doubt that Lee was a brilliant journalist who did not make the difficult transition to politics. But Enda Kenny as leader did not do enough to maximise the use of a potential national asset and some of that was down to concerns about offending his finance spokesman Richard Bruton. Now Lee's departure immediately fed renewed speculation that Kenny would be challenged as leader.

"Enda Kenny expected a leadership challenge at any stage from that moment onwards. In fact he had worked on the principle that, when you lead Fine Gael, you'll face a heave sooner or later. Remember he served under five leaders in all and two of them, Dukes and Bruton, were ousted.

"He was closely involved in defending up to five heaves against Bruton and they won one big one in 1994 and lost the last big one in 2001," is the assessment of one Fine Gael politician, who did not support Kenny's continued leadership in 2010.

But a challenge against Kenny was delayed as would-be rebels lacked a leader since Richard Bruton could not be persuaded to move against his boss. Equally, all of the parliamentary party were irked by the way Lee had quit and most felt an immediate heave would give him undeserved kudos. Finally, even if Bruton was willing, the timing was still off given Lee's accusations of having been frozen out by Bruton.

The weeks dragged on and speculation about the leadership heave persisted. The party faithful gathered in Killarney in March for a successful Ard Fheis. Kenny reiterated his surprise pledge of the previous October to abolish the Seanad – many parliamentary party members, especially long-serving senators, remained very disaffected by the abolition announcement.

As with John Bruton in January 2001, matters came to a head on the night of Thursday, June 11, 2010, when *The Irish Times* released its latest opinion poll results. They were a tale of continuing disaster for Fianna Fail, on a lamentable 17 per cent, and Taoiseach Brian Cowen, on 18 per cent.

But it was equally grim for Fine Gael and Enda Kenny. The party was down four per cent to 28 per cent – leaving it in the same place as the 2007 general election.

The real shocker was that Labour's surge continued and its 32 per cent score put the party in first place and could see it take 60 Dail seats if repeated in a general election. The 'Gilmore for Taoiseach' bandwagon was given impetus by Labour leader Eamon Gilmore's personal popularity rating of 46 per cent.

In a further twist, Kenny's deputy leader Richard Bruton was on RTE's Prime Time programme discussing the banking crisis when the survey results became known that evening. On live television Bruton dodged three opportunities to express confidence in Kenny and was also evasive a couple of hours later on TV3 with presenter Vincent Browne.

After Browne harangued him, Bruton managed a weak endorsement of Kenny but also conceded his own leadership ambitions, saying: "In the swag bag of every corporal there is a lieutenant's baton."

There would be a heave against Kenny – the only question was when. Earlier that same day, Kenny had tabled a Dail motion of no confidence in Taoiseach Brian Cowen, based on the ongoing banking debacle, which would be taken the following Tuesday and Wednesday. Fine Gael rebels later said they suspected he was taking defensive action based on leaked opinion poll figures, but Kenny supporters rejected these claims.

That weekend's newspapers were full of 'Fine Gael heave' speculation. The general assumption was that it would have to wait until some time after the Dail confidence vote in Taoiseach Brian Cowen.

But assumptions of delay were wrong. On Monday, June 14, Fionnan Sheahan's front page story on the *Irish Independent* headlined: 'Bruton Tells Kenny: I Have Lost confidence In You' dramatically showed that the pace had increased. Sheahan revealed that both men had spoken over the weekend and the only way an all-out heave could be stopped was if Kenny graciously stood aside.

It said a lot about politics that Kenny had spent nine years as Fine Gael chief whip stoutly defending Richard Bruton's older brother John. "Richard is a different type of person to John. He is brilliant academically, good but limited politically, and very deep and extraordinarily stubborn. Once he makes his mind up – that's it," a long-time Fine Gael insider explained.

Bruton had a strong vote in the June 2002 leadership election. In the media he was portrayed as able but lacking charisma. He had gained respect when his persistent warnings about the cost of public service pay "benchmarking" proved correct. Now by mid-2010, with reliability suddenly outweighing more flash attributes, even his low-key personality seemed a plus.

It emerged within hours that Kenny would not stand down under any circumstances – if 'Bruton & Company' wanted change they would have to unseat Enda Kenny in an all-out fight. Fine Gael was back doing what it had done best several times over the previous 20 years – it was tearing itself asunder again. The matter would be played out over the coming four days to the delight of Taoiseach Brian Cowen who was effectively, but temporarily, off the hook.

****

Kenny's defenders remained gleeful long afterwards at the lingering rumours of treachery among the challengers. But rumours were brushed aside that they had a 'mole' in the ranks of Richard Bruton's supporters.

"There was no need for a mole– though some of the other side had big mouths. Reality is that we had this one covered from way out. This was really about the extraordinary naivety of the 'officer corps'", one Kenny defender said.

The term 'officer corps' points up a very old 'them-and-us' divide in Fine Gael with the professional and better-off classes being differentiated from members drawn from ordinary working or middle class backgrounds. One Kenny supporter styled it "the tech versus the boarding school".

These were caricatures but had some basis to sustain them and were of use in a gut struggle. Bruton had attended the exclusive Clongowes Wood school and so did his supporter, Simon Coveney, while another 'Brutonite', Leo Varadkar, went to The King's Hospital, another 'posh' school. By contrast Michael Ring, once again a staunch Kenny supporter when the leadership chips were down, proudly boasted a 1973 All-Ireland football Vocational Schools competition medal.

As the drama unfolded, Kenny's opponents spoke of him missing the final vital ingredient to bring them to government. They acknowledged that he had rescued and rebuilt the party and won important gains in the local and European elections. But, to borrow a sporting comparison, Kenny could lead them to semi-finals and finals – but could not win the cup because people could not visualise him as Taoiseach.

"The public haven't faith in him. He's done a wonderful job for the party, but he doesn't seem able to make that bigger leap," Olwyn Enright, the party's social welfare spokeswoman summed up.

The Kenny camp was first to hit the phones as every backbench

TD, MEP and senator was canvassed. Carlow-Kilkenny TD Phil Hogan and another shrewd constituency operator, chief whip Paul Kehoe of Wexford, took the lead. Kenny's long-time Mayo collaborator, Senator Paddy Burke, spoke to all the senators.

Despite Kenny's peremptory announcement to abolish the Seanad, the vast bulk of senators came on board for him. Many had clear Dail ambitions for the next term and cared little about the Seanad's fate. Even those perceived as longer-term senators, such as Maurice Cummins of Waterford and Paul Coghlan of Killarney, backed Kenny.

Kenny's team made lists and then double-checked them. Waiverers were isolated for special attention. Michael Ring joined the others in reassuring backers that Kenny "had the numbers" among the 51 TDs, 15 senators and four MEPs who would vote to decide this issue.

The leader's powers to hire and fire and also his input into general election candidate selection were deployed to dissuade those thinking of voting for Richard Bruton's side. Kenny's lieutenant Phil Hogan was also very effective here.

"Being able to say who else might be on the Fine Gael ticket in your constituency and from which side of the constituency they would come helped 'clarify' matters for a lot of people," one Kenny insider said.

The four MEPs quickly came on board, with Dublin MEP Gay Mitchell telling colleagues they had to deal with the party's problems and not seek to change the leader every time opinion polls were bad. Many Bruton supporters were especially disappointed by a prompt declaration of support for Kenny from East MEP Mairead McGuinness.

Hogan and Kehoe also aggressively worked the media, denouncing the challenge and its timing, coming when they should be pinning down the Government. Bruton supporters delayed too long and hung too much on an assumption that Kenny would have to step down once he saw the bulk of his front bench were against him.

"I just thought once he saw that he had 'lost the dressing room' he would conclude that there was no point," one of Bruton's supporters explained.

Bruton's supporters were surprised by RTE reporter Valerie Cox when they tried to have a private breakfast meeting at the Green Isle Hotel, close to the southern motorway into Dublin, on day two of their campaign, Tuesday, June 15. They had come to hear an update from Richard Bruton and prepare for a planned walkout later at a Fine Gael frontbench meeting.

Kenny did the exact opposite to standing gracefully aside. He had drawn first blood by sacking Bruton from his front bench the previous day. Then he sacked the entire front bench before the majority could walk out on him.

The nine Bruton supporters then went on to the Leinster House plinth to make their opposition to Enda Kenny's leadership clear. They were Billy Timmins, Wicklow; Leo Varadkar, Dublin West; Brian Hayes, Dublin South West; Olivia Mitchell, Dublin South; Denis Naughten, Roscommon-South Leitrim; Simon Coveney, Cork South Central; Olwyn Enright, Laois-Offaly; Fergus O'Dowd, Louth and Michael Creed, Cork North West.

Next day things looked good for the Bruton camp. Kieran O'Donnell of Limerick East, chosen by Kenny to replace Bruton as finance spokesman, moved to the Bruton camp. He was joined by Charlie Flanagan, another big name.

Some in the media began to tilt towards calling a Bruton win in the following day's vote. But others were looking to lower-profile parliamentary figures who would decide the issue.

As with all such contests it was impossible to gauge who just might change their mind very late in proceedings – and just who was telling the truth about his or her allegiance to begin with. The best estimates at this stage were that Kenny had an advantage of up to seven votes as the 70 TDs, senators and MEPs gathered to decide his fate on Thursday, June 17, 2010.

The Kenny camp's final throw of the dice came on the eve of the vote. They warned that, if Kenny lost next day, one of his supporters would challenge Richard Bruton for the leadership, prolonging the party's internal turmoil. It all had echoes of February 2001 when Kenny stood against Noonan after John Bruton was ousted.

The meeting began at 11.30am. There was a small interruption for a Dail vote at 2.30pm and proceedings concluded around 4.45pm. Kenny proposed a vote of confidence in himself which allowed him to speak at the start and end of proceedings. There were a total of 47 speakers out of the 70 people present, many of whom exceeded their allotted four minutes.

All sides testified to the emotive strength of Kenny's contributions with his appeals for loyalty, a review of the distance he had taken the party and emphasis on how they were on the cusp of government. Some of those present were in tears.

He also tackled some of his opponents head-on and by name. Kenny made special mention of Leo Varadkar who had suggested during a television interview that there would be a strong role for Kenny under Taoiseach Richard Bruton, perhaps as Foreign Affairs Minister.

It was a secret ballot and only two people – party chairman Padraic McCormack, and secretary Paschal Donohoe – knew the final outcome which was not officially disclosed. Most of those present guessed Kenny won "by six or seven" – others, drawn from both camps, felt his victory margin was a bit higher and could have been "in or about 10 votes".

The failure of the challenge led to some ridicule of the group dubbed 'the Keystone conspirators' by *The Irish Times* writer Miriam Lord. It became apparent that Kenny's luck – evident on several occasions over the past decade – was in again. He was indeed lucky in the limitations of those who chose to try to oust him.

The rebels, however, now made it clear that there would be no more heaves and Kenny would lead Fine Gael into the next general election.

Kenny would delay appointing his new front bench, some rebels would be rehabilitated and others banished. But with a big rift in the Fine Gael team – of which he was supposed to be the 'chairman rather than the chief' – he knew he needed to be inclusive.

For many inside and outside Fine Gael the attempted heave was more about the party's ongoing failures to find an identity and role for itself in Irish politics. Since 1987 the party had periodically sought to change leaders as it offered itself as an alternative to Fianna Fail – an alternative voters decided they did not want.

But just because Kenny had won did not mean the arguments voiced by his opponents would evaporate. The harsh reality was that his engaging private personality did not come across in media and on television especially.

Henceforth, he and his advisors would have to be more selective about his media appearances. Enda Kenny would also have to do a much better job of briefing and preparing for media appearances and Dail debates.

The bigger dilemma for the Fine Gael leader – being able to say just what his party stood for – was in the process of resolving itself. He could happily continue to offer his party as an alternative to Fianna Fail's key members because Fianna Fail was continuing its process of comprehensively ruling itself out as a government option.

****

After the craziness of the previous year, the general election of February 25, 2011 was relatively tame. The main imponderables going into the campaign were how far Fianna Fail could fall and how would the Fine Gael versus Labour dynamic shake out.

Kenny and Fine Gael slowly but surely rallied after the June 2010 heave. Many relationships within the party were seriously strained. But Kenny showed a well-balanced approach to rebuilding his frontbench team, most of whom would feature in similar roles in his first Cabinet just eight months later.

Kenny's master stroke and hallmark of true political professionalism was his appointment of Michael Noonan as finance spokesman, when he unveiled his front bench on Friday July 1, 2010. Noonan had never, ever, rated Kenny and had been small-minded and short-sighted in omitting him from his own first team in February 2001, on his way to electoral meltdown as Fine Gael leader in May 2002.

Apart from his group of party friends, Noonan is respected rather than universally liked by Fine Gael colleagues. He justified his total silence on his voting intentions throughout the heave by saying he could not take sides as a former leader. But both the Kenny and Bruton camps agree that Noonan voted for Kenny – something which deeply irked some Bruton supporters as Noonan had never been known previously to speak up for his leader against others' criticisms.

"But these are professional relationships – they're not always or even often personal friendships. Kenny needed a strong and aggressive person to take on the Government and give a bit of popular fizz to Fine Gael economic policies. Time and place, Noonan was that person," one Fine Gael veteran explained.

The Limerick TD was impressive, drawing on a total of seven years' Cabinet experience in the 1980s and 1990s and many years as Fine Gael finance spokesman as well as chairman of the Public Accounts Committee. In May 2010 he had also revealed a moving personal story about 12 years spent nursing his wife Florence, as her Alzheimer's disease became progressively worse.

Kenny gave his vanquished rival Richard Bruton the number two economics job as enterprise spokesman. He also found space for rebels, Leo Varadkar, Simon Coveney, Fergus O'Dowd and Charlie Flanagan. But others on the Bruton side – Brian Hayes, Billy Timmins, Denis Naughten, Olwyn Enright, Olivia Mitchell and Michael Creed – were not on the first team.

It was a classic piece of divide and conquer designed to split the rebels copper-fastened by promoting politicians from the same constituency where he had dropped somebody. Alan Shatter's promotion offset Olivia Mitchell's banishment in Dublin South, Andrew Doyle's promotion balanced dropping Billy Timmins in Wicklow.

The loyalty and effectiveness of others was rewarded with first-time Dublin North TD and former Irish Medical Organisation president, Dr James Reilly, becoming deputy leader and health spokesman. Kenny was setting a lot of store in a novice TD in this appointment but he was banking on Reilly's trade union and medical experience and he also needed a Dublin-based deputy for balance.

Kerry North's Jimmy Deenihan became tourism, sport and culture spokesman, Alan Shatter justice spokesman, and Michael Ring was restored to social protection. The two anti-heave tough guys stayed put with their reputations enhanced; Phil Hogan added director of elections to his responsibility for environment and Paul Kehoe remained as chief whip.

****

The events of June 2010 also copper-fastened the power and influence of his principal adviser, Mark Kennelly, a Fine Gael 'lifer' who has worked for the party for over 22 years in one capacity or another. Enda Kenny is the third FG leader with whom he has worked very closely, having previously advised John Bruton and Michael Noonan.

Remarkably, Kennelly had survived the difficult circumstances in which Bruton and Noonan were each forced out of the leadership. He drew on those experiences to help Kenny see off a decisive heave against his leadership and noticeably increased his influence over the future Taoiseach and his reach is felt across the Fine Gael organisation.

Kennelly is originally from Killarney and a nephew of Brendan Kennelly, one of Ireland's most celebrated poets. His late father,

Colm Kennelly, played for Kerry in 1953 and 1955 All-Ireland football wins, and played alongside Enda Kenny's future father-in-law, Sean Kelly of Kilcummin, in the 1953 win.

After four years working for Fine Gael MEP John Cushnahan, in the summer of 1995 Kennelly was appointed special adviser to Minister for Transport, Energy and Communications, Michael Lowry, as part of the new Rainbow Government.

Less than 18 months later Lowry was forced out of office, but Lowry's replacement, the veteran Alan Dukes, kept Kennelly on his team.

Kennelly was called to give evidence to the McCracken and later Moriarty Tribunals which examined Lowry's affairs. But there has never been the smallest suggestion that Kennelly had any knowledge of Lowry's contentious links with businessmen Ben Dunne and Denis O'Brien.

After the Rainbow Government was ousted in June 1997, Kennelly moved to Leinster House to work on policy for Fine Gael. He worked closely with FG leader John Bruton, who was under continual pressure and was eventually ousted in March 2001. He then moved on to work for Michael Noonan and eventually Enda Kenny.

Kennelly's four years in Brussels helped him establish contacts for Kenny across the European Christian Democrat group, Fine Gael's European allies. It also helped him establish a very close rapport with the future Taoiseach and he was appointed chief of staff at Government Buildings after the 2011 election win.

****

Kenny and Fine Gael slowly rallied in the autumn of 2010. But more happily for them, the Fianna Fail Government just went from bad to worse.

On Tuesday September, 14, 2010, at a Fianna Fail pre-Dail think-in in Galway, Taoiseach Brian Cowen was accused of being drunk or hungover during an early morning interview on RTE's

Morning Ireland programme. Press conferences after a similar meeting by Cowen's Government partners, the Green Party, in Carlow later that week, on September 17, were dominated by journalists' questions about the so-called 'Garglegate'.

On September 30, 2010, the Central Bank Governor Patrick Honohan released what amounted to horrific figures for the cost of the bailout of the banks. The estimate was well over €50 billion, with Anglo Irish Bank costing something between €29 billion and €34 billion to phase out of existence in an ordered way. Bank debt would become public debt and the taxpayer would carry this enormous burden into future generations.

Some inside both Fianna Fail and the Green Party felt it was time to cut losses and fight a damage-limitation election. But the majority in both parties, who favoured soldiering on, prevailed. Mr Cowen began work on an austerity programme of economic rescue in conjunction with the European Commission.

But matters were beginning to spin utterly out of control. International money markets lost confidence in the Irish economy's ability to repay the enormous sums being swallowed up by the floundering banks. Reports began to emerge from Brussels and Frankfurt that the Irish Government was negotiating a bailout which would give direct supervision powers to the European Commission, the European Central Bank and the International Monetary Fund.

Some senior Fianna Fail ministers strongly denied these reports initially. When the EC-ECB-IMF finally arrived in town the Government bore a double shame. Irish sovereignty had been conceded on their watch and they also faced Opposition accusations of lying to the public.

Soon afterwards the Green Party announced that it would leave the Government as soon as the 2011 budget and the Finance Bill, which gave it legal force, were passed. There would be an election early in 2011 on a date yet to be named.

In January 2011, Brian Cowen came under pressure to explain revelations that he had played golf and dined with Sean

FitzPatrick, the boss of Anglo Irish Bank, in July 2008. The meeting was weeks before the Government extended its blanket guarantee to the banks and Anglo Irish Bank was the central actor in the wreck of the Irish banking system.

Again gathered at a party meeting, this time in Malahide, the Green Party came under renewed pressure as Cowen insisted that there was nothing untoward about his meeting with FitzPatrick. A war-weary Green Party leader, John Gormley, said: "First Garglegate — now Golfgate."

A long-threatened Fianna Fail leadership heave against Brian Cowen materialised and he faced it down. But Foreign Affairs Minister Micheal Martin resigned from the Cabinet.

This was followed by a botched attempt by Cowen to bring new people into the Cabinet, amid talk from Fianna Fail of the benefits of "a summer election". The Greens blocked the new appointments and Cowen signalled an election for March 11.

Cowen stood down as Fianna Fail leader but stayed on as Taoiseach. The Green Party left government and Cowen, announcing he was quitting politics, fixed an election for February 25, 2011.

****

Enda Kenny arrived at the Burlington Hotel for a small celebration on Saturday night, February 26, 2011, when the general shape of an extraordinary election win for Fine Gael was known.

He told emotional supporters that he had earlier received a phone call from his old boss and mentor, Liam Cosgrave, who had campaigned strongly 36 years previously for Kenny's election to the Dail. The former taoiseach was then 91 years old.

"I am an old man now but you have made me proud," Cosgrave told Kenny.

The former taoiseach also reminded Kenny of a little nugget of history. The new Dail would convene on March 9 – the very date in 1932 that Liam Cosgrave's father, WT Cosgrave, had handed over Government to Eamon de Valera and Fianna Fail.

Thus had begun eight decades of Fianna Fail dominance in Irish politics. Now the unthinkable had happened: Fianna Fail had been completely routed on a scale of defeat which was actually worse in terms of vote share than had happened to the old Irish Parliamentary Party in 1918. Fianna Fail had 17 per cent of the vote and just 20 TDs, only one of whom was in Dublin – and many constituencies across the country also had no Fianna Fail TD. The Green Party fared worse, losing all its six TDs.

Enda Kenny's Fine Gael had carried out a stunning piece of vote management. Everything the party had done wrong back in 2002 under Noonan, they did right in 2011 under the people Kenny had promoted and empowered, notably director of elections Phil Hogan and back room strategists Frank Flannery, Mark Mortell and Tom Curran.

The party's 36 per cent of the vote had guaranteed them a minimum of 60 Dail seats but their maximisation of vote share and transfers brought them 76 TDs. Mayo was the most outstanding example, where Enda Kenny brought in three running mates to take four out of the five seats, a feat never before achieved in Irish political history.

The Irish political landscape was completely changed. But it was hardly revolutionary – as claimed by some analysts. In fact the Irish voters had substituted one centre-right party for another.

Voters had wreaked a terrible vengeance on Fianna Fail, and blamed the party for smashing the economy with crazy policies that fuelled a property bubble and the arrival of the EU-IMF was really the final straw. They turned to Kenny's Fine Gael and accepted at face value his promise of a cleaner more upright style of politics.

On television, Kenny pledged a new era of transparency in politics – something the last Fine Gael taoiseach John Bruton, had done back in 1994, speaking of "governing behind a pane of glass". This time Kenny chose a more folksy, down-home phrase.

"The incoming Government is not going to leave our people in the dark. Paddy likes to know what the story is," the new Taoiseach-designate said. Many viewers hoped it was not going to be an era of referring to Irish people generically as 'Paddy'.

Eamon Gilmore's Labour Party did not achieve as much as it had hoped as it began the 24-day election campaign. Voters were clearly less than convinced by Gilmore's pledge, on just the third day of the campaign, that he would put manners on the European Central Bank in Frankfurt.

"It's Frankfurt's way or Labour's way," Gilmore said – and he dubbed the bank chairman Jean Claude Trichet "a mere civil servant". It was inappropriate and foolish bluster.

But Labour exceeded their own past record of 33 TDs under Dick Spring in 1992. Now Labour had 19 per cent of the vote, 37 TDs, and would be able to claim five Cabinet seats and six junior ministries, including one super-junior non-voting person at the Cabinet table, as part of Government negotiations. Gilmore easily brushed aside calls from a small minority of party members who wanted Labour to stay outside government and build for the longer term and an eventual overall Dail majority.

Sinn Fein also had its best election to date in the Republic with 10 per cent of the vote and 14 TDs, including party president Gerry Adams, who headed the poll in Louth. There was a wide scattering of independents and smaller groupings, notably the United Left Alliance which returned five TDs and promised a good deal of presence and controversy at Leinster House.

Enda Kenny had a good election campaign nationally, again crisscrossing the country. He stayed with his five-point plan and avoided all questions of detail as matters for later. Both he and his team also had the confidence to dictate the timing of debates – his perceived weakness in 2007.

In another bout of the 30-year-old periodic war with journalist Vincent Browne, he flatly refused to become involved. Browne had worsened matters between them in October 2010 when he said on TV3 that Kenny should be sent to a darkened room with a bottle of whiskey and a revolver.

The journalist's later abject apology did not redeem the situation. Kenny's flat refusal to participate in a TV3 debate did him or his party no harm.

The 'Mayo Taoiseach' phenomenon swelled Fine Gael support locally but posed an interesting challenge for the party's local director of elections, Michael Sloyan. The danger was that Enda Kenny could get the greater part of two quotas and ruin the chances of taking the four out of five Dail seats.

A good deal of Kenny territory was ceded to the fourth candidate, Michelle Mulherin of Ballina. A symbol of the unity of purpose in the Fine Gael camp was the image of Kenny's brother, Cllr Henry Kenny, canvassing for Mulherin in the village of Straide which was previously a happy hunting ground for the Kennys.

Kenny got almost 1.5 quotas with 17,472 votes. His old sparring partner Michael Ring also topped the quota on the first count for the first time ever and was duly elected. Both Mulherin and the other candidate, former football manager John O'Mahony, were elected on the eighth count. In total, Fine Gael got 48,000 votes or 65 per cent of the total in 'Kennyland'.

The only non-Fine Gael Mayo TD was former junior minister Dara Calleary of Fianna Fail. Dr Jerry Cowley, now standing for the Labour Party, failed to make an impact.

Michael Ring's supporters were elated at his performance and pointed to the successful transfer pact he had made with Michelle Mulherin as an example of his commitment to the team. Cllr Christy Hyland, a staunch Ring backer, speculated that a Cabinet place was surely on the cards for his hero – it would be a first for the town of Westport.

But Ring himself did not on this occasion use the media to push his application for promotion. "That's for another day. Today is about enjoying the victory," was all he would say.

Michael Ring was right to be cautious. He did not make Kenny's Cabinet, which was announced on the afternoon Enda Kenny was elected Taoiseach, March 9, 2011. In fact there was no other senior minister from Connacht or west of the Shannon.

As expected, Labour leader Eamon Gilmore became Tanaiste and Foreign Affairs Minister. The other Labour ministers were Ruairi Quinn, Education; Pat Rabbitte, Communications, Energy and Natural Resources; Brendan Howlin, Public Expenditure and Reform and Joan Burton, Social Protection.

Perhaps in a foretaste of the future, controversy from day one surrounded Labour, with the party accused of sexism and doing down its finance spokeswoman in opposition, Joan Burton. As expected the Finance Department had been split in two but Labour's portion went to Brendan Howlin.

Burton was extremely disappointed and there were rumblings in the Labour ranks at the failure to include other women such as Jan O'Sullivan, Roisin Shortall and Kathleen Lynch.

Kenny, as predicted, appointed Michael Noonan to the Finance Department and his deputy leader Dr James Reilly as Health Minister. Three rebels from the previous June were included in Kenny's Cabinet. His challenger, Richard Bruton got Jobs and Innovation; Leo Varadkar got Transport, Tourism and Sport and Simon Coveney got Agriculture, Marine and Food.

Frances Fitzgerald was the only woman he appointed to the Cabinet and she was given responsibility for Children and Youth Affairs. Giving the job full Cabinet rank was taken as a signal of seriousness in tackling Ireland's recent shameful past in this regard. His defenders in that heave the previous year were duly rewarded, with Phil Hogan taking on Environment; Jimmy Deenihan taking Arts, Heritage and Gaeltacht; Alan Shatter, Justice and Defence and Paul Kehoe, Government Chief Whip.

The Cabinet was heavily weighted towards Dublin but a west of Ireland Taoiseach did help offset that. The very next day he announced his team of junior ministers and blithely ignored a pledge of two years earlier to cut the number of junior ministers from 15 to 12. There was minimal comment and coverage as he pushed on and named his 15 juniors.

Eamon Gilmore tried to make amends to Labour women by

naming three among his five juniors. Both Kathleen Lynch and Roisin Shortall were appointed to the Health Department in support of Dr James Reilly, while Jan O'Sullivan went to Foreign Affairs. Gilmore also appointed Labour grassroots stalwart Willie Penrose, as 'super junior', and also included two young TDs, Alan Kelly and Sean Sherlock.

Kenny was also making amends and softened the no-Cabinet job blow to Michael Ring by giving him responsibility for tourism and sport – two sectors which would afford profile relevance to his home base of Westport.

Others from the western seaboard on the junior team were John Perry of Sligo-North Leitrim, small business; Dinny McGinley of Donegal South-West, Gaeltacht affairs; Ciaran Cannon of Galway East, training and skills.

Two more rebels, Brian Hayes and Fergus O'Dowd, were appointed to the junior ranks. Hayes got public service reform and the Office of Public Works, and Fergus O'Dowd became responsible for the so-called 'NewERA' group of new technology projects.

There was no place for veteran Laois-Offaly TD Charlie Flanagan, a rebel who had been on Kenny's post-heave front bench. Kenny did find a junior position for Meath East TD Shane McEntee, who had first been elected in the March 2005 by-election to replace John Bruton.

That same day Kenny also announced he was retaining Eoghan O Neachtain as Government Press Secretary, a tribute to the professionalism of a man who had served two very embattled Fianna Fail Taosigh, Bertie Ahern and Brian Cowen.

But the accolade of biggest winner, perhaps from all his Government appointments senior and junior, went to fellow Mayo person, Lucinda Creighton, who was given the prestigious job of Junior European Affairs Minister.

Lucinda Creighton, then aged 31, had not only supported Richard Bruton in the heave, she also had several well-publicised rows with her leader from soon after her election as a TD for

Dublin South East in summer 2007.

****

The Mayo faithful respected the new Taoiseach's request to not light up the county with homecoming bonfires which were the tradition for generations.

But Kenny's near neighbours at Lightford, just outside Castlebar, set fire to an old tree, which had been downed by a storm, to welcome home their hero in style with what they insisted was an "eco-friendly fire".

In his acceptance speech to the Dail the previous Wednesday, March 9, 2011, he had recalled all his predecessors who held the office as Taoiseach and saluted their service to the nation. Then he spoke of his late father, Henry Kenny, and his mother Ethna, who at the age of 93 was watching on television in Castlebar.

"They walk with me every step of this heart-stopping journey. For me, and for Fionnuala and the children, they represent the nobility and decency and very soul of the Irish people," the new Taoiseach said.

Now at home for the first time as Taoiseach, Enda Kenny and his wife Fionnuala showed up at their neighbours' bonfire at around 7.15 pm on that Saturday, March 12, 2011, and he joked about the changes his new role would bring to the area. Kenny pointed out that there were positives and negatives for the neighbours to having round-the-clock Garda security.

"The 'blue brigade' will see you're well protected from now onwards ... so get your driving licences and insurance sorted," he joked.

They stayed about half an hour at the bonfire and then it was on to the Royal Theatre at the Travellers' Friend, where 3,000 people were crammed in and waiting to fete the man they believed was Mayo's first true Taoiseach.

"It is always so nice to be home," he said, slowly emphasising each syllable, and drawing rapturous applause and cheers.

291

An accident of birth had given them Taoiseach Charlie Haughey, whose family left Castlebar when he was only four years old. Other national political leaders with local links included Clann na Talmhan leader Joe Blowick, and an early leader of the Labour Party, Thomas J O'Connell, who also had the distinction of being Labour's only TD for Mayo back in the late 1920s. The patrician James Dillon, who led Fine Gael from 1959 to 1965, had strong links with Ballaghaderreen, technically a Roscommon town, whose people play their football just across the countyline in Mayo.

"But this was completely different. Enda Kenny was one of our own – born, bred, schooled and living in Mayo. For 10 years the 'snoots' doubted and often made a mock of him. And now he held the highest office in the land. I heard people compare the welcome he got that night as 'Mayo Taoiseach' with the Pope's visit to Knock in 1979," one local Fine Gael veteran recalled with enormous pride.

Enda Kenny had been Taoiseach just four days on the evening of his triumphant return to Castlebar, the town where his political journey had begun on November 12, 1975, when he was declared an elected TD.

CONCLUSION

A LUCKY GENERAL

Enda Kenny has the essential quality Napoleon Bonaparte looked for in all his generals: he has been lucky many times over the past decade in politics.

Kenny was lucky he did not win the leadership of Fine Gael when he stood against Michael Noonan in February 2001. He was deeply wounded when Noonan did not appoint him to his front bench after that contest.

But when Fine Gael suffered meltdown and the loss of 23 TDs in the ensuing May 2002 general election, Enda Kenny was not leader, and in fact he was nowhere near the leadership team that had to bear the blame.

In that May 2002 election he was also very lucky indeed not to lose his Dail seat. His supporters had almost abandoned hope, and he was writing his resignation speech, when a few dozen votes and a lucky sequence of eliminations saw him hold on while his party rival Jim Higgins lost out.

After he took over as leader, Enda Kenny was lucky not to win the May 2007 general election. If he been elected Taoiseach at that point he would have been the one to face the economic meltdown when the global recession hit Ireland especially hard and led to the loss of economic sovereignty in November 2010.

While he went through a very rocky period as party leader in 2010, Enda Kenny was very lucky in the naivety and lack of preparation shown by those who conspired unsuccessfully against his leadership. He was additionally lucky in the strength of character and sound judgement of those who stood with him.

Kenny was also lucky that Fine Gael did not win an overall majority in the February 2011 general election. The 2:1 Fine Gael-Labour Dail configuration gives him additional political cover for the drastic fiscal medicine he must dish out. There is every chance that Labour could take the major political hit in the next election and Kenny could become the only Fine Gael taoiseach to be re-elected to two consecutive terms.

Ascribing luck to Enda Kenny is not an attempt to demean him – quite the opposite. All successful leaders need luck and if he has some more luck in his economic battles for Ireland in the coming years, the Irish people would certainly not carp.

Successful politicians usually also need another 'L' quality — longevity — which Enda Kenny has in abundance. November 12, 2012, marks the 37th anniversary of his first election to Dail Eireann in a by-election to replace his late father.

As others age, Enda Kenny remains the picture of health and fitness, capable of climbing mountains and cycling the Ring of Kerry. His ability to stand the demands and strains of public life across five decades has opened up additional possibilities of success and ascending to high office, especially since he was a late starter.

His good health and vigour are enhanced by a very positive demeanour and a flawless courtesy which make him an attractive character. He is unusual as a successful politician in having few if any enemies. He has at times over the years irked colleagues and adversaries, for lacking substance in their view– but nobody speaks of actually disliking him.

But he can also be ruthless and hard-hitting when required. This trait was on display when in 2004 he sacked Waterford dissident John Deasy from his front bench and later demoted his Mayo rival Michael Ring.

He again showed great toughness in his handling of the June 2010 frontbench heave against his leadership. The subsequent banishment of some rebels while retaining and promoting others in classic 'divide and conquer' mode was a further example.

Returning to our theme of luck, critics have grounds for arguing that his party's win in the February 2011 election was more about Fianna Fail totally discrediting and destroying itself. This and Ireland's deep recession left the voters with very few options.

But the counter-argument to this is that some other party or combination of parties rather than Fine Gael could have filled the gap left by Fianna Fail's implosion. It could have been the Labour Party and for a time it looked as if it might have been. Sinn Fein and/or a combination of far-left groups could have reaped a far larger dividend and claimed a share of government.

Pushing the argument that 'Fianna Fail lost – Fine Gael did not win' too far is to ignore 10 years of hard work by Kenny and others in rebuilding the party morale and structures and a steady graph of progress in every electoral contest since he took over as leader in June 2002. Certainly, he was lucky at the timing of economic collapse and Fianna Fail's astonishing self-destruction – but he had also prepared Fine Gael and placed it in a position capable of taking advantage of his adversaries' demise.

Enda Kenny has benefitted also from the gravitas the office of Taoiseach confers on politicians. The same thing occurred to his predecessor and former boss John Bruton, and also to his long-time opponent Bertie Ahern, who had to endure a decade of expressions of doubt about his ability before first being elected Taoiseach in June 1997.

But Kenny's potential for gaffes and less-than-serious presentation has not disappeared since he was elected Taoiseach on March 9, 2011. He at times also appears too heavily dependent on advisers who are loath to let him stray very far from their care. He has also been guilty of some hypocrisy by soft-pedalling public service reforms and breaching pay ceilings for some of the Government advisers.

But to his credit, he has restored some national morale since taking up office in Government Buildings. He has done this by dint of hard work and consistent projection of a positive image at home and abroad. His conduct of Ireland's six-month EU Presidency from January 2013 will be a further big test in that regard.

Ultimately, all of Kenny's bigger picture tests on his success or failure as Taoiseach lie in the revival of the Irish economy. But, as his second year in office draws towards a close, the economy is, according to Government think tank, the Economic and Social Research Institute, "bouncing along the bottom", with few signs of revival on the horizon.

Taoiseach Enda Kenny and his Government must restore confidence and stability. His first task is to wrest back economic sovereignty from the notorious Troika of the European Central Bank, the European Commission and the International Monetary Fund.

Then he must reduce unemployment, which currently remains depressingly high. This can only happen through a return to economic growth and some revival in the building and property sectors.

These are challenges which will require luck and, above all, an end to recession and to monetary instability in the Eurozone powerhouse economies.

In the absence of these developments, Enda Kenny will remain 'The Unlikely Taoiseach'.

Index

C

Caffrey 221
Caoimhghin O Caolain 199
Castlebar 7, 8, 13, 17, 19, 21,
    22, 27, 33, 36, 37, 42, 43,
    48, 49, 51, 53, 54, 55, 60,
    62, 65, 68, 77, 79-86, 88,
    98, 116, 118, 128, 129,
    131, 133, 134, 140, 141,
    145, 154, 155, 166, 168,
    170, 171, 179, 180-187,
    196, 198, 203-207, 218,
    226, 227, 237, 240-242,
    258, 261, 291, 292
Castlebar Mitchels 14, 25, 42
Celia Larkin 122
Charles Stewart Parnell 6
Charlie Bird 187
Charlie Flanagan 165, 167,
    190, 213, 222, 225, 278,
    281, 290, 291
Charlie Haughey 55, 76, 85-
    87, 98, 102, 105-111,
    114, 117, 131, 135-139,
    140, 142, 145, 146, 148,
    149, 155, 156-158, 191,
    197, 224, 291
Charlie McCreevy 94, 106,
    201, 210, 220, 244, 255
Chris Glennon 171
Christy Hyland 288
Ciaran Cannon 268, 290
Ciaran Conlon 249
Clann na Talmhan 3, 4, 6, 22,
    143, 291
Colm Kennelly 283

Conor Cruise O'Brien 31, 60,
    61, 62, 64
Conor McMorrow 40
Cornanool National School 24

D

Dail 5, 7, 16, 18, 23, 26, 27,
    28, 29, 30, 31, 32, 35, 39,
    40, 41, 43, 45, 46, 48, 52,
    61, 64, 67, 68, 69, 72, 75,
    76, 79, 80, 81, 85, 87-91,
    95-97, 101, 102, 109,
    113, 115, 125, 127, 128,
    130, 132, 134, 135, 139,
    140, 142, 143, 144, 147,
    148, 153, 155, 158, 161,
    162-166, 168, 170-176,
    178, 182, 183, 186, 187,
    190, 192, 195, 200, 203,
    207, 212, 213, 218, 225,
    226, 232, 233, 238-240,
    247, 250, 252, 253, 258,
    262, 268, 269, 272-275,
    277, 279, 280, 285-288,
    290, 291
Dana Rosemary Scallon 200,
    254
Dan Spring 11
Dara Calleary 261, 288
David Andrews 137
David Molony 82, 235
Declan Costello 32
Deirdre Clune 240
Democratic Left 160, 170,
    172, 175, 176, 177, 187,
    197, 198, 211
Democratic Socialist Party 94